HIDE
FOX,
AND ALL
AFTER

To
Dr P. J. Holt

HIDE
FOX,
AND ALL
AFTER

What lies concealed in
Shakespeare's *Hamlet*?

J. D. Winter

sussex
ACADEMIC
PRESS
Brighton • Portland • Toronto

2 4 6 8 10 9 7 5 3 1

First published in Great Britain in 2017 by
SUSSEX ACADEMIC PRESS
PO Box 139, Eastbourne BN24 9BP

Distributed in the United States of America by
SUSSEX ACADEMIC PRESS
International Specialized Book Services
920 NE 58th Ave #300
Portland, Oregon 97213

British Library Cataloguing in Publication Data

A CIP catalogue record for this book is available from the British Library.

Library of Congress Cataloging-in-Publication Data

Names: Winter, Joe, 1943– author.
Title: Hide fox, and all after : what lies concealed in Shakespeare's Hamlet? /
J. D. Winter.
Description: Brighton ; Portland : Sussex Academic Press, 2018.
Identifiers: LCCN 2017024605 | ISBN 9781845198879 (pbk : acid-free
paper)
Subjects: LCSH: Shakespeare, William, 1564–1616. Hamlet. | Shakespeare,
William, 1564–1616—Characters—Hamlet.
Classification: LCC PR2807 .W56 2018 | DDC 822.3/3—dc23
LC record available at https://lccn.loc.gov/2017024605

Typeset & designed by Sussex Academic Press, Brighton & Eastbourne.
Printed and bound by CPI Group (UK) Ltd, Croydon, CR0 4YY

Contents

Introduction

After accidentally killing Polonius Hamlet is required to see the king and cheerily consents, quipping, 'Hide fox, and all after'. It is not quite clear who the pursued is and who the pursuer. Virtually throughout the play nephew and uncle hunt each other down. The metaphor can however be taken further. There is a sense of elusiveness in the play's very make-up. Question after question is posed and not answered, while the audience is drawn in, as if closer to the stage, as with a part of their minds this or that conundrum is considered. The riddle of the prince's mental state is the most prominent of these; the nature (if any) of the queen's complicity in the crime committed before the play's start, perhaps the next; but there are a surprising number of less intrusive questions that nevertheless may bewilder and bother to an extent. The playwright must have his own reason for introducing these; there is a method to the drama's construction which itself may begin to emerge. But it is unlikely to yield to a mindset that likes a static solution, cut-and-dried. The play rests to a degree on an intuitive accommodation on the part of the audience, that can be teased out a little, no more.

Apart from a handful of readings from the First Quarto (1603), the text that follows is the generally accepted Second Quarto (1604-5), with a few well-known additions from the First Folio (1623). To add to the mass of commentary on it is a risky undertaking. *Hamlet* is notorious for both encouraging and resisting analysis. In any case a drama is an entertainment – is there a need for the travail of an exploratory process at all? The foremost purpose of my notes is to accompany a reading of the play at whatever level of familiarity. As scene by scene the to-and-fro of the stage is visited, a certain amount may or may not come to light relating to character and situation. My intent is to allow such matter to reveal itself, rather than try and identify it too neatly. To this end I adopt three further phrases from the text to give a certain direction to the journey.

The play's the thing

'The play's the thing / Wherein I'll catch the conscience of the king,' resolves the prince, as he prepares a trap for Claudius. I take the first words out of context to define a condition of my approach. I refer neither to any other literary work, by Shakespeare or otherwise, nor to any work of criticism. The discussion to follow seeks rather to operate as a spectator at a performance, observing what is in front of its nose, not the mass of comparative material or commentary below it. Nor do I attempt to follow up local historical or social questions, though several may have interested the first audiences, such as a possible caricature in the role of Polonius, or the topical passage on the child actors. Episode by episode, scene by scene it is my intention to serve as a kind of receptor for the developing action and interaction, at all times conscious that the notes that emerge stem from personal choices which others may not echo. It is a gamble, if one based not on pure chance. To adapt (audaciously) Hamlet's words on 'the purpose of playing', 'to show . . . the very age and body of the time his form and pressure' – it is the 'form and pressure' of the drama itself that has lain in my mind an age. My method is a heuristic one, based on the spectacle as it unfolds itself, and on that alone.

A rhapsody of words

'O, such a deed / As from the body of contraction plucks / The very soul, and sweet religion makes / A rhapsody of words.' Hamlet is furious at his mother for deserting the spirit of the marriage contract sealed with his father. "Rhapsody" there and then would have meant something like "rambling poetic effusion"; again I abstract a phrase from its immediate context, in this case from its time as well. With the stronger modern connotation of a tumbling thrilling gaiety, the old term (originally from the Greek for "to stitch") serves my purpose too well to ignore. Is not the cascade of poetry throughout an old-time drama in some respect 'a rhapsody of words'? The discussion for each scene, in the main at or towards its end, will include certain poetical effects. They may be something of particular interest in a word or phrase, an extra meaning or a meaning that may echo on a wider bandwidth in the play, so to speak. They may prompt a discussion of an outstanding or repeated image; but not, I shall hope, in such a way as to destroy its freshness. They may bring the staple fare of verse drama in English into consideration. In a Shakespearean play the sweep of the blank-verse iambic pentameter is an undeniable aspect in the working of the whole. Such effects can make certain passages immortal to the memory; and yet they are subsidiary to the dramatic action which they describe and from which they proceed.

The invisible event

'Witness this army of such mass and charge / Led by a delicate and tender prince, / Whose spirit with divine ambition puff'd / Makes mouths at the invisible event . . . '. On his (sanctioned) way across Danish territory to fight the Poles over 'a little patch of ground / That hath in it no profit but the name' (as the Norwegian officer has told Hamlet), Fortinbras is ready to risk all, to laugh in the face of the unforeseeable. Hamlet lashes himself for his own paralysis, as he sees it, his craven and dishonourable inaction. Again I borrow a phrase to indicate an aspect of the drama before us. A kind of blindness stamps its mark so heavily on the play as almost to define it. There is no prominent character whose role is not branded by it. Horatio alone is clear-seeing, a part which in its passivity tends to confirm the point at issue. For the blindness affecting others is in all cases related to the world of turbulent action, to the steps they take or have taken, to what they become and to what they do. Horatio's role, apart from a glimmer of forthright action at the start and the end, is to be a companion to Hamlet and to know him (itself no small thing). A misdirected and unseeing tendency is a part of any dramatic tragedy but in *Hamlet* it is ubiquitous. We are brought up close to human error, to witness a pattern of its working. Such is the power of theatre and of the modus operandi adopted by the playwright.

To enter a work of art requires more than clear-eyed thought. Whatever the complexity before it the mind will tend to seek a way in, as it were, by the sense of touch. There may be a way in which this is especially true of *Hamlet*. It is partly to chase up such an intimation that I have decided to throw caution to the winds and like so many others, to follow the fox into the thicket. Yet my deeper aim as a commentator is not analytical. I hope to open up the play a little to readers who may be interested in ideas on this or that character or aspect, whether or not they agree with them; to find out more about it myself; and by visiting something of the scale and depth of the creation, to celebrate it. I do not know if I hope the figure of Hamlet himself may become more knowable. In this respect a good acting performance is in any case worth a dozen commentaries. But there may be something to be gained by a background understanding. I do not offer such but perhaps a few directions in which it may be discovered, each mind for itself. Yet whatever illumination a reader comes to for him or herself, this most coruscating of stage scripts will always keep intact its dark source. No critic can say anything of the original creative process, describe how a single work of art has come to be.

THE TRAGICAL HISTORY OF HAMLET, PRINCE OF DENMARK

DRAMATIS PERSONAE
HAMLET, Prince of Denmark
GHOST of Hamlet's father, the late King Hamlet of Denmark
CLAUDIUS, King of Denmark, brother of the late King
GERTRUDE, Queen of Denmark, Hamlet's mother, now married
    to Claudius
POLONIUS, Claudius' counsellor
LAERTES, Polonius' son
OPHELIA, Polonius' daughter
REYNALDO, Polonius' servant
HORATIO, Hamlet's friend and fellow-student
ROSENCRANTZ and GUILDENSTERN, other fellow-students
BARNARDO, FRANCISCO and MARCELLUS, Sentinels
VOLTEMAND and CORNELIUS, Danish Ambassadors to Norway
OSRIC, a courtier
PLAYERS, playing Prologue, Player King, Player Queen and Lucianus
GRAVE-DIGGER, a Clown
SECOND MAN, another Clown
FORTINBRAS, Prince of Norway
CAPTAIN in Norwegian army
FOLLOWERS of Laertes
AMBASSADORS from England
PRIEST
MESSENGERS
LORDS
GENTLEMEN
SAILORS
Attendants, Courtiers, Officers, Norwegian Soldiers, Trumpets,
    Kettledrums, Drums

ACT I, SCENE 1

Elsinore: A platform before the castle

FRANCISCO at his post. Enter to him BARNARDO

BARNARDO Who's there?

FRANCISCO Nay, answer me: stand, and unfold yourself.

BARNARDO Long live the king!

FRANCISCO Barnardo?

BARNARDO He.

FRANCISCO You come most carefully upon your hour.

BARNARDO 'Tis now struck twelve; get thee to bed, Francisco.

FRANCISCO For this relief much thanks: 'tis bitter cold,
And I am sick at heart.

BARNARDO Have you had quiet guard?

FRANCISCO   Not a mouse stirring. 10

BARNARDO Well, good night.
If you do meet Horatio and Marcellus,
The rivals of my watch, bid them make haste.

FRANCISCO I think I hear them. Stand, ho! Who's there?

Enter HORATIO and MARCELLUS

HORATIO Friends to this ground.

MARCELLUS   And liegemen to the Dane.

FRANCISCO Give you good night.

MARCELLUS   O, farewell, honest soldier;
Who hath reliev'd you?

FRANCISCO   Barnardo has my place.
Give you good night.   *Exit*

MARCELLUS   Holla! Barnardo!

BARNARDO   Say,
What, is Horatio there?

HORATIO   A piece of him.

BARNARDO Welcome Horatio, welcome good Marcellus. 20

MARCELLUS What, has this thing appear'd again to-night?

BARNARDO I have seen nothing.

MARCELLUS Horatio says 'tis but our fantasy,
And will not let belief take hold of him

Touching this dreaded sight, twice seen of us.
Therefore I have entreated him along
With us to watch the minutes of this night;
That if again this apparition come,
He may approve our eyes and speak to it.
HORATIO Tush, tush, 'twill not appear.
BARNARDO   Sit down awhile;   30
And let us once again assail your ears,
That are so fortified against our story,
What we have two nights seen.
HORATIO   Well, sit we down,
And let us hear Barnardo speak of this.
BARNARDO Last night of all,
When yond same star that's westward from the pole
Had made his course to illume that part of heaven
Where now it burns, Marcellus and myself,
The bell then beating one –   *Enter GHOST*
MARCELLUS Peace, break thee off; look, where it comes again!   40
BARNARDO In the same figure, like the king that's dead.
MARCELLUS Thou art a scholar; speak to it, Horatio.
BARNARDO Looks it not like the king? mark it, Horatio.
HORATIO Most like – it harrows me with fear and wonder.
BARNARDO It would be spoke to.
MARCELLUS   Question it, Horatio.
HORATIO What art thou that usurp'st this time of night,
Together with that fair and warlike form
In which the majesty of buried Denmark
Did sometimes march? By heaven I charge thee, speak!
MARCELLUS It is offended.
BARNARDO   See, it stalks away!   50
HORATIO Stay! speak, speak! I charge thee, speak!   *Exit GHOST*
MARCELLUS 'Tis gone, and will not answer.
BARNARDO How now, Horatio! You tremble and look pale;
Is not this something more than fantasy?
What think you on't?
HORATIO Before my God, I might not this believe
Without the sensible and true avouch
Of mine own eyes.

MARCELLUS Is it not like the king?
HORATIO As thou art to thyself.   60
Such was the very armour he had on
When he the ambitious Norway combated;
So frown'd he once, when, in an angry parle,
He smote the sledded Polacks on the ice.
'Tis strange.
MARCELLUS Thus twice before, and jump at this dead hour,
With martial stalk hath he gone by our watch.
HORATIO In what particular thought to work I know not;
But in the gross and scope of my opinion,
This bodes some strange eruption to our state.   70
MARCELLUS Good now, sit down, and tell me, he that knows,
Why this same strict and most observant watch
So nightly toils the subject of the land,
And why such daily cast of brazen cannon,
And foreign mart for implements of war;
Why such impress of shipwrights, whose sore task
Does not divide the Sunday from the week;
What might be toward, that this sweaty haste
Doth make the night joint-labourer with the day:
Who is't that can inform me?
HORATIO   That can I;   80
At least, the whisper goes so. Our last king,
Whose image ev'n but now appear'd to us,
Was, as you know, by Fortinbras of Norway,
Thereto prick'd on by a most emulate pride,
Dar'd to the combat; in which our valiant Hamlet –
For so this side of our known world esteem'd him –
Did slay this Fortinbras; who by a seal'd compact,
Well ratified by law and heraldry,
Did forfeit, with his life, all those his lands
Which he stood seiz'd of, to the conqueror: 90
Against the which, a moiety competent
Was gagèd by our king; which had return'd
To the inheritance of Fortinbras,
Had he been vanquisher; as, by the same covenant,
And carriage of the article design'd,

His fell to Hamlet. Now sir, young Fortinbras,
Of unimprovèd mettle hot and full,
Hath in the skirts of Norway here and there
Shark'd up a list of lawless resolutes
For food and diet, to some enterprise   100
That hath a stomach in't; which is no other –
As it doth well appear unto our state –
But to recover of us, by strong hand
And terms compulsatory, those foresaid lands
So by his father lost. And this, I take it,
Is the main motive of our preparations,
The source of this our watch and the chief head
Of this post-haste and romage in the land.
BARNARDO I think it be no other but e'en so.
Well may it sort that this portentous figure   110
Comes armèd through our watch; so like the king
That was and is the question of these wars.
HORATIO A mote it is to trouble the mind's eye.
In the most high and palmy state of Rome,
A little ere the mightiest Julius fell,
The graves stood tenantless and the sheeted dead
Did squeak and gibber in the Roman streets;
As stars with trains of fire and dews of blood,
Disasters in the sun; and the moist star
Upon whose influence Neptune's empire stands   120
Was sick almost to doomsday with eclipse.
And even the like precurse of fierce events,
As harbingers preceding still the fates
And prologue to the omen coming on,
Have heaven and earth together demonstrated
Unto our climatures and countrymen.
But soft, behold! lo, where it comes again!
                              Re-enter GHOST
I'll cross it, though it blast me. Stay, illusion!
If thou hast any sound, or use of voice,
Speak to me!   130
If there be any good thing to be done,
That may to thee do ease and grace to me,

Speak to me!
If thou art privy to thy country's fate,
Which happily foreknowing may avoid,
O speak!
Or if thou hast uphoarded in thy life
Extorted treasure in the womb of earth,
For which, they say, you spirits oft walk in death,
Speak of it, stay and speak! *Cock crows* Stop it, Marcellus!   140
MARCELLUS Shall I strike at it with my partisan?
HORATIO Do, if it will not stand.
BARNARDO   'Tis here!
HORATIO   'Tis here!   *Exit GHOST*
MARCELLUS 'Tis gone!
We do it wrong, being so majestical,
To offer it the show of violence;
For it is as the air, invulnerable,
And our vain blows malicious mockery.
BARNARDO It was about to speak when the cock crew.
HORATIO And then it started like a guilty thing
Upon a fearful summons. I have heard,   150
The cock, that is the trumpet to the morn,
Doth with his lofty and shrill-sounding throat
Awake the god of day; and at his warning,
Whether in sea or fire, in earth or air,
The extravagant and erring spirit hies
To his confine – and of the truth herein
This present object made probation.
MARCELLUS It faded on the crowing of the cock.
Some say that ever 'gainst that season comes
Wherein our Saviour's birth is celebrated,   160
The bird of dawning singeth all night long.
And then, they say, no spirit dare stir abroad;
The nights are wholesome; then no planets strike,
No fairy takes, nor witch hath power to charm,
So hallow'd and so gracious is the time.
HORATIO So have I heard and do in part believe it.
But look, the morn in russet mantle clad
Walks o'er the dew of yon high eastern hill.

Break we our watch up; and by my advice
Let us impart what we have seen tonight   170
Unto young Hamlet; for upon my life
This spirit, dumb to us, will speak to him.
Do you consent we shall acquaint him with it,
As needful in our loves, fitting our duty?
MARCELLUS   Let's do't, I pray; and I this morning know
Where we shall find him most conveniently.

Exeunt

ACT I, SCENE 2

A room of state in the castle

Enter KING CLAUDIUS, QUEEN GERTRUDE, HAMLET,
POLONIUS, LAERTES, VOLTEMAND, CORNELIUS,
Lords and Attendants
KING   Though yet of Hamlet our dear brother's death
The memory be green, and that it us befitted
To bear our hearts in grief and our whole kingdom
To be contracted in one brow of woe,
Yet so far hath discretion fought with nature
That we with wisest sorrow think on him,
Together with remembrance of ourselves.
Therefore our sometime sister, now our queen,
The imperial jointress to this warlike state,
Have we, as 'twere with a defeated joy –   10
With an auspicious and a dropping eye,
With mirth in funeral and with dirge in marriage,
In equal scale weighing delight and dole –
Taken to wife; nor have we herein barr'd
Your better wisdoms, which have freely gone
With this affair along. For all, our thanks.
Now follows, that you know, young Fortinbras,
Holding a weak supposal of our worth,
Or thinking by our late dear brother's death
Our state to be disjoint and out of frame,   20
Colleaguèd with the dream of his advantage,
He hath not fail'd to pester us with message
Importing the surrender of those lands
Lost by his father, with all bonds of law,
To our most valiant brother. So much for him.
Now for ourself and for this time of meeting,
Thus much the business is: we have here writ
To Norway, uncle of young Fortinbras,
Who, impotent and bed-rid, scarcely hears
Of this his nephew's purpose, to suppress   30
His further gait herein; in that the levies,

12

The lists and full proportions, are all made
Out of his subject: and we here dispatch
You, good Cornelius, and you, Voltemand,
For bearers of this greeting to old Norway;
Giving to you no further personal power
To business with the king, more than the scope
Of these delated articles allow.
Farewell, and let your haste commend your duty.
CORNELIUS, VOLTEMAND   In that and all things will
                                we show our duty.   40
KING   We doubt it nothing; heartily farewell.

Exeunt VOLTEMAND and CORNELIUS

And now, Laertes, what's the news with you?
You told us of some suit; what is't, Laertes?
You cannot speak of reason to the Dane,
And lose your voice: what wouldst thou beg, Laertes,
That shall not be my offer, not thy asking?
The head is not more native to the heart,
The hand more instrumental to the mouth,
Than is the throne of Denmark to thy father.
What wouldst thou have, Laertes?
LAERTES   Dread my lord,   50
Your leave and favour to return to France;
From whence though willingly I came to Denmark
To show my duty in your coronation,
Yet now, I must confess, that duty done,
My thoughts and wishes bend again toward France
And bow them to your gracious leave and pardon.
KING   Have you your father's leave? What says Polonius?
POLONIUS   He hath, my lord, wrung from me my slow leave
By laboursome petition, and at last
Upon his will I seal'd my hard consent.   60
I do beseech you, give him leave to go.
KING   Take thy fair hour, Laertes; time be thine,
And thy best graces spend it at thy will.
But now, my cousin Hamlet, and my son –
HAMLET   *aside*   A little more than kin, and less than kind.

KING   How is it that the clouds still hang on you?
HAMLET   Not so, my lord; I am too much i'the sun.
QUEEN   Good Hamlet, cast thy nighted colour off,
And let thine eye look like a friend on Denmark.
Do not for ever with thy vailèd lids   70
Seek for thy noble father in the dust.
Thou know'st 'tis common, all that lives must die,
Passing through nature to eternity.
HAMLET   Ay, madam, it is common.
QUEEN   If it be,
Why seems it so particular with thee?
HAMLET   Seems, madam! nay it is, I know not 'seems'.
'Tis not alone my inky cloak, good mother,
Nor customary suits of solemn black,
Nor windy suspiration of forc'd breath,
No, nor the fruitful river in the eye,   80
Nor the dejected 'haviour of the visage,
Together with all forms, moods, shapes of grief,
That can denote me truly; these indeed seem,
For they are actions that a man might play.
But I have that within which passeth show;
These but the trappings and the suits of woe.
KING   'Tis sweet and commendable in your nature, Hamlet,
To give these mourning duties to your father.
But you must know your father lost a father,
That father lost, lost his, and the survivor bound   90
In filial obligation for some term
To do obsequious sorrow; but to persever
In obstinate condolement is a course
Of impious stubbornness. 'Tis unmanly grief;
It shows a will most incorrect to heaven,
A heart unfortified, a mind impatient,
An understanding simple and unschool'd.
For what we know must be and is as common
As any the most vulgar thing to sense –
Why should we in our peevish opposition   100
Take it to heart? Fie! 'tis a fault to heaven,
A fault against the dead, a fault to nature,

To reason most absurd, whose common theme
Is death of fathers, and who still hath cried,
From the first corse till he that died to-day,
'This must be so.' We pray you, throw to earth
This unprevailing woe, and think of us
As of a father; for let the world take note,
You are the most immediate to our throne;
And with no less nobility of love   110
Than that which dearest father bears his son
Do I impart toward you. For your intent
In going back to school in Wittenberg,
It is most retrograde to our desire;
And we beseech you, bend you to remain
Here, in the cheer and comfort of our eye,
Our chiefest courtier, cousin, and our son.
QUEEN Let not thy mother lose her prayers, Hamlet:
I pray thee, stay with us; go not to Wittenberg.
HAMLET I shall in all my best obey you, madam.   120
KING Why, 'tis a loving and a fair reply.
Be as ourself in Denmark. Madam, come;
This gentle and unforc'd accord of Hamlet
Sits smiling to my heart; in grace whereof,
No jocund health that Denmark drinks to-day,
But the great cannon to the clouds shall tell,
And the king's rouse the heavens shall bruit again,
Re-speaking earthly thunder. Come away.

Exeunt all but HAMLET

HAMLET O that this too too solid flesh would melt,
Thaw and resolve itself into a dew!   130
Or that the Everlasting had not fix'd
His canon 'gainst self-slaughter! O God! O God!
How weary, stale, flat and unprofitable
Seem to me all the uses of this world!
Fie on't! ah fie! 'tis an unweeded garden
That grows to seed; things rank and gross in nature
Possess it merely. That it should come to this!
But two months dead – nay, not so much, not two –

So excellent a king, that was, to this,
Hyperion to a satyr; so loving to my mother   140
That he might not beteem the winds of heaven
Visit her face too roughly. Heaven and earth!
Must I remember? why, she would hang on him
As if increase of appetite had grown
By what it fed on; and yet, within a month –
Let me not think on't – Frailty, thy name is woman! –
A little month, or ere those shoes were old
With which she follow'd my poor father's body,
Like Niobe, all tears; why she, even she –
O, God! a beast, that wants discourse of reason,   150
Would have mourn'd longer – married with my uncle,
My father's brother, but no more like my father
Than I to Hercules. Within a month,
Ere yet the salt of most unrighteous tears
Had left the flushing in her gallèd eyes,
She married. O most wicked speed, to post
With such dexterity to incestuous sheets!
It is not nor it cannot come to good.
But break, my heart, for I must hold my tongue!

Enter HORATIO, MARCELLUS and BARNARDO

HORATIO Hail to your lordship!
HAMLET   I am glad to see you well,   160
Horatio, or I do forget myself.
HORATIO The same, my lord, and your poor servant ever.
HAMLET Sir, my good friend; I'll change that name with you.
And what make you from Wittenberg, Horatio?
Marcellus?
MARCELLUS My good lord –
HAMLET I am very glad to see you.
(*To Barnardo*) Good even, sir.
But what, in faith, make you from Wittenberg?
HORATIO A truant disposition, good my lord.   170
HAMLET I would not hear your enemy say so,
Nor shall you do mine ear that violence,
To make it truster of your own report

Against yourself; I know you are no truant.
But what is your affair in Elsinore?
We'll teach you to drink deep ere you depart.
HORATIO My lord, I came to see your father's funeral.
HAMLET I pray thee, do not mock me, fellow-student;
I think it was to see my mother's wedding.
HORATIO Indeed, my lord, it follow'd hard upon.   180
HAMLET Thrift, thrift, Horatio! the funeral bak'd meats
Did coldly furnish forth the marriage tables.
Would I had met my dearest foe in heaven
Or ever I had seen that day, Horatio!
My father, methinks I see my father.
HORATIO O where, my lord?
HAMLET   In my mind's eye, Horatio.
HORATIO I saw him once; he was a goodly king.
HAMLET He was a man, take him for all in all,
I shall not look upon his like again.
HORATIO My lord, I think I saw him yesternight.   190
HAMLET Saw who?
HORATIO My lord, the king your father.
HAMLET   The king my father!
HORATIO Season your admiration for awhile
With an attent ear, till I may deliver,
Upon the witness of these gentlemen,
This marvel to you.
HAMLET   For God's love, let me hear.
HORATIO Two nights together had these gentlemen,
Marcellus and Barnardo, on their watch,
In the dead vast and middle of the night,
Been thus encounter'd. A figure like your father,   200
Armèd at point exactly, cap-a-pe,
Appears before them, and with solemn march
Goes slow and stately by them; thrice he walk'd
By their oppress'd and fear-surprisèd eyes
Within his truncheon's length; whilst they, distill'd
Almost to jelly with the act of fear,
Stand dumb and speak not to him. This to me
In dreadful secrecy impart they did;

And I with them the third night kept the watch;
Where, as they had deliver'd, both in time,   210
Form of the thing, each word made true and good,
The apparition comes. I knew your father;
These hands are not more like.
HAMLET   But where was this?
MARCELLUS My lord, upon the platform where we watch'd.
HAMLET Did you not speak to it?
HORATIO   My lord, I did;
But answer made it none; yet once methought
It lifted up its head and did address
Itself to motion, like as it would speak;
But even then the morning cock crew loud,
And at the sound it shrunk in haste away   220
And vanish'd from our sight.
HAMLET   'Tis very strange.
HORATIO As I do live, my honour'd lord, 'tis true;
And we did think it writ down in our duty
To let you know of it.
HAMLET Indeed, indeed, sirs, but this troubles me.
Hold you the watch to-night?
MARCELLUS, BARNARDO We do, my lord.
HAMLET Arm'd, say you?
MARCELLUS, BARNARDO Arm'd, my lord.
HAMLET   From top to toe?
MARCELLUS, BARNARDO My lord, from head to foot.
HAMLET Then saw you not his face?
HORATIO O, yes, my lord; he wore his beaver up.   230
HAMLET What, look'd he frowningly?
HORATIO A countenance more in sorrow than in anger.
HAMLET Pale or red?
HORATIO Nay, very pale.
HAMLET   And fix'd his eyes upon you?
HORATIO Most constantly.
HAMLET   I would I had been there.
HORATIO It would have much amaz'd you.
HAMLET Very like, very like. Stay'd it long?
HORATIO While one with moderate haste might tell a hundred.

MARCELLUS, BARNARDO   Longer, longer.
HORATIO   Not when I saw't.
HAMLET   His beard was grizzl'd, no?   240
HORATIO   It was, as I have seen it in his life,
A sable silver'd.
HAMLET   I will watch to-night;
Perchance 'twill walk again.
HORATIO   I warrant it will.
HAMLET   If it assume my noble father's person,
I'll speak to it, though hell itself should gape
And bid me hold my peace. I pray you all,
If you have hitherto conceal'd this sight,
Let it be tenable in your silence still;
And whatsoever else shall hap to-night,
Give it an understanding, but no tongue.   250
I will requite your loves. So, fare you well;
Upon the platform, 'twixt eleven and twelve,
I'll visit you.
ALL   Our duty to your honour.
HAMLET   Your loves, as mine to you: farewell.

Exeunt all but HAMLET

My father's spirit in arms! all is not well;
I doubt some foul play. Would the night were come!
Till then, sit still, my soul. Foul deeds will rise,
Though all the earth o'erwhelm them, to men's eyes.

Exit

ACT I, SCENE 3

A room in Polonius' house

Enter LAERTES and OPHELIA

LAERTES My necessaries are embark'd; farewell.
And sister, as the winds give benefit
And convoy is assistant, do not sleep,
But let me hear from you.
OPHELIA   Do you doubt that?
LAERTES For Hamlet and the trifling of his favour,
Hold it a fashion and a toy in blood,
A violet in the youth of primy nature,
Forward, not permanent, sweet, not lasting,
The perfume and suppliance of a minute;
No more.
OPHELIA No more but so?
LAERTES   Think it no more;   10
For nature, crescent, does not grow alone
In thews and bulk, but as this temple waxes,
The inward service of the mind and soul
Grows wide withal. Perhaps he loves you now,
And now no soil nor cautel doth besmirch
The virtue of his will; but you must fear,
His greatness weigh'd, his will is not his own;
For he himself is subject to his birth.
He may not, as unvalued persons do,
Carve for himself, for on his choice depends   20
The safety and the health of this whole state;
And therefore must his choice be circumscrib'd
Unto the voice and yielding of that body
Whereof he is the head. Then if he says he loves you,
It fits your wisdom so far to believe it
As he in his particular act and place
May give his saying deed; which is no further
Than the main voice of Denmark goes withal.
Then weigh what loss your honour may sustain
If with too credent ear you list his songs,   30

Or lose your heart, or your chaste treasure open
To his unmaster'd importunity.
Fear it, Ophelia, fear it, my dear sister,
And keep you in the rear of your affection,
Out of the shot and danger of desire.
The chariest maid is prodigal enough
If she unmask her beauty to the moon.
Virtue itself 'scapes not calumnious strokes;
The canker galls the infants of the spring
Too oft before their buttons be disclos'd;   40
And in the morn and liquid dew of youth
Contagious blastments are most imminent.
Be wary then; best safety lies in fear;
Youth to itself rebels, though none else near.
OPHELIA I shall the effect of this good lesson keep
As watchman to my heart. But, good my brother,
Do not, as some ungracious pastors do,
Show me the steep and thorny way to heaven,
Whiles, like a puff'd and reckless libertine,
Himself the primrose path of dalliance treads   50
And recks not his own rede.
LAERTES   O, fear me not.
I stay too long: but here my father comes.   *Enter POLONIUS*
A double blessing is a double grace,
Occasion smiles upon a second leave.
POLONIUS Yet here, Laertes! aboard, aboard, for shame!
The wind sits in the shoulder of your sail,
And you are stay'd for. There, my blessing with thee!
And these few precepts in thy memory
See thou character. Give thy thoughts no tongue,
Nor any unproportion'd thought his act.   60
Be thou familiar, but by no means vulgar.
Those friends thou hast, and their adoption tried,
Grapple them to thy soul with hoops of steel;
But do not dull thy palm with entertainment
Of each new-hatch'd, unfledg'd comrade. Beware
Of entrance to a quarrel, but being in,
Bear't that the opposèd may beware of thee.

Give every man thy ear, but few thy voice;
Take each man's censure, but reserve thy judgment.
Costly thy habit as thy purse can buy,   70
But not express'd in fancy; rich, not gaudy;
For the apparel oft proclaims the man,
And they in France of the best rank and station
Are most select and generous, chief in that.
Neither a borrower nor a lender be;
For loan oft loses both itself and friend,
And borrowing dulls the edge of husbandry.
This above all: to thine own self be true,
And it must follow, as the night the day,
Thou canst not then be false to any man.   80
Farewell, my blessing season this in thee!
LAERTES Most humbly do I take my leave, my lord.
POLONIUS The time invites you; go, your servants tend.
LAERTES Farewell, Ophelia, and remember well
What I have said to you.
OPHELIA   'Tis in my memory lock'd,
And you yourself shall keep the key of it.
LAERTES Farewell.   *Exit*
POLONIUS What is't, Ophelia, he hath said to you?
OPHELIA So please you, something touching the Lord Hamlet.
POLONIUS Marry, well bethought.   90
'Tis told me, he hath very oft of late
Giv'n private time to you; and you yourself
Have of your audience been most free and bounteous.
If it be so, as so 'tis put on me,
And that in way of caution, I must tell you
You do not understand yourself so clearly
As it behoves my daughter and your honour.
What is between you? Give me up the truth.
OPHELIA He hath, my lord, of late made many tenders
Of his affection to me.   100
POLONIUS Affection! pooh! you speak like a green girl,
Unsifted in such perilous circumstance.
Do you believe his tenders, as you call them?
OPHELIA I do not know, my lord, what I should think.

POLONIUS Marry, I'll teach you: think yourself a baby,
That you have ta'en these tenders for true pay,
Which are not sterling. Tender yourself more dearly;
Or – not to crack the wind of the poor phrase,
Running it thus – you'll tender me a fool.
OPHELIA My lord, he hath importun'd me with love   110
In honourable fashion.
POLONIUS Ay, fashion you may call it; go to, go to.
OPHELIA And hath given countenance to his speech, my lord,
With almost all the holy vows of heaven.
POLONIUS Ay, springes to catch woodcocks. I do know,
When the blood burns, how prodigal the soul
Lends the tongue vows. These blazes, daughter,
Giving more light than heat, extinct in both,
Even in their promise, as it is a-making,
You must not take for fire. From this time   120
Be somewhat scanter of your maiden presence;
Set your entreatments at a higher rate
Than a command to parley. For Lord Hamlet,
Believe so much in him, that he is young,
And with a larger tether may he walk
Than may be given you. In few, Ophelia,
Do not believe his vows, for they are brokers
Not of that dye which their investments show,
But mere implorators of unholy suits,
Breathing like sanctified and pious bawds,   130
The better to beguile. This is for all:
I would not, in plain terms, from this time forth,
Have you so slander any moment's leisure,
As to give words or talk with the Lord Hamlet.
Look to't, I charge you. Come your ways.
OPHELIA I shall obey, my lord.

Exeunt

ACT I, SCENE 4

The platform

Enter HAMLET, HORATIO and MARCELLUS
HAMLET   The air bites shrewdly; it is very cold.
HORATIO   It is a nipping and an eager air.
HAMLET   What hour now?
HORATIO   I think it lacks of twelve.
MARCELLUS   No, it is struck.
HORATIO   Indeed? I heard it not.
It then draws near the season
Wherein the spirit held his wont to walk.

A flourish of trumpets, and ordnance shot off, within

What does this mean, my lord?
HAMLET   The king doth wake to-night and takes his rouse,
Keeps wassail, and the swaggering up-spring reels;
And, as he drains his draughts of Rhenish down,   10
The kettle-drum and trumpet thus bray out
The triumph of his pledge.
HORATIO   Is it a custom?
HAMLET   Ay, marry, is't:
But to my mind, though I am native here
And to the manner born, it is a custom
More honour'd in the breach than the observance.
This heavy-headed revel east and west
Makes us traduc'd and tax'd of other nations:
They clepe us drunkards, and with swinish phrase
Soil our addition; and indeed it takes   20
From our achievements, though perform'd at height,
The pith and marrow of our attribute.
So oft it chances in particular men
That for some vicious mole of nature in them –
As, in their birth, wherein they are not guilty,
Since nature cannot choose his origin;
By the o'ergrowth of some complexion,
Oft breaking down the pales and forts of reason;

24

Or by some habit that too much o'er-leavens
The form of plausive manners – that these men,   30
Carrying, I say, the stamp of one defect,
Being nature's livery, or fortune's star –
Their virtues else, be they as pure as grace,
As infinite as man may undergo,
Shall in the general censure take corruption
From that particular fault. The dram of eale
Doth all the noble substance of a doubt
To his own scandal –   *Enter Ghost*
HORATIO   Look, my lord, it comes!
HAMLET Angels and ministers of grace defend us!
Be thou a spirit of health or goblin damn'd,   40
Bring with thee airs from heaven or blasts from hell,
Be thy intents wicked or charitable,
Thou com'st in such a questionable shape
That I will speak to thee. I'll call thee Hamlet,
King, father, royal Dane: O, answer me!
Let me not burst in ignorance; but tell
Why thy canoniz'd bones, hearsèd in death,
Have burst their cerements; why the sepulchre,
Wherein we saw thee quietly inurn'd,
Hath op'd his ponderous and marble jaws   50
To cast thee up again. What may this mean,
That thou, dead corse, again in complete steel
Revisit'st thus the glimpses of the moon,
Making night hideous; and we fools of nature
So horridly to shake our disposition
With thoughts beyond the reaches of our souls?
Say, why is this? Wherefore? What should we do?

Ghost beckons HAMLET

HORATIO It beckons you to go away with it,
As if it some impartment did desire
To you alone.   60
MARCELLUS Look, with what courteous action
It waves you to a more removèd ground;
But do not go with it.

HORATIO   No, by no means.

HAMLET   It will not speak; then I will follow it.

HORATIO   Do not, my lord.

HAMLET   Why, what should be the fear?
I do not set my life at a pin's fee;
And for my soul, what can it do to that,
Being a thing immortal as itself?
It waves me forth again: I'll follow it.

HORATIO   What if it tempt you toward the flood, my lord,   70
Or to the dreadful summit of the cliff
That beetles o'er his base into the sea,
And there assume some other horrible form,
Which might deprive your sovereignty of reason
And draw you into madness? Think of it.
The very place puts toys of desperation,
Without more motive, into every brain
That looks so many fathoms to the sea
And hears it roar beneath.

HAMLET   It waves me still. Go on, I'll follow thee.   80

MARCELLUS   You shall not go, my lord.

HAMLET   Hold off your hands!

HORATIO   Be rul'd; you shall not go.

HAMLET   My fate cries out,
And makes each petty artery in this body
As hardy as the Nemean lion's nerve.
Still am I call'd. Unhand me, gentlemen!
By heaven, I'll make a ghost of him that lets me!
I say, away! Go on, I'll follow thee.

Exeunt Ghost and HAMLET

HORATIO   He waxes desperate with imagination.

MARCELLUS   Let's follow; 'tis not fit thus to obey him.

HORATIO   Have after. To what issue will this come?   90

MARCELLUS   Something is rotten in the state of Denmark.

HORATIO   Heaven will direct it.

MARCELLUS   Nay, let's follow him.

Exeunt

ACT I, SCENE 5

Another part of the platform

Enter GHOST and HAMLET
HAMLET Where wilt thou lead me? Speak! I'll go no further.
GHOST   Mark me.
HAMLET   I will.
GHOST   My hour is almost come
When I to sulphurous and tormenting flames
Must render up myself.
HAMLET   Alas, poor ghost!
GHOST   Pity me not, but lend thy serious hearing
To what I shall unfold.
HAMLET   Speak: I am bound to hear.
GHOST   So art thou to revenge, when thou shalt hear.
HAMLET What?
GHOST   I am thy father's spirit,
Doom'd for a certain term to walk the night,   10
And for the day confin'd to fast in fires,
Till the foul crimes done in my days of nature
Are burnt and purg'd away. But that I am forbid
To tell the secrets of my prison-house,
I could a tale unfold whose lightest word
Would harrow up thy soul, freeze thy young blood,
Make thy two eyes, like stars, start from their spheres,
Thy knotted and combinèd locks to part
And each particular hair to stand on end
Like quills upon the fretful porpentine.   20
But this eternal blazon must not be
To ears of flesh and blood. List, list, O, list!
If thou didst ever thy dear father love –
HAMLET O God!
GHOST   Revenge his foul and most unnatural murder.
HAMLET Murder!
GHOST   Murder most foul, as in the best it is;
But this most foul, strange and unnatural.
HAMLET Haste me to know't that I, with wings as swift

As meditation or the thoughts of love 30
May sweep to my revenge.
GHOST   I find thee apt;
And duller shouldst thou be than the fat weed
That rots itself in ease on Lethe wharf,
Wouldst thou not stir in this. Now, Hamlet, hear:
'Tis given out that, sleeping in my orchard,
A serpent stung me; so the whole ear of Denmark
Is by a forgèd process of my death
Rankly abus'd. But know, thou noble youth,
The serpent that did sting thy father's life
Now wears his crown.
HAMLET   O my prophetic soul! 40
My uncle!
GHOST Ay, that incestuous, that adulterate beast,
With witchcraft of his wit, with traitorous gifts –
O wicked wit and gifts, that have the power
So to seduce! – won to his shameful lust
The will of my most seeming-virtuous queen.
O Hamlet, what a falling-off was there!
From me, whose love was of that dignity
That it went hand in hand even with the vow
I made to her in marriage, and to decline 50
Upon a wretch whose natural gifts were poor
To those of mine!
But virtue, as it never will be mov'd,
Though lewdness court it in a shape of heaven,
So lust, though to a radiant angel link'd,
Will sate itself in a celestial bed,
And prey on garbage.
But, soft! methinks I scent the morning air;
Brief let me be. Sleeping within my orchard,
My custom always of the afternoon, 60
Upon my secure hour thy uncle stole
With juice of cursèd hebona in a vial,
And in the porches of my ears did pour
The leperous distilment; whose effect
Holds such an enmity with blood of man

That swift as quicksilver it courses through
The natural gates and alleys of the body,
And with a sudden vigour it doth posset
And curd, like eager droppings into milk,
The thin and wholesome blood. So did it mine;   70
And a most instant tetter bark'd about
Most lazar-like, with vile and loathsome crust,
All my smooth body.
Thus was I, sleeping, by a brother's hand
Of life, of crown, of queen, at once dispatch'd;
Cut off even in the blossoms of my sin,
Unhousel'd, disappointed, unanel'd,
No reckoning made, but sent to my account
With all my imperfections on my head.
O horrible! O horrible! most horrible!   80
If thou hast nature in thee, bear it not!
Let not the royal bed of Denmark be
A couch for luxury and damnèd incest.
But, howsoever thou pursuest this act,
Taint not thy mind, nor let thy soul contrive
Against thy mother aught; leave her to heaven,
And to those thorns that in her bosom lodge
To prick and sting her. Fare thee well at once!
The glow-worm shows the matin to be near,
And 'gins to pale his uneffectual fire.   90
Adieu, adieu! Hamlet, remember me.   *Exit*
HAMLET   O all you host of heaven! O earth! what else?
And shall I couple hell? O fie! Hold, hold, my heart,
And you, my sinews, grow not instant old,
But bear me stiffly up. Remember thee!
Ay, thou poor ghost, while memory holds a seat
In this distracted globe. Remember thee!
Yea, from the table of my memory
I'll wipe away all trivial fond records,
All saws of books, all forms, all pressures past   100
That youth and observation copied there;
And thy commandment all alone shall live
Within the book and volume of my brain,

Unmix'd with baser matter: yes, by heaven!
O most pernicious woman!
O villain, villain, smiling, damnèd villain!
My tables – meet it is I set it down,
That one may smile, and smile, and be a villain;
At least I'm sure it may be so in Denmark.   *Writing*
So, uncle, there you are. Now to my word –   110
It is 'Adieu, adieu! remember me.'
I have sworn't.
HORATIO *within* My lord, my lord –
MARCELLUS *within*   Lord Hamlet –
HORATIO *within*   Heaven secure him!
HAMLET So be it.
HORATIO *within* Hillo, ho, ho, my lord!
HAMLET Hillo, ho, ho, boy! come, bird, come.

Enter HORATIO and MARCELLUS

MARCELLUS How is't, my noble lord?
HORATIO   What news, my lord?
HAMLET O, wonderful!
HORATIO Good my lord, tell it.
HAMLET   No; you will reveal it.
HORATIO Not I, my lord, by heaven.
MARCELLUS   Nor I, my lord.
HAMLET How say you, then; would heart of man once think it? 120
But you'll be secret?
HORATIO, MARCELLUS Ay, by heaven, my lord.
HAMLET There's ne'er a villain dwelling in all Denmark
But he's an arrant knave.
HORATIO There needs no ghost, my lord, come from the grave
To tell us this.
HAMLET Why, right; you are i'the right;
And so, without more circumstance at all,
I hold it fit that we shake hands and part;
You, as your business and desire shall point you,
For every man has business and desire,   130
Such as it is; and for mine own poor part,
Look you, I'll go pray.

HORATIO   These are but wild and whirling words, my lord.

HAMLET   I'm sorry they offend you, heartily;
Yes 'faith, heartily.

HORATIO   There's no offence, my lord.

HAMLET   Yes, by Saint Patrick, but there is, Horatio,
And much offence too. Touching this vision here,
It is an honest ghost, that let me tell you.
For your desire to know what is between us,
O'ermaster't as you may. And now, good friends,   140
As you are friends, scholars and soldiers,
Give me one poor request.

HORATIO   What is't, my lord? we will.

HAMLET   Never make known what you have seen tonight.

HORATIO, MARCELLUS   My lord, we will not.

HAMLET   Nay, but swear't.

HORATIO   In faith,
My lord, not I.

MARCELLUS   Nor I, my lord, in faith.

HAMLET   Upon my sword.

MARCELLUS   We have sworn, my lord, already.

HAMLET   Indeed, upon my sword, indeed.

GHOST   *beneath*   Swear.

HAMLET   Aha, boy! say'st thou so? art thou there, truepenny?
Come on – you hear this fellow in the cellarage –   150
Consent to swear.

HORATIO   Propose the oath, my lord.

HAMLET   Never to speak of this that you have seen,
Swear by my sword.

GHOST   *beneath*   Swear.

HAMLET   *Hic et ubique*? Then we'll shift our ground.
Come hither, gentlemen,
And lay your hands again upon my sword.
Never to speak of this that you have heard,
Swear by my sword.

GHOST   *beneath*   Swear.   160

HAMLET   Well said, old mole! canst work i'the earth so fast?
A worthy pioner! Once more remove, good friends.

HORATIO   O day and night, but this is wondrous strange!

HAMLET   And therefore as a stranger give it welcome.
There are more things in heaven and earth, Horatio,
Than are dreamt of in your philosophy.
But come:
Here, as before, never, so help you mercy,
How strange or odd soe'er I bear myself,
As I perchance hereafter shall think meet   170
To put an antic disposition on,
That you, at such times seeing me, never shall,
With arms encumber'd thus, or this headshake,
Or by pronouncing of some doubtful phrase,
As 'Well, well, we know,' or 'We could, an if we would,'
Or 'If we list to speak,' or 'There be, an if they might,'
Or such ambiguous giving out, to note
That you know aught of me: this not to do,
So grace and mercy at your most need help you,
Swear.   180
Ghost *beneath*   Swear.   *They swear*
HAMLET   Rest, rest, perturbèd spirit! So, gentlemen,
With all my love I do commend me to you;
And what so poor a man as Hamlet is
May do, to express his love and friending to you,
God willing, shall not lack. Let us go in together;
And still your fingers on your lips, I pray.
The time is out of joint: O cursèd spite,
That ever I was born to set it right!
Nay, come, let's go together.   190

Exeunt

ACT II, SCENE 1

A room in Polonius' house

Enter POLONIUS and REYNALDO
POLONIUS Give him this money and these notes, Reynaldo.
REYNALDO I will, my lord.
POLONIUS You shall do marvellous wisely, good Reynaldo,
Before you visit him, to make inquiry
Of his behaviour.
REYNALDO My lord, I did intend it.
POLONIUS Marry, well said; very well said. Look you, sir,
Inquire me first what Danskers are in Paris;
And how, and who, what means, and where they keep,
What company, at what expense; and finding
By this encompassment and drift of question   10
That they do know my son, come you more nearer
Than your particular demands will touch it.
Take you, as 'twere, some distant knowledge of him;
As thus, 'I know his father and his friends,
And in part him.' Do you mark this, Reynaldo?
REYNALDO Ay, very well, my lord.
POLONIUS 'And in part him; but', you may say, 'not well;
But, if't be he I mean, he's very wild,
Addicted so and so;' and there put on him
What forgeries you please. Marry, none so rank   20
As may dishonour him; take heed of that;
But, sir, such wanton, wild and usual slips
As are companions noted and most known
To youth and liberty.
REYNALDO   As gaming, my lord?
POLONIUS Ay, or drinking, fencing, swearing,
Quarrelling, drabbing; you may go so far.
REYNALDO My lord, that would dishonour him.
POLONIUS 'Faith, no; as you may season it in the charge.
You must not put another scandal on him,
That he is open to incontinency –   30
That's not my meaning – but breathe his faults so quaintly

That they may seem the taints of liberty,
The flash and outbreak of a fiery mind,
A savageness in unreclaimèd blood,
Of general assault.
REYNALDO   But, my good lord –
POLONIUS Wherefore should you do this?
REYNALDO   Ay, my lord,
I would know that.
POLONIUS   Marry, sir, here's my drift;
And I believe it is a fetch of warrant.
You laying these slight sullies on my son,
As 'twere a thing a little soil'd i'the working,   40
Mark you,
Your party in converse, him you would sound,
Having ever seen in the prenominate crimes
The youth you breathe of guilty, be assur'd
He closes with you in this consequence;
'Good sir,' or so, or 'friend,' or 'gentleman,'
According to the phrase or the addition
Of man and country.
REYNALDO   Very good, my lord.
POLONIUS And then, sir, does he this – he does – what was I
about to say? By the mass, I was about to say something; where   50
did I leave?
REYNALDO At 'closes in the consequence,' at 'friend or so,'
and 'gentleman.'
POLONIUS At 'closes in the consequence,' ay, marry.
He closes thus: 'I know the gentleman;
I saw him yesterday, or t'other day,
Or then, or then; with such, or such; and, as you say,
There was 'a gaming; there o'ertook in's rouse;
There falling out at tennis;' or perchance,
'I saw him enter such a house of sale,'   60
Videlicet a brothel, or so forth.
See you now:
Your bait of falsehood takes this carp of truth;
And thus do we of wisdom and of reach,
With windlasses and with assays of bias,

By indirections find directions out.
So by my former lecture and advice
Shall you my son. You have me, have you not?
REYNALDO   My lord, I have.
POLONIUS   God be wi'you; fare you well.
REYNALDO   Good my lord!   70
POLONIUS   Observe his inclination in yourself.
REYNALDO   I shall, my lord.
POLONIUS   And let him ply his music.
REYNALDO   Well, my lord.
POLONIUS   Farewell.

Exit REYNALDO   Enter OPHELIA

                          How now, Ophelia! what's the matter?
OPHELIA   Alas my lord, I have been so affrighted!
POLONIUS   With what, i'the name of God?
OPHELIA   My lord, as I was sewing in my closet
Lord Hamlet, with his doublet all unbrac'd,
No hat upon his head; his stockings foul'd,
Ungarter'd, and down-gyvèd to his ankle;   80
Pale as his shirt; his knees knocking each other;
And with a look so piteous in purport
As if he had been loosèd out of hell
To speak of horrors – he comes before me.
POLONIUS   Mad for thy love?
OPHELIA   My lord, I do not know;
But truly, I do fear it.
POLONIUS   What said he?
OPHELIA   He took me by the wrist and held me hard;
Then goes he to the length of all his arm;
And, with his other hand thus o'er his brow,
He falls to such perusal of my face   90
As he would draw it. Long stay'd he so;
At last, a little shaking of mine arm,
And thrice his head thus waving up and down,
He raised a sigh so piteous and profound
As it did seem to shatter all his bulk
And end his being. That done, he lets me go,

And with his head over his shoulder turn'd,
He seem'd to find his way without his eyes;
For out o'doors he went without their help,
And to the last bended their light on me.   100
POLONIUS   Come, go with me; I will go seek the king.
This is the very ecstasy of love
Whose violent property fordoes itself,
And leads the will to desperate undertakings,
As oft as any passion under heaven
That does afflict our natures. I am sorry.
What, have you given him any hard words of late?
OPHELIA   No, my good lord, but as you did command,
I did repel his letters and denied
His access to me.
POLONIUS   That hath made him mad.   110
I am sorry that with better heed and judgment
I had not quoted him. I fear'd he did but trifle,
And meant to wreck thee; but beshrew my jealousy!
By heaven, it is as proper to our age
To cast beyond ourselves in our opinions,
As it is common for the younger sort
To lack discretion. Come, go we to the king.
This must be known; which, being kept close, might move
More grief to hide than hate to utter love.
Come.   120

Exeunt

ACT II, SCENE 2

A room in the castle

*Enter KING, QUEEN, ROSENCRANTZ, GUILDENSTERN
and Attendants*

KING Welcome, dear Rosencrantz and Guildenstern!
Moreover that we much did long to see you,
The need we have to use you did provoke
Our hasty sending. Something have you heard
Of Hamlet's transformation; so I call it,
Sith nor the exterior nor the inward man
Resembles that it was. What it should be,
More than his father's death, that thus hath put him
So much from th'understanding of himself
I cannot dream of. I entreat you both   10
That, being of so young days brought up with him,
And sith so neighbour'd to his youth and humour,
That you vouchsafe your rest here in our court
Some little time; so by your companies
To draw him on to pleasures; and to gather
So much as from occasion you may glean,
Whether aught to us unknown afflicts him thus,
That open'd, lies within our remedy.
QUEEN Good gentlemen, he hath much talk'd of you;
And sure I am two men there are not living   20
To whom he more adheres. If it will please you
To show us so much gentry and good will
As to expend your time with us awhile
For the supply and profit of our hope,
Your visitation shall receive such thanks
As fits a king's remembrance.
ROSENCRANTZ   Both your majesties
Might, by the sovereign power you have of us,
Put your dread pleasures more into command
Than to entreaty.
GUILDENSTERN But we both obey,
And here give up ourselves in the full bent   30

To lay our service freely at your feet,
To be commanded.
KING   Thanks, Rosencrantz and gentle Guildenstern.
QUEEN   Thanks, Guildenstern and gentle Rosencrantz;
And I beseech you instantly to visit
My too much changèd son. Go, some of you,
And bring these gentlemen where Hamlet is.
GUILDENSTERN   Heavens make our presence and our practices
Pleasant and helpful to him!
QUEEN   Ay, amen!

Exeunt ROSENCRANTZ, GUILDENSTERN and some Attendants
Enter POLONIUS

POLONIUS   The ambassadors from Norway, my good lord,   40
Are joyfully return'd.
KING   Thou still hast been the father of good news.
POLONIUS   Have I, my lord? Assure you, my good liege,
I hold my duty, as I hold my soul,
Both to my God and to my gracious king;
And I do think, or else this brain of mine
Hunts not the trail of policy so sure
As it hath us'd to do, that I have found
The very cause of Hamlet's lunacy.
KING   O, speak of that; that do I long to hear.   50
POLONIUS   Give first admittance to the ambassadors;
My news shall be the fruit to that great feast.
KING   Thyself do grace to them, and bring them in.

Exit POLONIUS

He tells me, my dear Gertrude, he hath found
The head and source of all your son's distemper.
QUEEN   I doubt it is no other but the main;
His father's death, and our o'erhasty marriage.
KING   Well, we shall sift him.

Re-enter POLONIUS, with VOLTEMAND and CORNELIUS

                              Welcome, my good friends!
Say, Voltemand, what from our brother Norway?

VOLTEMAND   Most fair return of greetings and desires.   60
Upon our first, he sent out to suppress
His nephew's levies; which to him appear'd
To be a preparation 'gainst the Polack;
But, better look'd into, he truly found
It was against your highness: whereat griev'd
That so his sickness, age and impotence
Was falsely borne in hand, sends out arrests
On Fortinbras; which he, in brief, obeys;
Receives rebuke from Norway, and in fine
Makes vow before his uncle never more   70
To give the assay of arms against your majesty.
Whereon old Norway, overcome with joy,
Gives him three thousand crowns in annual fee,
And his commission to employ those soldiers,
So levied as before, against the Polack;
With an entreaty, herein further shown,   *Giving a paper*
That it might please you to give quiet pass
Through your dominions for this enterprise,
On such regards of safety and allowance
As therein are set down.
KING   It likes us well;   80
And at our more consider'd time we'll read,
Answer, and think upon this business.
Meantime we thank you for your well-took labour.
Go to your rest; at night we'll feast together.
Most welcome home!

Exeunt VOLTEMAND and CORNELIUS

POLONIUS   This business is well ended.
My liege and madam, to expostulate
What majesty should be, what duty is,
Why day is day, night night, and time is time,
Were nothing but to waste night, day and time.
Therefore, since brevity is the soul of wit,   90
And tediousness the limbs and outward flourishes,
I will be brief: your noble son is mad.
Mad call I it; for to define true madness,

What is't but to be nothing else but mad?
But let that go.
QUEEN   More matter, with less art.
POLONIUS   Madam, I swear I use no art at all.
That he is mad, 'tis true; 'tis true 'tis pity;
And pity 'tis 'tis true: a foolish figure –
But farewell it, for I will use no art.
Mad let us grant him then; and now remains   100
That we find out the cause of this effect,
Or rather say, the cause of this defect,
For this effect defective comes by cause;
Thus it remains, and the remainder thus.
Perpend.
I have a daughter, have while she is mine;
Who, in her duty and obedience, mark,
Hath given me this: now gather and surmise.   (reads)
To the celestial and my soul's idol, the most beautified Ophelia.
That's an ill phrase, a vile phrase; 'beautified' is a vile phrase: 110
but you shall hear. Thus: (reads)
In her excellent white bosom, these, & c.
QUEEN   Came this from Hamlet to her?
POLONIUS   Good madam, stay awhile; I will be faithful.
(reads)
Doubt thou the stars are fire;
Doubt that the sun doth move;
Doubt truth to be a liar;
But never doubt I love.
O dear Ophelia, I am ill at these numbers. I have not art to reckon
my groans: but that I love thee best, O most best, believe it. Adieu.   120
Thine evermore, most dear lady, whilst this machine is to him,
Hamlet.
This in obedience hath my daughter shown me;
And more above, hath his solicitings,
As they fell out by time, by means and place,
All given to mine ear.
KING   But how hath she
Receiv'd his love?
POLONIUS   What do you think of me?

KING   As of a man faithful and honourable.
POLONIUS   I would fain prove so. But what might you think
When I had seen this hot love on the wing –   130
As I perceiv'd it, I must tell you that,
Before my daughter told me – what might you,
Or my dear majesty your queen here, think
If I had play'd the desk or table-book,
Or giv'n my heart a winking, mute and dumb,
Or look'd upon this love with idle sight;
What might you think? No, I went round to work,
And my young mistress thus I did bespeak:
'Lord Hamlet is a prince, out of thy star;
This must not be.' And then I precepts gave her,   140
That she should lock herself from his resort,
Admit no messengers, receive no tokens;
Which done, she took the fruits of my advice;
And he, repulsèd – a short tale to make –
Fell into a sadness, then into a fast,
Thence to a watch, thence into a weakness,
Thence to a lightness, and, by this declension,
Into the madness wherein now he raves,
And all we mourn for.
KING   Do you think 'tis this?
QUEEN   It may be, very likely.   150
POLONIUS   Hath there been such a time – I'd fain know that –
That I have positively said ' 'Tis so,'
When it prov'd otherwise?
KING   Not that I know.
POLONIUS *pointing to his head and shoulder*
Take this from this, if this be otherwise.
If circumstances lead me, I will find
Where truth is hid, though it were hid indeed
Within the centre.
KING   How may we try it further?
POLONIUS   You know, sometimes he walks four hours together
Here in the lobby.
QUEEN   So he does indeed.
POLONIUS   At such a time I'll loose my daughter to him.   160

41

Be you and I behind an arras then.
Mark the encounter: if he love her not,
And be not from his reason fall'n thereon,
Let me be no assistant for a state,
But keep a farm and carters.
KING   We will try it.
QUEEN But look, where sadly the poor wretch comes reading.
POLONIUS Away, I do beseech you, both away;
I'll board him presently. O, give me leave.

Exeunt KING, QUEEN and Attendants. Enter HAMLET, reading

How does my good Lord Hamlet?
HAMLET   Well, God-a-mercy.
POLONIUS Do you know me, my lord?   170
HAMLET Excellent well; you are a fishmonger.
POLONIUS Not I, my lord.
HAMLET Then I would you were so honest a man.
POLONIUS Honest, my lord?
HAMLET Ay, sir; to be honest, as this world goes,
is to be one man pick'd out of ten thousand.
POLONIUS That's very true, my lord.
HAMLET For if the sun breed maggots in a dead dog, being a
god kissing carrion ... Have you a daughter?
POLONIUS I have, my lord.   180
HAMLET Let her not walk i'the sun. Conception is a blessing,
but not as your daughter may conceive. Friend, look to't.
POLONIUS *aside* How say you by that? Still harping on my
daughter: yet he knew me not at first; he said I was a fishmonger:
he is far gone, far gone: and truly in my youth I suffered much
extremity for love; very near this. I'll speak to him again. What
do you read, my lord?
HAMLET Words, words, words.
POLONIUS What is the matter, my lord?
HAMLET Between who?   190
POLONIUS I mean the matter that you read, my lord.
HAMLET Slanders sir, for the satirical rogue says here that old
men have grey beards, that their faces are wrinkl'd, their eyes
purging thick amber and plum-tree gum, and that they have a

plentiful lack of wit, together with most weak hams: all which, sir, though I most powerfully and potently believe, yet I hold it not honesty to have it thus set down; for yourself, sir, should be old as I am, if like a crab you could go backward.

POLONIUS *aside* Though this be madness, yet there is method in't. Will you walk out of the air, my lord?   200

HAMLET Into my grave.

POLONIUS Indeed, that is out o'the air. *Aside* How pregnant sometimes his replies are! a happiness that often madness hits on, which reason and sanity could not so prosperously be deliver'd of. I will leave him, and suddenly contrive the means of meeting between him and my daughter. My honourable lord, I will most humbly take my leave of you.

HAMLET You cannot, sir, take from me anything that I will more willingly part withal: except my life, except my life, except my life.   210

POLONIUS Fare you well, my lord.   *Going*

HAMLET These tedious old fools!

Enter ROSENCRANTZ and GUILDENSTERN

POLONIUS You go to seek the Lord Hamlet? There he is.

ROSENCRANTZ *to Polonius* God save you, sir!   *Exit POLONIUS*

GUILDENSTERN My honoured lord!

ROSENCRANTZ My most dear lord!

HAMLET My excellent good friends! How dost thou, Guildenstern? Ah, Rosencrantz! Good lads, how do ye both?

ROSENCRANTZ As the indifferent children of the earth.

GUILDENSTERN Happy in that we are not over-happy;   220
On Fortune's cap we are not the very button.

HAMLET Nor the soles of her shoe?

ROSENCRANTZ Neither, my lord.

HAMLET Then you live about her waist, or in the middle of her favours?

GUILDENSTERN 'Faith, her privates we.

HAMLET In the secret parts of Fortune? O, most true; she is a strumpet. What's the news?

ROSENCRANTZ None, my lord, but that the world's grown honest.   230

HAMLET Then is doomsday near; but your news is not true. Let me question more in particular. What have you, my good friends, deserved at the hands of Fortune, that she sends you to prison hither?

GUILDENSTERN Prison, my lord?

HAMLET Denmark's a prison.

ROSENCRANTZ Then is the world one.

HAMLET A goodly one; in which there are many confines, wards and dungeons, Denmark being one o'the worst.

ROSENCRANTZ We think not so, my lord.   240

HAMLET Why, then, 'tis none to you; for there is nothing either good or bad, but thinking makes it so. To me it is a prison.

ROSENCRANTZ Why then, your ambition makes it one; 'tis too narrow for your mind.

HAMLET O God, I could be bounded in a nutshell and count myself a king of infinite space, were it not that I have bad dreams.

GUILDENSTERN Which dreams indeed are ambition, for the very substance of the ambitious is merely the shadow of a dream.   250

HAMLET A dream itself is but a shadow.

ROSENCRANTZ Truly, and I hold ambition of so airy and light a quality that it is but a shadow's shadow.

HAMLET Then are our beggars bodies, and our monarchs and outstretch'd heroes the beggars' shadows. Shall we to the court? for, by my fay, I cannot reason.

ROSENCRANTZ, GUILDENSTERN We'll wait upon you.

HAMLET No such matter: I will not sort you with the rest of my servants, for to speak to you like an honest man, I am most dreadfully attended. But, in the beaten way of friendship, what   260 make you at Elsinore?

ROSENCRANTZ To visit you, my lord; no other occasion.

HAMLET Beggar that I am, I am even poor in thanks; but I thank you: and sure, dear friends, my thanks are too dear a halfpenny. Were you not sent for? Is it your own inclining? Is it a free visitation? Come, deal justly with me: come, come; nay, speak.

GUILDENSTERN What should we say, my lord?

HAMLET   Why anything, but to the purpose. You were sent for;
and there is a kind of confession in your looks which your   270
modesties have not craft enough to colour. I know the good king
and queen have sent for you.
ROSENCRANTZ   To what end, my lord?
HAMLET   That you must teach me. But let me conjure you,
by the rights of our fellowship, by the consonancy of our youth,
by the obligation of our ever-preserv'd love, and by what more
dear a better proposer could charge you withal, be even and
direct with me – whether you were sent for, or no?
ROSENCRANTZ   *aside to Guildenstern*   What say you?
HAMLET   Nay, then, I have an eye of you. If you love me,   280
hold not off.
GUILDENSTERN   My lord, we were sent for.
HAMLET   I will tell you why; so shall my anticipation prevent
your discovery, and your secrecy to the king and queen moult
no feather. I have of late – but wherefore I know not – lost all
my mirth, forgone all custom of exercises; and indeed it goes so
heavily with my disposition that this goodly frame, the earth,
seems to me a sterile promontory; this most excellent canopy,
the air, look you, this brave o'erhanging firmament, this
majestical roof fretted with golden fire, why, it appears no other   290
thing to me than a foul and pestilent congregation of vapours.
What a piece of work is a man! How noble in reason! how
infinite in faculty! in form and moving how express and
admirable! in action how like an angel! in apprehension how
like a god! the beauty of the world! the paragon of animals!
And yet, to me, what is this quintessence of dust? Man delights
not me: no, nor woman neither, though by your smiling you
seem to say so.
ROSENCRANTZ   My lord, there was no such stuff in my
thoughts.   300
HAMLET   Why did you laugh then, when I said man delights
not me?
ROSENCRANTZ   To think, my lord, if you delight not in man,
what lenten entertainment the players shall receive from you.
We coted them on the way, and hither are they coming, to offer
you service.

HAMLET He that plays the king shall be welcome. His majesty
shall have tribute of me, the adventurous knight shall use his
foil and target, the lover shall not sigh gratis, the humorous man
shall end his part in peace, the clown shall make those laugh   310
whose lungs are tickl'd o'the sere, and the lady shall say her
mind freely, or the blank verse shall halt for't. What players
are they?
ROSENCRANTZ Even those you were wont to take delight in,
the tragedians of the city.
HAMLET How chances it they travel? Their residence, both in
reputation and profit, was better both ways.
ROSENCRANTZ I think their inhibition comes by the means of
the late innovation.
HAMLET Do they hold the same estimation they did when I   320
was in the city? are they so follow'd?
ROSENCRANTZ No, indeed are they not.
HAMLET How comes it? do they grow rusty?
ROSENCRANTZ Nay, their endeavour keeps in the wonted
pace; but there is, sir, an aery of children, little eyases, that cry
out on the top of question, and are most tyrannically clapp'd
for't. These are now the fashion, and so berattle the common
stages – so they call them – that many wearing rapiers are afraid
of goose-quills, and dare scarce come thither.
HAMLET What, are they children? Who maintains 'em? How   330
are they escoted? Will they pursue the quality no longer than
they can sing? Will they not say afterwards, if they should grow
themselves to common players – as it is most like, if their means
are no better – their writers do them wrong, to make them
exclaim against their own succession?
ROSENCRANTZ 'Faith, there has been much to-do on both
sides, and the nation holds it no sin to tarre them to controversy.
There was, for a while, no money bid for argument, unless the
poet and the player went to cuffs in the question.
HAMLET Is't possible?   340
GUILDENSTERN O, there has been much throwing about
of brains.
HAMLET Do the boys carry it away?

ROSENCRANTZ   Ay, that they do, my lord; Hercules and his
load too.

HAMLET   It is not very strange; for mine uncle is King of
Denmark, and those that would make mows at him while my
father liv'd, give twenty, forty, fifty, an hundred ducats a-piece
for his picture in little. 'Sblood, there is something in this more
than natural, if philosophy could find it out.   350

Flourish of trumpets within

GUILDENSTERN   There are the players.

HAMLET   Gentlemen, you are welcome to Elsinore. Your hands,
come then! The appurtenance of welcome is fashion and
ceremony. Let me comply with you in this garb, lest my extent
to the players, which, I tell you, must show fairly outward,
should more appear like entertainment than yours. You are
welcome – but my uncle-father and aunt-mother are deceiv'd.

GUILDENSTERN   In what, my dear lord?

HAMLET   I am but mad north-north-west: when the wind is
southerly I know a hawk from a hernshaw.   *Enter POLONIUS*   360

POLONIUS   Well be with you, gentlemen!

HAMLET   Hark you, Guildenstern, and you too; at each ear a
hearer. That great baby you see there is not yet out of his
swaddling-clouts.

ROSENCRANTZ   Happily he's the second time come to them;
for they say an old man is twice a child.

HAMLET   I will prophesy he comes to tell me of the players;
mark it. You say right, sir: o'Monday morning; 'twas so indeed.

POLONIUS   My lord, I have news to tell you.

HAMLET   My lord, I have news to tell you. When Roscius was   370
an actor in Rome –

POLONIUS   The actors are come hither, my lord.

HAMLET   Buzz, buzz!

POLONIUS   Upon mine honour –

HAMLET   Then came each actor on his ass –

POLONIUS   The best actors in the world, either for tragedy,
comedy, history, pastoral, pastoral-comical, historical-pastoral,
tragical-historical, tragical-comical-historical-pastoral, scene
individable or poem unlimited. Seneca cannot be too heavy nor

Plautus too light. For the law of writ and the liberty, these are   380
the only men.
POLONIUS   O Jephthah, judge of Israel, what a treasure hadst thou!
POLONIUS   What a treasure had he, my lord?
HAMLET   Why,
> One fair daughter and no more,
> The which he lovèd passing well.

POLONIUS   *aside*   Still on my daughter.
HAMLET   Am I not i'the right, old Jephthah?
POLONIUS   If you call me Jephthah, my lord, I have a daughter
that I love passing well.   390
HAMLET   Nay, that follows not.
POLONIUS   What follows, then, my lord?
HAMLET   Why, *As by lot, God wot*, and then, you know,
It came to pass, as most like it was –
The first row of the pious chanson will show you more; for look,
where my abridgement comes.

Enter four or five PLAYERS

You are welcome, masters, welcome all. I am glad to see thee
well. Welcome, good friends. O, my old friend! thy face is
valanc'd since I saw thee last; com'st thou to beard me in
Denmark? What, my young lady and mistress! By'r lady, your   400
ladyship is nearer to heaven than when I saw you last, by the
altitude of a chopine. Pray God your voice, like a piece of
uncurrent gold, be not crack'd within the ring. Masters, you are
all welcome. We'll e'en to't like French falconers – fly at
anything we see. We'll have a speech straight. Come, give us a
taste of your quality; come, a passionate speech.
FIRST PLAYER   What speech, my lord?
HAMLET   I heard thee speak me a speech once, but it was never
acted; or, if it was, not above once; for the play, I remember,
pleas'd not the million. 'Twas caviare to the general; but it was –   410
as I receiv'd it, and others, whose judgments in such matters
cried in the top of mine – an excellent play, well digested in the
scenes, set down with as much modesty as cunning. I remember,
one said there were no sallets in the lines to make the matter
savoury, nor no matter in the phrase that might indict the author

of affectation; but called it an honest method, as wholesome
as sweet, and by very much more handsome than fine. One speech
in it I chiefly lov'd, 'twas Aeneas' tale to Dido, and thereabout
of it especially where he speaks of Priam's slaughter. If it live in
your memory, begin at this line: let me see, let me see –   420
The rugged Pyrrhus, like th'Hyrcanian beast –
it is not so – it begins with Pyrrhus –
The rugged Pyrrhus, he whose sable arms,
Black as his purpose, did the night resemble
When he lay couchèd in the ominous horse,
Hath now this dread and black complexion smear'd
With heraldry more dismal. Head to foot
Now is he total gules; horridly trick'd
With blood of fathers, mothers, daughters, sons,
Bak'd and impasted with the parching streets,   430
That lend a tyrannous and damnèd light
To their lord's murder: roasted in wrath and fire,
And thus o'er-sizèd with coagulate gore,
With eyes like carbuncles, the hellish Pyrrhus
Old grandsire Priam seeks.
So, proceed you.

POLONIUS 'Fore God, my lord, well spoken, with good accent
and good discretion.

FIRST PLAYER *Anon he finds him*
Striking too short at Greeks; his antique sword,   440
Rebellious to his arm, lies where it falls,
Repugnant to command. Unequal match'd,
Pyrrhus at Priam drives; in rage strikes wide;
But with the whiff and wind of his fell sword
The unnervèd father falls. Then senseless Ilium,
Seeming to feel this blow, with flaming top
Stoops to his base, and with a hideous crash
Takes prisoner Pyrrhus' ear. For lo! his sword,
Which was declining on the milky head
Of reverend Priam, seem'd i'the air to stick.   450
So, as a painted tyrant, Pyrrhus stood,
And like a neutral to his will and matter
Did nothing.

But as we often see against some storm
A silence in the heavens, the rack stand still,
The bold winds speechless and the orb below
As hush as death, anon the dreadful thunder
Doth rend the region; so, after Pyrrhus' pause,
Arousèd vengeance sets him new a-work;
And never did the Cyclops' hammers fall   460
On Mars's armour forg'd for proof eterne,
With less remorse than Pyrrhus' bleeding sword
Now falls on Priam.
Out, out, thou strumpet Fortune! All you gods
In general synod take away her power,
Break all the spokes and fellies from her wheel,
And bowl the round nave down the hill of heaven
As low as to the fiends!

POLONIUS This is too long.

HAMLET It shall to the barber's with your beard. Prithee,   470
say on: he's for a jig or a tale of bawdry, or he sleeps. Say on;
come to Hecuba.

FIRST PLAYER *But who, O, who had seen the mobl'd queen –*

HAMLET 'The mobl'd queen'?

POLONIUS That's good; 'mobl'd queen' is good.

FIRST PLAYER *Run barefoot up and down, threatening the flames*
With bisson rheum; a clout upon that head
Where late the diadem stood, and for a robe,
About her lank and all o'er-teemèd loins,
A blanket, in the alarm of fear caught up;   480
Who this had seen, with tongue in venom steep'd,
'Gainst Fortune's state would treason have pronounc'd.
But if the gods themselves did see her then
When she saw Pyrrhus make malicious sport
In mincing with his sword her husband's limbs,
The instant burst of clamour that she made,
Unless things mortal move them not at all,
Would have made milch the burning eyes of heaven,
And passion in the gods.

POLONIUS Look, whether he has not turned his colour and   490
has tears in's eyes. Pray you, no more.

HAMLET 'Tis well; I'll have thee speak out the rest soon. Good my lord, will you see the players well bestow'd? Do you hear, let them be well us'd; for they are the abstract and brief chronicles of the time. After your death you were better have a bad epitaph than their ill report while you live.

POLONIUS My lord, I will use them according to their desert.

HAMLET God's bodikins, man, much better. Use every man after his desert and who should 'scape whipping? Use them after your own honour and dignity: the less they deserve, the more merit is in your bounty. Take them in.   500

POLONIUS Come, sirs.

HAMLET Follow him, friends; we'll hear a play to-morrow.

Exit POLONIUS with all the PLAYERS but the First

Dost thou hear me, old friend; can you play *The Murder of Gonzago?*

FIRST PLAYER Ay, my lord.

HAMLET We'll ha't tomorrow night. You could, for a need, study a speech of some dozen or sixteen lines, which I would set down and insert in't, could you not?

FIRST PLAYER Ay, my lord.

HAMLET Very well. Follow that lord; and look you mock   510
him not.

Exit FIRST PLAYER

My good friends, I'll leave you till night. You are welcome to Elsinore.

ROSENCRANTZ Good my lord!

HAMLET Ay, so, God be wi'ye.

Exeunt ROSENCRANTZ and GUILDENSTERN

Now I am alone.
O, what a rogue and peasant slave am I!
Is it not monstrous that this player here,
But in a fiction, in a dream of passion,
Could force his soul so to his own conceit   520
That from her working all his visage wann'd,
Tears in his eyes, distraction in's aspect,
A broken voice, and his whole function suiting

With forms to his conceit? and all for nothing!
For Hecuba!
What's Hecuba to him, or he to Hecuba,
That he should weep for her? What would he do,
Had he the motive and the cue for passion
That I have? He would drown the stage with tears
And cleave the general ear with horrid speech,   530
Make mad the guilty and appal the free,
Confound the ignorant, and amaze indeed
The very faculties of eyes and ears.
Yet I,
A dull and muddy-mettl'd rascal, peak
Like John-a-dreams, unpregnant of my cause,
And can say nothing; no, not for a king,
Upon whose property and most dear life
A damn'd defeat was made. Am I a coward?
Who calls me villain? breaks my pate across?   540
Plucks off my beard and blows it in my face?
Tweaks me by the nose? gives me the lie i'the throat,
As deep as to the lungs? Who does me this?
Ha!
'Swounds, I should take it, for it cannot be
But I am pigeon-liver'd and lack gall
To make oppression bitter, or ere this
I should have fatted all the region kites
With this slave's offal. Bloody, bawdy villain!
Remorseless, treacherous, lecherous, kindless villain!   550
O vengeance!
Why, what an ass am I! This is most brave,
That I, the son of a dear father murder'd,
Prompted to my revenge by heaven and hell,
Must like a whore unpack my heart with words,
And fall a-cursing like a very drab,
A scullion!
Fie upon't! foh! About, my brain! I have heard
That guilty creatures sitting at a play
Have by the very cunning of the scene   560
Been struck so to the soul that presently

They have proclaim'd their malefactions;
For murder, though it have no tongue, will speak
With most miraculous organ. I'll have these players
Play something like the murder of my father
Before mine uncle; I'll observe his looks;
I'll tent him to the quick: if he but blench,
I know my course. The spirit that I have seen
May be the devil, and the devil hath power
To assume a pleasing shape; yea, and perhaps   570
Out of my weakness and my melancholy,
As he is very potent with such spirits,
Abuses me to damn me. I'll have grounds
More relative than this. The play's the thing
Wherein I'll catch the conscience of the king.

Exit

ACT III, SCENE 1

A room in the castle

Enter KING, QUEEN, POLONIUS, OPHELIA, ROSENCRANTZ and
GUILDENSTERN

KING   And can you, by no drift of circumstance,
Get from him why he puts on this confusion,
Grating so harshly all his days of quiet
With turbulent and dangerous lunacy?
ROSENCRANTZ   He does confess he feels himself distracted;
But from what cause he will by no means speak.
GUILDENSTERN   Nor do we find him forward to be sounded,
But, with a crafty madness, keeps aloof
When we would bring him on to some confession
Of his true state.
QUEEN   Did he receive you well?   10
ROSENCRANTZ   Most like a gentleman.
GUILDENSTERN   But with much forcing of his disposition.
ROSENCRANTZ   Niggard of question, but of our demands
Most free in his reply.
QUEEN   Did you assay him
To any pastime?
ROSENCRANTZ   Madam, it so fell out, that certain players
We o'er-raught on the way; of these we told him;
And there did seem in him a kind of joy
To hear of it. They are about the court,
And, as I think, they have already order   20
This night to play before him.
POLONIUS   'Tis most true;
And he beseech'd me to entreat your majesties
To hear and see the matter.
KING   With all my heart; and it doth much content me
To hear him so inclin'd.
Good gentlemen, give him a further edge,
And drive his purpose on to these delights.
ROSENCRANTZ   We shall, my lord.
Exeunt ROSENCRANTZ and GUILDENSTERN

KING   Sweet Gertrude, leave us too;   30
For we have closely sent for Hamlet hither,
That he, as 'twere by accident, may here
Affront Ophelia.
Her father and myself, lawful espials,
Will so bestow ourselves that, seeing unseen,
We may of their encounter frankly judge,
And gather by him, as he is behav'd,
If't be the affliction of his love or no
That thus he suffers for.
QUEEN   I shall obey you.
And for your part, Ophelia, I do wish
That your good beauties be the happy cause   40
Of Hamlet's wildness; so shall I hope your virtues
Will bring him to his wonted way again,
To both your honours.
OPHELIA   Madam, I wish it may.
Exit QUEEN
POLONIUS   Ophelia, walk you here. Gracious, so please you,
We will bestow ourselves.   *To OPHELIA*
                          Read on this book,
That show of such an exercise may colour
Your loneliness. We are oft to blame in this –
'Tis too much prov'd – that with devotion's visage
And pious action we do sugar o'er
The devil himself.
KING   *aside*   O, 'tis too true!   50
How smart a lash that speech doth give my conscience!
The harlot's cheek, beautied with plastering art,
Is not more ugly to the thing that helps it
Than is my deed to my most painted word.
O heavy burden!
POLONIUS   I hear him coming; let's withdraw, my lord.

Exeunt KING and POLONIUS.   Enter HAMLET

HAMLET   To be, or not to be, that is the question:
Whether 'tis nobler in the mind to suffer
The slings and arrows of outrageous fortune,

Or to take arms against a sea of troubles, 60
And by opposing end them. To die, to sleep –
No more – and by a sleep to say we end
The heart-ache and the thousand natural shocks
That flesh is heir to – 'tis a consummation
Devoutly to be wish'd. To die, to sleep –
To sleep, perchance to dream. Ay, there's the rub;
For in that sleep of death what dreams may come
When we have shuffl'd off this mortal coil
Must give us pause. There's the respect
That makes calamity of so long life; 70
For who would bear the whips and scorns of time,
The oppressor's wrong, the proud man's contumely,
The pangs of dispriz'd love, the law's delay,
The insolence of office and the spurns
That patient merit of the unworthy takes,
When he himself might his quietus make
With a bare bodkin? Who would fardels bear,
To grunt and sweat under a weary life,
But that the dread of something after death,
The undiscover'd country from whose bourn 80
No traveller returns, puzzles the will,
And makes us rather bear those ills we have
Than fly to others that we know not of?
Thus conscience does make cowards of us all;
And thus the native hue of resolution
Is sicklied o'er with the pale cast of thought,
And enterprises of great pith and moment
With this regard their currents turn awry,
And lose the name of action. Soft you now!
The fair Ophelia! Nymph, in thy orisons 90
Be all my sins remember'd.
OPHELIA   Good my lord,
How does your honour for this many a day?
HAMLET   I humbly thank you; well, well, well.
OPHELIA   My lord, I have remembrances of yours,
That I have longèd long to re-deliver;
I pray you, now receive them.

HAMLET   No, not I;
I never gave you aught.

OPHELIA   My honour'd lord, you know right well you did;
And, with them, words of so sweet breath compos'd
As made the things more rich. Their perfume lost,   100
Take these again; for to the noble mind
Rich gifts wax poor when givers prove unkind.
There, my lord.

HAMLET   Ha, ha! are you honest?

OPHELIA   My lord?

HAMLET   Are you fair?

OPHELIA   What means your lordship?

HAMLET   That if you be honest and fair, your honesty should
admit no discourse to your beauty.

OPHELIA   Could beauty, my lord, have better commerce than   110
with honesty?

HAMLET   Ay, truly; for the power of beauty will sooner
transform honesty from what it is to a bawd than the force of
honesty can translate beauty into his likeness. This was sometime
a paradox, but now the time gives it proof. I did love you once.

OPHELIA   Indeed, my lord, you made me believe so.

HAMLET   You should not have believ'd me; for virtue cannot so
inoculate our old stock but we shall relish of it. I lov'd you not.

OPHELIA   I was the more deceiv'd.

HAMLET   Get thee to a nunnery: why wouldst thou be a breeder   120
of sinners? I am myself indifferent honest; but yet I could accuse
me of such things that it were better my mother had not borne
me. I am very proud, revengeful, ambitious, with more offences
at my beck than I have thoughts to put them in, imagination to
give them shape, or time to act them in. What should such
fellows as I do crawling between earth and heaven? We are
arrant knaves, all; believe none of us. Go thy ways to a nunnery.
Where's your father?

OPHELIA   At home, my lord.

HAMLET   Let the doors be shut upon him, that he may play the   130
fool nowhere but in's own house. Farewell.

OPHELIA   O help him, you sweet heavens!

HAMLET   If thou dost marry, I'll give thee this plague for thy

dowry: be thou as chaste as ice, as pure as snow, thou shalt not
escape calumny. Get thee to a nunnery, go, farewell. Or, if thou
wilt needs marry, marry a fool; for wise men know well enough
what monsters you make of them. To a nunnery, go, and quickly
too. Farewell.

OPHELIA O heavenly powers, restore him!

HAMLET I have heard of your paintings too, well enough; God   140
has given you one face, and you make yourselves another. You
jig, you amble and you lisp, and nickname God's creatures, and
make your wantonness your ignorance. Go to, I'll no more on't;
it hath made me mad. I say, we will have no more marriages!
Those that are married already, all but one, shall live; the rest
shall keep as they are. To a nunnery, go!   *Exit*

OPHELIA O, what a noble mind is here o'erthrown!
The courtier's, soldier's, scholar's, eye, tongue, sword;
The expectancy and rose of the fair state,
The glass of fashion and the mould of form,   150
The observ'd of all observers, quite, quite down!
And I, of ladies most deject and wretched,
That suck'd the honey of his music vows,
Now see that noble and most sovereign reason,
Like sweet bells jangl'd, out of tune and harsh;
That unmatch'd form and feature of blown youth
Blasted with ecstasy. O, woe is me,
To have seen what I have seen, see what I see!

Re-enter KING and POLONIUS

KING Love! his affections do not that way tend;
Nor what he spake, though it lack'd form a little,   160
Was not like madness. There's something in his soul
O'er which his melancholy sits on brood;
And I do doubt the hatch and the disclose
Will be some danger; which for to prevent,
I have in quick determination
Thus set it down: he shall with speed to England,
For the demand of our neglected tribute.
Haply the seas and countries different
With variable objects shall expel

This something-settl'd matter in his heart,   170
Whereon his brains still beating puts him thus
From fashion of himself. What think you on't?
POLONIUS   It shall do well; but yet do I believe
The origin and commencement of his grief
Sprung from neglected love. How now, Ophelia!
You need not tell us what Lord Hamlet said;
We heard it all. My lord, do as you please;
But, if you hold it fit, after the play
Let his queen mother all alone entreat him
To show his grief: let her be round with him;   180
And I'll be plac'd, so please you, in the ear
Of all their conference. If she find him not,
To England send him, or confine him where
Your wisdom best shall think.
KING   It shall be so.
Madness in great ones must not unwatch'd go.

Exeunt

ACT III, SCENE 2

A hall in the castle

Enter HAMLET and Players

HAMLET Speak the speech, I pray you, as I pronounc'd it to you, trippingly on the tongue; but if you mouth it, as many of your players do, I had as lief the town-crier spoke my lines. Nor do not saw the air too much with your hand, thus, but use all gently; for in the very torrent, tempest, and, as I may say, the whirlwind of passion, you must acquire and beget a temperance that may give it smoothness. O, it offends me to the soul to hear a robustious periwig-pated fellow tear a passion to tatters, to very rags, to split the ears of the groundlings, who for the most part are capable of nothing but inexplicable dumbshows and noise. I would have such a fellow whipp'd for o'erdoing Termagant; it out-Herods Herod. Pray you avoid it. 10

FIRST PLAYER I warrant your honour.

HAMLET Be not too tame neither, but let your own discretion be your tutor; suit the action to the word, the word to the action, with this special observance, that you o'erstep not the modesty of nature. For anything so overdone is from the purpose of playing, whose end, both at the first and now, was and is to hold as 'twere the mirror up to nature; to show virtue her own feature, scorn her own image, and the very age and body of the time his form and pressure. Now this overdone, or come tardy off, though it make the unskilful laugh, cannot but make the judicious grieve; the censure of which one must in your allowance o'erweigh a whole theatre of others. O, there be players that I have seen play, and heard others praise, and that highly, not to speak it profanely, that, neither having the accent of Christians nor the gait of Christian, pagan, nor man, have so strutted and bellow'd that I have thought some of nature's journeymen had made men and not made them well, they imitated humanity so abominably. 20

FIRST PLAYER I hope we have reform'd that indifferently with us, sir. 30

HAMLET O, reform it altogether! And let those that play your clowns speak no more than is set down for them; for there be of

them that will themselves laugh, to set on some quantity of
barren spectators to laugh too; though in the meantime some
necessary question of the play be then to be consider'd. That's
villainous, and shows a most pitiful ambition in the fool that
uses it. Go, make you ready.

Exeunt Players
Enter POLONIUS, ROSENCRANTZ and GUILDENSTERN

How now, my lord! Will the king hear this piece of work?
POLONIUS   And the queen too, and that presently.   40
HAMLET   Bid the players make haste.   *Exit POLONIUS*
Will you two help to hasten them?
ROSENCRANTZ, GUILDENSTERN   We will, my lord.

Exeunt ROSENCRANTZ and GUILDENSTERN

HAMLET   What ho! Horatio!   *Enter HORATIO*
HORATIO   Here, sweet lord, at your service.
HAMLET   Horatio, thou art e'en as just a man
As e'er my conversation cop'd withal.
HORATIO   O my dear lord —
HAMLET   Nay, do not think I flatter;
For what advancement may I hope from thee
That no revenue hast but thy good spirits   50
To feed and clothe thee? Why should the poor be flatter'd?
No, let the candied tongue lick absurd pomp,
And crook the pregnant hinges of the knee,
Where thrift may follow fawning. Dost thou hear?
Since my dear soul was mistress of her choice
And could of men distinguish, her election
Hath seal'd thee for herself; for thou hast been
As one, in suffering all, that suffers nothing,
A man that fortune's buffets and rewards
Hast ta'en with equal thanks: and blest are those   60
Whose blood and judgment are so well commingl'd,
That they are not a pipe for fortune's finger
To sound what stop she please. Give me that man
That is not passion's slave, and I will wear him
In my heart's core, ay, in my heart of heart,

As I do thee. Something too much of this.
There is a play tonight before the king;
One scene of it comes near the circumstance
Which I have told thee of my father's death.
I prithee, when thou seest that act afoot,   70
Even with the very comment of thy soul
Observe mine uncle; if his occulted guilt
Do not itself unkennel in one speech,
It is a damnèd ghost that we have seen,
And my imaginations are as foul
As Vulcan's stithy. Give him heedful note;
For I mine eyes will rivet to his face,
And after we will both our judgments join
In censure of his seeming.
HORATIO   Well, my lord;
If he steal aught the whilst this play is playing,   80
And 'scape detecting, I will pay the theft.
HAMLET They are coming to the play; I must be idle:
Get you a place.

*Danish march. A flourish. Enter KING, QUEEN, POLONIUS,
OPHELIA, ROSENCRANTZ, GUILDENSTERN and others*

KING How fares our cousin Hamlet?
HAMLET Excellent, i'faith, of the chameleon's dish. I eat
the air, promise-cramm'd – you cannot feed capons so.
KING I have nothing with this answer, Hamlet; these
words are not mine.
HAMLET No, nor mine now. *To POLONIUS*
My lord, you play'd once i'the university, you say?   90
POLONIUS That did I, my lord, and was accounted a good
actor.
HAMLET What did you enact?
POLONIUS I did enact Julius Caesar: I was kill'd i'the Capitol;
Brutus kill'd me.
HAMLET It was a brute part of him to kill so capital a calf there.
Be the players ready?
ROSENCRANTZ Ay, my lord; they stay upon your patience.
QUEEN Come hither, my dear Hamlet, sit by me.

HAMLET   No, good mother, here's metal more attractive.   100
POLONIUS   *To KING*   O ho! do you mark that?
HAMLET   Lady, shall I lie in your lap?

Lying down at OPHELIA's feet

OPHELIA   No, my lord.
HAMLET   I mean, my head upon your lap?
OPHELIA   Ay, my lord.
HAMLET   Do you think I meant country matters?
OPHELIA   I think nothing, my lord.
HAMLET   That's a fair thought to lie between maids' legs.
OPHELIA   What is, my lord?
HAMLET   Nothing.   110
OPHELIA   You are merry, my lord.
HAMLET   Who, I?
OPHELIA   Ay, my lord.
HAMLET   O God, your only jig-maker. What should a man do
but be merry? for, look you, how cheerfully my mother looks,
and my father died within's two hours.
OPHELIA   Nay, 'tis twice two months, my lord.
HAMLET   So long? Nay then, let the devil wear black, for I'll
have a suit of sables. O heavens! die two months ago, and not
forgotten yet? Then there's hope a great man's memory may   120
outlive his life half a year; but, by'r lady, he must build churches
then, or else shall he suffer not thinking on, with the hobby-horse,
whose epitaph is 'For O, for O, the hobby-horse is forgot.'

Hautboys play. The dumb-show enters

*Enter a King and a Queen very lovingly; the Queen embracing him.
She kneels and makes show of protestation unto him. He takes her up
and declines his head upon her neck: lays him down upon a bank of
flowers: she, seeing him asleep, leaves him. Anon comes in a fellow,
takes off his crown, kisses it, and pours poison in the King's ears, and
exit. The Queen returns; finds the King dead and makes passionate
action. The Poisoner, with some two or three Mutes, comes in again,
seeming to lament with her. The dead body is carried away. The
Poisoner woos the Queen with gifts: she seems loath and unwilling
awhile, but in the end accepts his love.*

Exeunt

OPHELIA   What means this, my lord?

HAMLET   Marry, this is miching mallecho; it means mischief.

OPHELIA   Belike this show imports the argument of the play.

Enter PROLOGUE

HAMLET   We shall know by this fellow; the players cannot
keep counsel, they'll tell all.

OPHELIA   Will he tell us what this show meant?

HAMLET   Ay, or any show that you'll show him; be not you   130
asham'd to show, he'll not shame to tell you what it means.

OPHELIA   You are naught, you are naught. I'll mark the play.

PROLOGUE   For us, and for our tragedy,
Here stooping to your clemency,
We beg your hearing patiently.   *Exit*

HAMLET   Is this a prologue, or the posy of a ring?

OPHELIA   'Tis brief, my lord.

HAMLET   As woman's love.

Enter two Players, King and Queen

PLAYER KING   Full thirty times hath Phoebus' cart gone round
Neptune's salt wash and Tellus' orbèd ground,   140
And thirty dozen moons with borrow'd sheen
About the world have times twelve thirties been,
Since love our hearts and Hymen did our hands
Unite commutual in most sacred bands.

PLAYER QUEEN   So many journeys may the sun and moon
Make us again count o'er ere love be done!
But, woe is me, you are so sick of late,
So far from cheer and from your former state,
That I distrust you. Yet, though I distrust,
Discomfort you, my lord, it nothing must: 150
For women's fear and love holds quantity;
In neither aught, or in extremity.
Now what my love is, proof hath made you know;
And as my love is siz'd, my fear is so.
Where love is great, the littlest doubts are fear;
Where little fears grow great, great love grows there.

PLAYER KING   'Faith, I must leave thee, love, and shortly too;
My operant powers their functions leave to do:

And thou shalt live in this fair world behind,
Honour'd, belov'd; and haply one as kind   160
For husband shalt thou –
PLAYER QUEEN   O, confound the rest!
Such love must needs be treason in my breast –
In second husband let me be accurst!
None wed the second but who kill'd the first.
HAMLET *aside* Wormwood, wormwood.
PLAYER QUEEN   The instances that second marriage move
Are base respects of thrift, but none of love.
A second time I kill my husband dead
When second husband kisses me in bed.
PLAYER KING   I do believe you think what now you speak;   170
But what we do determine oft we break.
Purpose is but the slave to memory,
Of violent birth, but poor validity;
Which now, like fruit unripe, sticks on the tree;
But fall unshaken when they mellow be.
Most necessary 'tis that we forget
To pay ourselves what to ourselves is debt;
What to ourselves in passion we propose,
The passion ending, doth the purpose lose.
The violence of either grief or joy   180
Their own enactures with themselves destroy.
Where joy most revels, grief doth most lament;
Grief joys, joy grieves, on slender accident.
This world is not for aye, nor 'tis not strange
That even our loves should with our fortunes change;
For 'tis a question left us yet to prove
Whe'r love lead fortune, or else fortune love.
The great man down, you mark his favourite flies;
The poor advanc'd makes friends of enemies.
And hitherto doth love on fortune tend;   190
For who not needs shall never lack a friend,
And who in want a hollow friend doth try,
Directly seasons him his enemy.
But, orderly to end where I begun,
Our wills and fates do so contrary run

That our devices still are overthrown;
Our thoughts are ours, their ends none of our own.
So think thou wilt no second husband wed;
But die thy thoughts when thy first lord is dead.
PLAYER QUEEN Nor earth to me give food, nor heaven light, 200
Sport and repose lock from me day and night,
To desperation turn my trust and hope,
An anchor's cheer in prison be my scope!
Each opposite that blanks the face of joy
Meet what I would have well and it destroy!
Both here and hence pursue me lasting strife,
If, once a widow, ever I be wife!
HAMLET If she should break it now!
PLAYER KING 'Tis deeply sworn. Sweet, leave me here awhile;
My spirits grow dull, and fain I would beguile 210
The tedious day with sleep.   *Sleeps*
PLAYER QUEEN   Sleep rock thy brain,
And never come mischance between us twain!   *Exit*
HAMLET Madam, how like you this play?
QUEEN The lady doth protest too much, methinks.
HAMLET O, but she'll keep her word.
KING Have you heard the argument? Is there no offence in't?
HAMLET No, no, they do but jest, poison in jest; no offence
i'the world.
KING What do you call the play?
HAMLET *The Mouse-trap*. Marry, how? Tropically: this play is 220
the image of a murder done in Vienna. Gonzago is the duke's
name, his wife, Baptista: you shall see anon; 'tis a knavish piece
of work, but what of that? Your majesty and we that have free
souls, it touches us not; let the gallèd jade wince, our withers are
unwrung.

Enter LUCIANUS

This is one Lucianus, nephew to the king.
OPHELIA You are as good as a chorus, my lord.
HAMLET I could interpret between you and your love, if I
could see the puppets dallying.
OPHELIA You are keen, my lord, you are keen. 230

HAMLET   It would cost you a groaning to take off my edge.

OPHELIA   Still better, and worse.

HAMLET   So you must take your husbands. Begin, murderer;
pox, leave thy damnable faces, and begin. Come: 'The croaking
raven doth bellow for revenge.'

LUCIANUS   Thoughts black, hands apt, drugs fit,
                                                and time agreeing;
Confederate season, else no creature seeing;
Thou mixture rank, of midnight weeds collected,
With Hecate's ban thrice blasted, thrice infected,
Thy natural magic and dire property   240
On wholesome life usurp immediately.

Pours the poison into the sleeper's ears

HAMLET   He poisons him i'the garden for's estate. His name's
Gonzago; the story is extant, and writ in very choice Italian. You
shall see anon how the murderer gets the love of Gonzago's wife.

OPHELIA   The king rises.

HAMLET   What, frighted with false fire?

QUEEN   How fares my lord?

POLONIUS   Give o'er the play.

KING   Give me some light, away!

ALL   Lights, lights, lights!   250

Exeunt all but HAMLET and HORATIO

HAMLET   Why, let the stricken deer go weep,
                       The hart ungallèd play;
                 For some must watch, while some must sleep:
                       So runs the world away.
Would not this, sir, and a forest of feathers – if the rest of my
fortunes turn Turk with me – with two Provincial roses on my
raz'd shoes, get me a fellowship in a cry of players, sir?

HORATIO   Half a share.

HAMLET   A whole one, ay.

For thou dost know, O Damon dear,   260
       This realm dismantl'd was
Of Jove himself; and now reigns here
       A very, very – pajock.

HORATIO You might have rhym'd.

HAMLET O good Horatio, I'll take the ghost's word for a
thousand pound. Didst perceive?

HORATIO Very well, my lord.

HAMLET Upon the talk of the poisoning?

HORATIO I did very well note him.

HAMLET Aha! Come, some music! come, the recorders!   270
For if the king like not the comedy,
Why then, belike he likes it not, perdy.
Come, some music!

Re-enter ROSENCRANTZ and GUILDENSTERN

GUILDENSTERN Good my lord, vouchsafe me a word with you.

HAMLET Sir, a whole history.

GUILDENSTERN The king, sir –

HAMLET Ay, sir, what of him?

GUILDENSTERN Is in his retirement marvellous distemper'd.

HAMLET With drink, sir?

GUILDENSTERN No, my lord, rather with choler.   280

HAMLET Your wisdom should show itself more richer to signify
this to his doctor. For me to put him to his purgation would
perhaps plunge him into far more choler.

GUILDENSTERN Good my lord, put your discourse into some
frame, and start not so wildly from my affair.

HAMLET I am tame, sir: pronounce.

GUILDENSTERN The queen, your mother, in most great
affliction of spirit hath sent me to you.

HAMLET You are welcome.

GUILDENSTERN Nay, good my lord, this courtesy is not of the   290
right breed. If it shall please you to make me a wholesome answer,
I will do your mother's commandment; if not, your pardon and
my return shall be the end of my business.

HAMLET Sir, I cannot.

GUILDENSTERN What, my lord?

HAMLET Make you a wholesome answer; my wit's diseas'd: but
sir, such answer as I can make, you shall command; or rather, as
you say, my mother: therefore no more, but to the matter: my
mother, you say –

ROSENCRANTZ Then thus she says: your behaviour hath struck 300
her into amazement and admiration.
HAMLET O wonderful son, that can so astonish a mother! But is
there no sequel at the heels of this mother's admiration? Impart.
ROSENCRANTZ She desires to speak with you in her closet, ere
you go to bed.
HAMLET We shall obey, were she ten times our mother. Have
you any further trade with us?
ROSENCRANTZ My lord, you once did love me.
HAMLET So I do still, by these pickers and stealers.
ROSENCRANTZ Good my lord, what is your cause of distemper? 310
You do surely bar the door upon your own liberty, if you deny
your griefs to your friend.
HAMLET Sir, I lack advancement.
ROSENCRANTZ How can that be, when you have the voice of
the king himself for your succession in Denmark?
HAMLET Ay, but sir, 'While the grass grows' – the proverb is
something musty.   *Re-enter Players with recorders*
O, the recorders! let me see one. To withdraw with you: why do
you go about to recover the wind of me, as if you would drive me
into a toil?   320
GUILDENSTERN O, my lord, if my duty be too bold, my love is
too unmannerly.
HAMLET I do not well understand that. Will you play upon
this pipe?
GUILDENSTERN My lord, I cannot.
HAMLET I pray you.
GUILDENSTERN Believe me, I cannot.
HAMLET I do beseech you.
GUILDENSTERN I know no touch of it, my lord.
HAMLET 'Tis as easy as lying: govern these ventages with your 330
fingers and thumb, give it breath with your mouth, and it will
discourse most eloquent music. Look you, these are the stops.
GUILDENSTERN But these cannot I command to any utterance of
harmony; I have not the skill.
HAMLET Why, look you now, how unworthy a thing you make
of me! You would play upon me; you would seem to know my

stops; you would pluck out the heart of my mystery; you would
sound me from my lowest note to the top of my compass: and
there is much music, excellent voice, in this little organ; yet
cannot you make it speak. 'Sblood, do you think I am easier to be   340
play'd on than a pipe? Call me what instrument you will, though
you can fret me, yet you cannot play upon me.   *Enter POLONIUS*
God bless you, sir!

POLONIUS My lord, the queen would speak with you, and
presently.

HAMLET   Do you see yonder cloud that's almost in shape of
a camel?

POLONIUS   By the mass, and 'tis like a camel, indeed.

HAMLET   Methinks it is like a weasel.

POLONIUS   It is back'd like a weasel.   350

HAMLET   Or like a whale?

POLONIUS   Very like a whale.

HAMLET   Then I will come to my mother by and by.
aside   They fool me to the top of my bent.
                             – I will come by and by.

POLONIUS   I will say so.

HAMLET   'By and by' is easily said.   *Exit POLONIUS*
Leave me, friends.   *Exeunt all but HAMLET*
'Tis now the very witching time of night,
When churchyards yawn and hell itself breathes out   360
Contagion to this world. Now could I drink hot blood,
And do such bitter business as the day
Would quake to look on. Soft, now to my mother.
O heart, lose not thy nature; let not ever
The soul of Nero enter this firm bosom.
Let me be cruel, not unnatural –
I will speak daggers to her but use none;
My tongue and soul in this be hypocrites.
How in my words soever she be shent,
To give them seals never, my soul, consent!   370

Exit

ACT III, SCENE 3

A room in the castle

Enter KING, ROSENCRANTZ and GUILDENSTERN
KING I like him not, nor stands it safe with us
To let his madness range. Therefore prepare you;
I your commission will forthwith dispatch,
And he to England shall along with you.
The terms of our estate may not endure
Hazard so dangerous as doth hourly grow
Out of his lunacies.
GUILDENSTERN We will ourselves provide.
Most holy and religious fear it is
To keep those many many bodies safe
That live and feed upon your majesty.   10
ROSENCRANTZ The single and peculiar life is bound,
With all the strength and armour of the mind,
To keep itself from noyance; but much more
That spirit upon whose weal depend and rest
The lives of many. The cease of majesty
Dies not alone; but, like a gulf, doth draw
What's near it with it: it is a massy wheel,
Fix'd on the summit of the highest mount,
To whose huge spokes ten thousand lesser things
Are mortis'd and adjoin'd; which, when it falls,   20
Each small annexment, petty consequence,
Attends the boisterous ruin. Never alone
Did the king sigh, but with a general groan.
KING Arm you, I pray you, to this speedy voyage;
For we will fetters put upon this fear
Which now goes too free-footed.
ROSENCRANTZ, GUILDENSTERN We will haste us.

Exeunt ROSENCRANTZ and GUILDENSTERN Enter POLONIUS

POLONIUS My lord, he's going to his mother's closet;
Behind the arras I'll convey myself
To hear the process. I'll warrant she'll tax him home:

And, as you said, and wisely was it said,   30
'Tis meet that some more audience than a mother,
Since nature makes them partial, should o'erhear
The speech of vantage. Fare you well, my liege;
I'll call upon you ere you go to bed,
And tell you what I know.
KING   Thanks, dear my lord.   *Exit POLONIUS*
O, my offence is rank, it smells to heaven;
It hath the primal eldest curse upon't,
A brother's murder! Pray can I not,
Though inclination be as sharp as will:
My stronger guilt defeats my strong intent;   40
And like a man to double business bound,
I stand in pause where I shall first begin,
And both neglect. What if this cursèd hand
Were thicker than itself with brother's blood,
Is there not rain enough in the sweet heavens
To wash it white as snow? Whereto serves mercy
But to confront the visage of offence?
And what's in prayer but this two-fold force,
To be forestallèd ere we come to fall,
Or pardon'd being down? Then I'll look up;   50
My fault is past. But O, what form of prayer
Can serve my turn? 'Forgive me my foul murder'?
That cannot be, since I am still possess'd
Of those effects for which I did the murder,
My crown, mine own ambition and my queen.
May one be pardon'd and retain the offence?
In the corrupted currents of this world
Offence's gilded hand may shove by justice,
And oft 'tis seen the wicked prize itself
Buys out the law: but 'tis not so above;   60
There is no shuffling, there the action lies
In his true nature; and we ourselves compell'd,
Even to the teeth and forehead of our faults,
To give in evidence. What then? what rests?
Try what repentance can – what can it not? –
Yet what can it when one cannot repent?

O wretched state! O bosom black as death!
O limèd soul, that struggling to be free,
Art more engag'd! Help, angels, make assay.
Bow, stubborn knees, and heart with strings of steel,   70
Be soft as sinews of the new-born babe.
All may be well.   *Retires and kneels   Enter HAMLET*
HAMLET   Now might I do it pat, now he is praying;
And now I'll do't. And so he goes to heaven;
And so am I reveng'd. That would be scann'd:
A villain kills my father; and for that,
I, his sole son, do this same villain send
To heaven.
O this is hire and salary, not revenge.
He took my father grossly, full of bread,   80
With all his crimes broad blown, as flush as May;
And how his audit stands who knows save heaven?
But in our circumstance and course of thought,
'Tis heavy with him. And am I then reveng'd
To take him in the purging of his soul,
When he is fit and season'd for his passage?
No.
Up sword, and know thou a more horrid hent;
When he is drunk asleep, or in his rage,
Or in th'incestuous pleasure of his bed;   90
At gaming, swearing, or about some act
That has no relish of salvation in't.
Then trip him, that his heels may kick at heaven,
And that his soul may be as damn'd and black
As hell, whereto it goes. My mother stays;
This physic but prolongs thy sickly days.   *Exit*
KING *rising*   My words fly up, my thoughts remain below.
Words without thoughts never to heaven go.

Exit

ACT III, SCENE 4

The Queen's closet

Enter QUEEN and POLONIUS
POLONIUS   He will come straight; look you lay home to him.
Tell him his pranks have been too broad to bear with,
And that your grace hath screen'd and stood between
Much heat and him. I'll silence me e'en here.
Pray you, be round with him.
QUEEN   I'll warrant you,
Fear me not. Withdraw, I hear him coming.

POLONIUS hides behind the arras   Enter HAMLET

HAMLET   Now, mother, what's the matter?
QUEEN   Hamlet, thou hast thy father much offended.
HAMLET   Mother, you have my father much offended.
QUEEN   Come, come, you answer with an idle tongue.   10
HAMLET   Go, go, you question with a wicked tongue.
QUEEN   Why, how now, Hamlet!
HAMLET   What's the matter now?
QUEEN   Have you forgot me?
HAMLET   No, by the rood, not so:
You are the queen, your husband's brother's wife;
And – would it were not so! – you are my mother.
QUEEN   Nay, then, I'll set those to you that can speak.
HAMLET   Come, come, and sit you down; you shall not budge.
You go not till I set you up a glass
Where you may see the inmost part of you.
QUEEN   What wilt thou do? thou wilt not murder me?   20
Help, help, ho!
POLONIUS *behind*   What, ho! help, help, help!
HAMLET *drawing*   How now! a rat? Dead, for a ducat, dead!
Makes a pass through the arras
POLONIUS *behind*   O, I am slain!   *Falls and dies*
QUEEN   O me, what hast thou done?
HAMLET   Nay, I know not: is it the king?

QUEEN O, what a rash and bloody deed is this!
HAMLET A bloody deed! almost as bad, good mother,
As kill a king and marry with his brother.
QUEEN As kill a king!
HAMLET   Ay, lady, 'twas my word.   30

Lifts up the arras and discovers POLONIUS

Thou wretched, rash, intruding fool, farewell!
I took thee for thy better. Take thy fortune;
Thou find'st to be too busy is some danger.
Leave wringing of your hands: peace! sit you down,
And let me wring your heart; for so I shall,
If it be made of penetrable stuff,
If damnèd custom have not brass'd it so
That it is proof and bulwark against sense.
QUEEN What have I done, that thou dar'st wag thy tongue
In noise so rude against me?
HAMLET   Such an act   40
That blurs the grace and blush of modesty,
Calls virtue hypocrite, takes off the rose
From the fair forehead of an innocent love
And sets a blister there, makes marriage-vows
As false as dicers' oaths. O, such a deed
As from the body of contraction plucks
The very soul, and sweet religion makes
A rhapsody of words. Heaven's face doth glow;
Yea, this solidity and compound mass,
With tristful visage, as against the doom,   50
Is thought-sick at the act.
QUEEN   Ay me, what act,
That roars so loud, and thunders in the index?
HAMLET Look here, upon this picture, and on this –
The counterfeit presentment of two brothers.
See, what a grace was seated on this brow:
Hyperion's curls; the front of Jove himself;
An eye like Mars to threaten and command;
A station like the herald Mercury
New-lighted on a heaven-kissing hill;

A combination and a form indeed   60
Where every god did seem to set his seal,
To give the world assurance of a man.
This was your husband. Look you now, what follows:
Here is your husband, like a mildew'd ear
Blasting his wholesome brother. Have you eyes?
Could you on this fair mountain leave to feed
And batten on this moor? Ha! have you eyes?
You cannot call it love; for at your age
The heyday in the blood is tame, it's humble,
And waits upon the judgment: and what judgment   70
Would step from this to this? Sense, sure, you have,
Else could you not have motion; but sure that sense
Is apoplex'd; for madness would not err,
Nor sense to ecstasy was ne'er so thrall'd
But it reserved some quantity of choice
To serve in such a difference. What devil was't
That thus hath cozen'd you at hoodman-blind?
Eyes without feeling, feeling without sight,
Ears without hands or eyes, smelling sans all,
Or but a sickly part of one true sense   80
Could not so mope.
O shame! where is thy blush? Rebellious hell,
If thou canst mutine in a matron's bones,
To flaming youth let virtue be as wax,
And melt in her own fire. Proclaim no shame
When the compulsive ardour gives the charge,
Since frost itself as actively doth burn,
And reason pardons will.
QUEEN   O Hamlet, speak no more.
Thou turn'st mine eyes into my very soul,
And there I see such black and grainèd spots   90
As will not leave their tinct.
HAMLET   Nay, but to live
In the rank sweat of an enseamèd bed,
Stew'd in corruption, honeying and making love
Over the nasty sty –

QUEEN   O speak to me no more!
These words, like daggers, enter in mine ears.
No more, sweet Hamlet!
HAMLET   A murderer and a villain;
A slave that is not twentieth part the tithe
Of your precedent lord; a vice of kings;
A cutpurse of the empire and the rule,
That from a shelf the precious diadem stole,   100
And put it in his pocket –
QUEEN   No more!
HAMLET   A king of shreds and patches –   *Enter Ghost*
Save me and hover o'er me with your wings,
You heavenly guards! What would your gracious figure?
QUEEN   Alas! he's mad.
HAMLET   Do you not come your tardy son to chide,
That laps'd in time and passion, lets go by
The important acting of your dread command?
O, say!
GHOST   Do not forget. This visitation   110
Is but to whet thy almost blunted purpose.
But, look, amazement on thy mother sits –
O, step between her and her fighting soul.
Conceit in weakest bodies strongest works.
Speak to her, Hamlet.
HAMLET   How is it with you, lady?
QUEEN   Alas, how is't with you,
That you do bend your eye on vacancy
And with the incorporal air do hold discourse?
Forth at your eyes your spirits wildly peep;
And, as the sleeping soldiers in the alarm,   120
Your bedded hair, like life in excrements,
Starts up and stands on end. O gentle son,
Upon the heat and flame of thy distemper
Sprinkle cool patience. Whereon do you look?
HAMLET   On him, on him! Look you, how pale he glares!
His form and cause conjoin'd, preaching to stones
Would make them capable. Do not look upon me;
Lest with this piteous action you convert

My stern effects: then what I have to do
Will want true colour; tears perchance for blood.   130
QUEEN   To whom do you speak this?
HAMLET   Do you see nothing there?
QUEEN   Nothing at all; yet all that is I see.
HAMLET   Nor did you nothing hear?
QUEEN   No, nothing but ourselves.
HAMLET   Why, look you there! look, how it steals away!
My father, in his habit as he lived!
Look, where he goes, even now, out at the portal!   *Exit Ghost*
QUEEN   This is the very coinage of your brain.
This bodiless creation ecstasy   140
Is very cunning in.
HAMLET   Ecstasy!
My pulse, as yours, doth temperately keep time,
And makes as healthful music. It is not madness
That I have utter'd; bring me to the test,
And I the matter will re-word, which madness
Would gambol from. Mother, for love of grace,
Lay not that flattering unction to your soul,
That not your trespass, but my madness speaks.
It will but skin and film the ulcerous place,
Whilst rank corruption, mining all within,   150
Infects unseen. Confess yourself to heaven,
Repent what's past, avoid what is to come,
And do not spread the compost on the weeds
To make them ranker. Forgive me this my virtue;
For in the fatness of these pursy times
Virtue itself of vice must pardon beg,
Yea, curb and woo for leave to do him good.
QUEEN   O Hamlet, thou hast cleft my heart in twain!
HAMLET   O throw away the worser part of it,
And live the purer with the other half.   160
Good night: but go not to mine uncle's bed;
Assume a virtue, if you have it not.
That monster, custom, who all sense doth eat,
Of habits devil, is angel yet in this,
That to the use of actions fair and good

He likewise gives a frock or livery,
That aptly is put on. Refrain tonight,
And that shall lend a kind of easiness
To the next abstinence, the next more easy;
For use almost can change the stamp of nature,   170
And master e'en the devil or throw him out
With wondrous potency. Once more, good night;
And when you are desirous to be bless'd,
I'll blessing beg of you. For this same lord,   *pointing*
I do repent; but heaven hath pleas'd it so
To punish me with this and this with me,
That I must be their scourge and minister.
I will bestow him, and will answer well
The death I gave him. So again, good night.
I must be cruel only to be kind.   180
Thus bad begins and worse remains behind.
One word more, good lady.
QUEEN   What shall I do?
HAMLET   Not this, by no means, that I bid you do –
Let the bloat king tempt you again to bed;
Pinch wanton on your cheek; call you his mouse;
And let him, for a pair of reechy kisses,
Or paddling in your neck with his damn'd fingers,
Make you to ravel all this matter out,
That I essentially am not in madness,
But mad in craft. 'Twere good you let him know;   190
For who that's but a queen – fair, sober, wise –
Would from a paddock, from a bat, a gib,
Such dear concernings hide? who would do so?
No, in despite of sense and secrecy,
Unpeg the basket on the house's top,
Let the birds fly, and like the famous ape,
To try conclusions in the basket creep,
And break your own neck down.
QUEEN   Be thou assur'd, if words be made of breath,
And breath of life, I have no life to breathe   200
What thou hast said to me.
HAMLET   I must to England; you know that?

QUEEN   Alack,
I had forgot; 'tis so concluded on.
HAMLET   There's letters seal'd; and my two schoolfellows,
Whom I will trust as I will adders fang'd,
They bear the mandate; they must sweep my way,
And marshal me to knavery. Let it work:
For 'tis the sport to have the enginer
Hoist with his own petard; and't shall go hard
But I will delve one yard below their mines,   210
And blow them at the moon. O, 'tis most sweet
When in one line two crafts directly meet!
This man shall set me packing;
I'll lug the guts into the neighbour room.
Mother, good night. Indeed this counsellor
Is now most still, most secret and most grave,
Who was in life a foolish prating knave.
Come, sir, to draw toward an end with you.
Good night, mother.

Exeunt severally; HAMLET dragging in POLONIUS

ACT IV, SCENE 1

A room in the castle

Enter KING, QUEEN, ROSENCRANTZ and GUILDENSTERN
KING There's matter in these sighs, these profound heaves.
You must translate; 'tis fit we understand them.
Where is your son?
QUEEN Bestow this place on us a little while.

Exeunt ROSENCRANTZ and GUILDENSTERN

Ah, my good lord, what have I seen tonight!
KING What, Gertrude? How does Hamlet?
QUEEN Mad as the sea and wind, when both contend
Which is the mightier. In his lawless fit,
Behind the arras hearing something stir,
Whips out his rapier, cries, 'A rat, a rat!'   10
And in this brainish apprehension kills
The unseen good old man.
KING   O heavy deed!
It had been so with us had we been there.
His liberty is full of threats to all;
To you yourself, to us, to everyone.
Alas, how shall this bloody deed be answer'd?
It will be laid to us, whose providence
Should have kept short, restrain'd and out of haunt,
This mad young man. But so much was our love,
We would not understand what was most fit;   20
But like the owner of a foul disease,
To keep it from divulging, let it feed
Even on the pith of life. Where is he gone?
QUEEN To draw apart the body he hath kill'd;
O'er whom his very madness, like some ore
Among a mineral of metals base
Shows itself pure; he weeps for what is done.
KING O Gertrude, come away!
The sun no sooner shall the mountains touch
But we will ship him hence; and this vile deed   30

We must, with all our majesty and skill,
Both countenance and excuse. Ho, Guildenstern!

Re-enter ROSENCRANTZ and GUILDENSTERN

Friends both, go join you with some further aid:
Hamlet in madness hath Polonius slain,
And from his mother's closet hath he dragg'd him.
Go seek him out; speak fair, and bring the body
Into the chapel. I pray you, haste in this.

Exeunt ROSENCRANTZ and GUILDENSTERN

Come, Gertrude, we'll call up our wisest friends
And let them know, both what we mean to do,
And what's untimely done. So haply slander,   40
Whose whisper o'er the world's diameter
As level as the cannon to his blank
Transports his poison'd shot, may miss our name
And hit the woundless air. O come away!
My soul is full of discord and dismay.

Exeunt

ACT IV, SCENE 2

Another room in the castle

Enter HAMLET

HAMLET Safely stow'd.

ROSENCRANTZ, GUILDENSTERN Hamlet! Lord Hamlet!

HAMLET What noise? Who calls on Hamlet?
O, here they come.

Enter ROSENCRANTZ and GUILDENSTERN

ROSENCRANTZ What have you done, my lord, with the
dead body?

HAMLET Compounded it with dust, whereto 'tis kin.

ROSENCRANTZ Tell us where 'tis, that we may take it thence
And bear it to the chapel.

HAMLET Do not believe it.

ROSENCRANTZ Believe what?   10

HAMLET That I can keep your counsel and not mine own.
Besides, to be demanded of a sponge! what replication should be
made by the son of a king?

ROSENCRANTZ Take you me for a sponge, my lord?

HAMLET Ay, sir, that soaks up the king's countenance, his
rewards, his authorities. But such officers do the king best service
in the end: he keeps them, like an ape, in the corner of his jaw;
first mouth'd, to be last swallow'd. When he needs what you
have glean'd, it is but squeezing you, and, sponge, you shall be
dry again.   20

ROSENCRANTZ I understand you not, my lord.

HAMLET I am glad of it; a knavish speech sleeps in a foolish ear.

ROSENCRANTZ My lord, you must tell us where the body is, and
go with us to the king.

HAMLET The body is with the king, but the king is not with the
body. The king is a thing –

GUILDENSTERN A thing, my lord!

HAMLET Of nothing: bring me to him. Hide fox, and all after.

Exeunt

ACT IV, SCENE 3

Another room in the castle

Enter KING, attended
KING I have sent to seek him, and to find the body.
How dangerous is it that this man goes loose!
Yet must not we put the strong law on him:
He's lov'd of the distracted multitude,
Who like not in their judgment, but their eyes;
And where 'tis so, the offender's scourge is weigh'd,
But never the offence. To bear all smooth and even,
This sudden sending him away must seem
Deliberate pause. Diseases desperate grown
By desperate appliance are reliev'd,   10
Or not at all.   *Enter ROSENCRANTZ*
                    How now! what hath befall'n?
ROSENCRANTZ Where the dead body is bestow'd, my lord,
We cannot get from him.
KING   But where is he?
ROSENCRANTZ Without, my lord; guarded, to know
                              your pleasure.
KING Bring him before us.
ROSENCRANTZ Ho, Guildenstern! bring in my lord.

Enter HAMLET and GUILDENSTERN

KING Now Hamlet, where's Polonius?
HAMLET At supper.
KING At supper! where?
HAMLET Not where he eats, but where he is eaten; a certain   20
convocation of politic worms are e'en at him. Your worm is your
only emperor for diet; we fat all creatures else to fat us, and we
fat ourselves for maggots. Your fat king and your lean beggar
is but variable service, two dishes, but to one table: that's
the end.
KING Alas, alas!
HAMLET A man may fish with the worm that hath eat of a king,
and eat of the fish that hath fed of that worm.

KING   What dost thou mean by this?

HAMLET   Nothing, but to show you how a king may go a   30
progress through the guts of a beggar.

KING   Where is Polonius?

HAMLET   In heaven; send thither to see. If your messenger find
him not there, seek him i'the other place yourself. But indeed,
if you find him not within this month, you shall nose him as
you go up the stairs into the lobby.

KING   *to some attendants*   Go seek him there.

HAMLET   He will stay till you come.   *Exeunt Attendants*

KING   Hamlet, this deed, for thine especial safety,
Which we do tender, as we dearly grieve   40
For that which thou hast done, must send thee hence
With fiery quickness. Therefore prepare thyself;
The bark is ready, and the wind at help,
The associates tend, and everything is bent
For England.

HAMLET   For England!

KING   Ay, Hamlet.

HAMLET   Good.

KING   So is it, if thou knew'st our purposes.

HAMLET   I see a cherub that sees them. But come, for England!
Farewell, dear mother.

KING   Thy loving father, Hamlet.

HAMLET   My mother. Father and mother is man and wife; man   50
and wife is one flesh; and so, my mother. Come, for England! *Exit*

KING   Follow him at foot, tempt him with speed aboard,
Delay it not; I'll have him hence to-night.
Away! for everything is seal'd and done
That else leans on the affair. Pray you, make haste.

Exeunt ROSENCRANTZ and GUILDENSTERN

And England, if my love thou hold'st at aught,
As my great power thereof may give thee sense,
Since yet thy cicatrice looks raw and red
After the Danish sword, and thy free awe
Pays homage to us – thou mayst not coldly set   60
Our sovereign process, which imports at full,

By letters congruing to that effect,
The present death of Hamlet. Do it, England;
For like the hectic in my blood he rages,
And thou must cure me. Till I know 'tis done,
Howe'er my haps, my joys were ne'er begun.

Exit

ACT IV, SCENE 4

A plain in Denmark

Enter FORTINBRAS, a Captain, and Soldiers marching
FORTINBRAS   Go, captain, from me greet the Danish king;
Tell him that by his licence Fortinbras
Craves the conveyance of a promis'd march
Over his kingdom. You know the rendezvous.
If that his majesty would aught with us,
We shall express our duty in his eye;
And let him know so.
CAPTAIN   I will do't, my lord.
FORTINBRAS   Go softly on.

Exeunt FORTINBRAS and Soldiers
Enter HAMLET, ROSENCRANTZ, GUILDENSTERN and others

HAMLET   Good sir, whose powers are these?
CAPTAIN   They are of Norway, sir.   10
HAMLET   How purpos'd, sir, I pray you?
CAPTAIN   Against some part of Poland.
HAMLET   Who commands them, sir?
CAPTAIN   The nephew to old Norway, Fortinbras.
HAMLET   Goes it against the main of Poland, sir,
Or for some frontier?
CAPTAIN   Truly to speak, and with no addition,
We go to gain a little patch of ground
That hath in it no profit but the name.
To pay five ducats, five, I would not farm it;   20
Nor will it yield to Norway or the Pole
A ranker rate, should it be sold in fee.
HAMLET   Why, then the Polack never will defend it.
CAPTAIN   Yes, it is already garrison'd.
HAMLET   Two thousand souls and twenty thousand ducats
Will not debate the question of this straw.
This is th'impostume of much wealth and peace
That inward breaks, and shows no cause without
Why the man dies. I humbly thank you, sir.

CAPTAIN   God be wi'you, sir.   *Exit*
ROSENCRANTZ   Will't please you go, my lord?   30
HAMLET   I'll be with you straight. Go a little before.

Exeunt all except HAMLET

How all occasions do inform against me
And spur my dull revenge! What is a man,
If his chief good and market of his time
Be but to sleep and feed? a beast, no more.
Sure, he that made us with such large discourse,
Looking before and after, gave us not
That capability and god-like reason
To fust in us unus'd. Now whether it be
Bestial oblivion, or some craven scruple   40
Of thinking too precisely on the event,
A thought which, quarter'd, hath but one part wisdom
And ever three parts coward, I do not know
Why yet I live to say this thing's to do,
Sith I have cause and will and strength and means
To do't. Examples gross as earth exhort me:
Witness this army of such mass and charge
Led by a delicate and tender prince,
Whose spirit with divine ambition puff'd
Makes mouths at the invisible event,   50
Exposing what is mortal and unsure
To all that fortune, death and danger dare,
Even for an eggshell. Rightly to be great
Is not to stir without great argument,
But greatly to find quarrel in a straw
When honour's at the stake. How stand I then,
That have a father kill'd, a mother stain'd,
Excitements of my reason and my blood,
And let all sleep? while, to my shame, I see
The imminent death of twenty thousand men,   60
That for a fantasy and trick of fame
Go to their graves like beds, fight for a plot
Whereon the numbers cannot try the cause,
Which is not tomb enough and continent

To hide the slain. O, from this time forth,
My thoughts be bloody, or be nothing worth!

Exit

ACT IV, SCENE 5

Elsinore: a room in the castle

Enter QUEEN, HORATIO and a Gentleman

QUEEN   I will not speak with her.

GENTLEMAN   She is importunate, indeed distract;
Her mood will needs be pitied.

QUEEN   What would she have?

GENTLEMAN   She speaks much of her father; says she hears
There's tricks i'the world; and hems, and beats her heart;
Spurns enviously at straws; speaks things in doubt,
That carry but half sense. Her speech is nothing,
Yet the unshapèd use of it doth move
The hearers to collection; they aim at it,
And botch the words up fit to their own thoughts;   10
Which as her winks and nods and gestures yield them,
Indeed would make one think there might be thought,
Though nothing sure, yet much unhappily.
'Twere good she were spoken with; for she may strew
Dangerous conjectures in ill-breeding minds.

QUEEN   Let her come in.   *Exit GENTLEMAN*
To my sick soul, as sin's true nature is,
Each toy seems prologue to some great amiss.
So full of artless jealousy is guilt,
It spills itself in fearing to be spilt.   20

Re-enter GENTLEMAN with OPHELIA

OPHELIA   Where is the beauteous majesty of Denmark?

QUEEN   How now, Ophelia!

OPHELIA   *(sings)   How should I your true love know*
                    From another one?
                By his cockle hat and staff,
                    And his sandal shoon.

QUEEN   Alas, sweet lady, what imports this song?

OPHELIA   Say you? nay, pray you, mark.
(sings)   *He is dead and gone, lady,*
                    He is dead and gone;   30

> At his head a grass-green turf,
>> At his heels a stone.

QUEEN Nay, but, Ophelia –

OPHELIA Pray you, mark.

(sings)   White his shroud as the mountain snow –

Enter KING

QUEEN Alas, look here, my lord.

OPHELIA (sings)   Larded with sweet flowers,
>> Which bewept to the grave did go
>> With true-love showers.

KING How do you, pretty lady?   40

OPHELIA Well, God 'ild you! They say the owl was a baker's daughter. Lord, we know what we are, but know not what we may be. God be at your table!

KING Conceit upon her father.

OPHELIA Pray you, let's have no words of this; but when they ask you what it means, say you this.

(sings)   To-morrow is Saint Valentine's day,
>> All in the morning betime,
>> And I a maid at your window,
>> To be your Valentine.   50
>> Then up he rose, and donn'd his clothes,
>> And dupp'd the chamber-door –
>> Let in the maid, that out a maid
>> Never departed more.

KING Pretty Ophelia!

OPHELIA Indeed, la, without an oath, I'll make an end on't:

(sings)   By Gis and by Saint Charity,
>> Alack, and fie for shame!
>> Young men will do't, if they come to't;
>> By Cock they are to blame.   60
>> Quoth she, before you tumbl'd me,
>> You promis'd me to wed.
>> So would I ha' done, by yonder sun,
>> An thou hadst not come to my bed.

KING How long hath she been thus?

OPHELIA I hope all will be well. We must be patient, but I cannot choose but weep, to think they should lay him i'the cold

ground. My brother shall know of it – and so I thank you for
your good counsel. Come, my coach! Good night ladies, good
night sweet ladies, good night, good night.   *Exit*   70
KING   Follow her close; give her good watch, I pray you.

Exit GENTLEMAN

O, this is the poison of deep grief; it springs
All from her father's death. O Gertrude, Gertrude,
When sorrows come, they come not single spies
But in battalions. First her father slain;
Next your son gone; and he most violent author
Of his own just remove. The people muddied,
Thick and unwholesome in their thoughts and whispers,
For good Polonius' death; and we have done but greenly
In hugger-mugger to inter him. Poor Ophelia   80
Divided from herself and her fair judgment,
Without the which we are pictures, or mere beasts.
Last, and as much containing as all these,
Her brother is in secret come from France;
Feeds on his wonder, keeps himself in clouds,
And wants not buzzers to infect his ear
With pestilent speeches of his father's death;
Wherein necessity, of matter beggar'd,
Will nothing stick our person to arraign
In ear and ear. O my dear Gertrude, this,   90
Like to a murdering-piece, in many places
Gives me superfluous death.   *A noise within*
QUEEN   Alack, what noise is this?
KING   Where are my Switzers? Let them guard the door.

Enter another Gentleman

What is the matter?
GENTLEMAN   Save yourself, my lord;
The ocean, overpeering of his list,
Eats not the flats with more impetuous haste
Than young Laertes, in a riotous head,
O'erbears your officers. The rabble call him lord;
And, as the world were now but to begin,   100

Antiquity forgot, custom not known,
The ratifiers and props of every word,
They cry 'Choose we: Laertes shall be king!'
Caps, hands and tongues applaud it to the clouds –
'Laertes shall be king, Laertes king!'
QUEEN   How cheerfully on the false trail they cry!
O this is counter, you false Danish dogs!
KING   The doors are broke.   *Noise within*

Enter LAERTES, armed; Danes following

LAERTES   Where is this king? Sirs, stand you all without.
DANES   No, let's come in.
LAERTES   I pray you, give me leave.   110
DANES   We will, we will.   *They retire without the door*
LAERTES   I thank you, keep the door. O thou vile king,
Give me my father!
QUEEN   Calmly, good Laertes.
LAERTES   That drop of blood that's calm proclaims me bastard,
Cries cuckold to my father, brands the harlot
Even here, between the chaste unsmirchèd brow
Of my true mother.
KING   What is the cause, Laertes,
That thy rebellion looks so giant-like?
Let him go, Gertrude; do not fear our person.
There's such divinity doth hedge a king   120
That treason can but peep to what it would,
Acts little of his will. Tell me, Laertes,
Why thou art thus incens'd. Let him go, Gertrude.
Speak, man.
LAERTES   Where is my father?
KING   Dead.
QUEEN   But not by him.
KING   Let him demand his fill.
LAERTES   How came he dead? I'll not be juggl'd with.
To hell, allegiance! Vows, to the blackest devil!
Conscience and grace, to the profoundest pit!
I dare damnation. To this point I stand,   130
That both the worlds I give to negligence,

Let come what comes; only I'll be reveng'd
Most throughly for my father.
KING   Who shall stay you?
LAERTES   My will, not all the world;
And for my means, I'll husband them so well,
They shall go far with little.
KING   Good Laertes,
If you desire to know the certainty
Of your dear father's death – is't writ in your revenge,
That swoopstake you will draw both friend and foe,
Winner and loser?   140
LAERTES   None but his enemies.
KING   Will you know them then?
LAERTES   To his good friends thus wide I'll ope my arms;
And like the kind life-rendering pelican,
Repast them with my blood.
KING   Why, now you speak
Like a good child and a true gentleman.
That I am guiltless of your father's death,
And am most sensible in grief for it,
It shall as level to your judgment pierce
As day does to your eye.
DANES *within*   Let her come in.
LAERTES   How now! what noise is that?   150

Re-enter OPHELIA

O heat, dry up my brains! tears seven times salt,
Burn out the sense and virtue of mine eye!
By heaven, thy madness shall be paid by weight,
Till our scale turn the beam. O rose of May!
Dear maid, kind sister, sweet Ophelia!
O heavens! is't possible, a young maid's wits
Should be as mortal as an old man's life?
OPHELIA *(sings)*   *They bore him barefac'd on the bier,*
                     Hey non nonny, nonny, hey nonny,
                     And in his grave rain'd many a tear –   160
Fare you well, my dove!

LAERTES   Hadst thou thy wits, and didst persuade revenge,
It could not move thus.

OPHELIA   *(sings)*   *You must sing a-down a-down,*
                            An you call him a-down-a.

O, how the wheel becomes it! It is the false steward that stole
his master's daughter.

LAERTES   This nothing's more than matter.

OPHELIA   There's rosemary, that's for remembrance, pray,
love, remember; and there is pansies. that's for thoughts.   170

LAERTES   A document in madness, thoughts and
remembrance fitted.

OPHELIA   There's fennel for you, and columbines; there's rue
for you, and here's some for me: we may call it herb-grace
o'Sundays. O you must wear your rue with a difference. There's
a daisy. I would give you some violets, but they wither'd all
when my father died. They say he made a good end –

      (sings)   *For bonny sweet Robin is all my joy.*

LAERTES   Thought and affliction, passion, hell itself,
She turns to favour and to prettiness.   180

OPHELIA   *(sings)*   *And will he not come again?*
                          And will he not come again?
                             No, no, he is dead,
                             Go to thy death-bed,
                          He never will come again.
                          His beard was as white as snow,
                            All flaxen was his poll,
                             He is gone, he is gone,
                             And we cast away moan.
                          God ha' mercy on his soul!   190

And of all Christian souls, I pray God. God be wi'ye.   *Exit*

LAERTES   Do you see this, O God?

KING   Laertes, I must commune with your grief,
Or you deny me right. Go but apart,
Make choice of whom your wisest friends you will,
And they shall hear and judge 'twixt you and me.
If by direct or by collateral hand
They find us touch'd, we will our kingdom give,
Our crown, our life, and all that we call ours

To you in satisfaction; but if not,   200
Be you content to lend your patience to us,
And we shall jointly labour with your soul
To give it due content.
LAERTES   Let this be so.
His means of death, his obscure funeral –
No trophy, sword, nor hatchment o'er his bones,
No noble rite nor formal ostentation –
Cry to be heard, as 'twere from heaven to earth,
That I must call't in question.
KING   So you shall;
And where the offence is let the great axe fall.
I pray you, go with me.   210

Exeunt

ACT IV, SCENE 6

Another room in the castle

Enter HORATIO and a Servant
HORATIO What are they that would speak with me?
SERVANT Sailors, sir. They say they have letters for you.
HORATIO Let them come in.   *Exit Servant*
I do not know from what part of the world
I should be greeted, if not from Lord Hamlet. *Enter Sailors*
FIRST SAILOR God bless you, sir.
HORATIO   Let him bless thee too.
FIRST SAILOR He shall, sir, an't please him. There's a letter
for you, sir; it comes from the ambassador that was bound for
England; if your name be Horatio, as I am let to know it is.
HORATIO *(reads) Horatio, when thou shalt have overlook'd this,*   10
give these fellows some means to the king: they have letters for him. Ere
we were two days old at sea, a pirate of very warlike appointment gave
us chase. Finding ourselves too slow of sail, we put on a compell'd valour,
and in the grapple I boarded them; on the instant they got clear of our
ship, so I alone became their prisoner. They have dealt with me like
thieves of mercy, but they knew what they did; I am to do a good turn
for them. Let the king have the letters I have sent, and repair thou to
me with as much speed as thou wouldst fly death. I have words to speak
in thine ear will make thee dumb; yet are they much too light for the
bore of the matter. These good fellows will bring thee where I am.   20
Rosencrantz and Guildenstern hold their course for England: of them
I have much to tell thee. Farewell. He that thou knowest thine, Hamlet.
Come, I will make you way for these your letters;
And do't the speedier, that you may direct me
To him from whom you brought them.

Exeunt

ACT IV, SCENE 7

Another room in the castle

Enter KING and LAERTES

KING Now must your conscience my acquittance seal,
And you must put me in your heart for friend,
Sith you have heard, and with a knowing ear,
That he which hath your noble father slain
Pursued my life.

LAERTES   It well appears; but tell me
Why you proceeded not against these feats,
So crimeful and so capital in nature,
As by your safety, wisdom, all things else,
You mainly were stirr'd up.

KING   O, for two special reasons;
Which may to you, perhaps, seem much unsinew'd,   10
But yet to me they are strong. The queen his mother
Lives almost by his looks; and for myself –
My virtue or my plague, be it either which –
She's so conjunctive to my life and soul,
That as the star moves not but in his sphere,
I could not but by her. The other motive,
Why to a public count I might not go,
Is the great love the general gender bear him;
Who, dipping all his faults in their affection,
Would, like the spring that turneth wood to stone,   20
Convert his gyves to graces; so that my arrows,
Too slightly timber'd for so loud a wind,
Would have reverted to my bow again,
And not where I had aim'd them.

LAERTES   And so have I a noble father lost;
A sister driven into desperate terms,
Whose worth, if praises may go back again,
Stood challenger on mount of all the age
For her perfections. But my revenge will come.

KING Break not your sleeps for that; you must not think   30
That we are made of stuff so flat and dull

That we can let our beard be shook with danger
And think it pastime. You shortly shall hear more.
I lov'd your father, and we love ourself,
And that, I hope, will teach you to imagine –

Enter a Messenger

How now! what news?
MESSENGER   Letters, my lord, from Hamlet:
This to your majesty; this to the queen.
KING   From Hamlet! who brought them?
MESSENGER   Sailors, my lord, they say; I saw them not.
They were given me by Claudio; he receiv'd them   40
Of him that brought them.
KING   Laertes, you shall hear them.
Leave us.   *Exit Messenger*
(*reads*) *High and mighty, You shall know I am set naked on your*
kingdom. Tomorrow shall I beg leave to see your kingly eyes, when
I shall, first asking your pardon thereunto, recount the occasion of my
sudden and more strange return. Hamlet.
What should this mean? Are all the rest come back?
Or is it some abuse, and no such thing?
LAERTES   Know you the hand?
KING   'Tis Hamlet's character. 'Naked',
And in a postscript here, he says 'alone.'   50
Can you advise me?
LAERTES   I'm lost in it, my lord. But let him come.
It warms the very sickness in my heart,
That I shall live and tell him to his teeth,
'Thus diest thou.'
KING   If it be so, Laertes –
As how should it be so? how otherwise? –
Will you be rul'd by me?
LAERTES   Ay, my lord;
So you will not o'errule me to a peace.
KING   To thine own peace. If he be now return'd,
As checking at his voyage, and that he means   60
No more to undertake it, I will work him
To an exploit, now ripe in my device,

Under the which he shall not choose but fall.
And for his death no wind of blame shall breathe,
But even his mother shall uncharge the practice
And call it accident.
LAERTES   My lord, I will be rul'd;
The rather, if you could devise it so,
That I might be the organ.
KING   It falls right.
You have been talk'd of since your travel much,
And that in Hamlet's hearing, for a quality   70
Wherein, they say, you shine. Your sum of parts
Did not together pluck such envy from him
As did that one; and that, in my regard,
Of the unworthiest siege.
LAERTES What part is that, my lord?
KING A very riband in the cap of youth,
Yet needful too; for youth no less becomes
The light and careless livery that it wears
Than settl'd age his sables and his weeds,
Importing health and graveness. Two months since   80
Here was a gentleman of Normandy.
I've seen myself, and serv'd against the French,
And they can well on horseback; but this gallant
Had witchcraft in't; he grew unto his seat,
And to such wondrous doing brought his horse,
As he had been incorps'd and demi-natur'd
With the brave beast. So far he topp'd my thought
That I, in forgery of shapes and tricks,
Come short of what he did.
LAERTES   A Norman was't?
KING A Norman.   90
LAERTES Upon my life, Lamord!
KING   The very same.
LAERTES I know him well. He is the brooch indeed
And gem of all the nation.
KING He made confession of you,
And gave you such a masterly report
For art and exercise in your defence

And for your rapier most especially,
That he cried out, 'twould be a sight indeed
If one could match you; the scrimers of their nation,
He swore, had neither motion, guard, nor eye,   100
If you oppos'd them. Sir, this report of his
Did Hamlet so envenom with his envy
That he could nothing do but wish and beg
Your sudden coming o'er, to play with him.
Now, out of this —
LAERTES   What out of this, my lord?
KING Laertes, was your father dear to you?
Or are you like the painting of a sorrow,
A face without a heart?
LAERTES   Why ask you this?
KING Not that I think you did not love your father,
But that I know love is begun by time,   110
And that I see, in passages of proof,
Time qualifies the spark and fire of it.
There lives within the very flame of love
A kind of wick or snuff that will abate it;
And nothing is at a like goodness still,
For goodness, growing to a plurisy,
Dies in his own too-much. That we would do
We should do when we would; for this 'would' changes
And hath abatements and delays as many
As there are tongues, are hands, are accidents;   120
And then this 'should' is like a spendthrift sigh
That hurts by easing. But to the quick o'the ulcer —
Hamlet comes back: what would you undertake
To show yourself your father's son in deed
More than in words?
LAERTES   To cut his throat i'the church.
KING No place, indeed, should murder sanctuarize;
Revenge should have no bounds. But good Laertes,
Will you do this, keep close within your chamber.
Hamlet return'd shall know you are come home;
We'll put on those shall praise your excellence   130
And set a double varnish on the fame

The Frenchman gave you; bring you in fine together,
And wager on your heads. He, being remiss,
Most generous and free from all contriving,
Will not peruse the foils; so that with ease,
Or with a little shuffling, you may choose
A sword unbated, and in a pass of practice
Requite him for your father.
LAERTES   I will do't:
And, for that purpose, I'll anoint my sword.
I bought an unction of a mountebank,   140
So mortal that, but dip a knife in it,
Where it draws blood no cataplasm so rare,
Collected from all simples that have virtue
Under the moon, can save the thing from death
That is but scratch'd withal. I'll touch my point
With this contagion, that, if I gall him slightly,
It may be death.
KING   Let's further think of this;
Weigh what convenience both of time and means
May fit us to our shape. If this should fail,
And that our drift look through our bad performance,   150
'Twere better not assay'd; therefore this project
Should have a back or second, that might hold
If this should blast in proof. Soft! let me see:
We'll make a solemn wager on your cunnings –
I ha't!
When in your motion you are hot and dry –
As make your bouts more violent to that end –
And that he calls for drink, I'll have prepar'd him
A chalice for the nonce, whereon but sipping,
If he by chance escape your venom'd stuck,   160
Our purpose may hold there. But stay, what noise?

Enter QUEEN

How now, sweet queen!
QUEEN One woe doth tread upon another's heel,
So fast they follow. Your sister's drown'd, Laertes.
LAERTES Drown'd! O, where?
QUEEN There is a willow grows aslant a brook

That shows his hoar leaves in the glassy stream;
There with fantastic garlands did she come
Of crow-flowers, nettles, daisies, and long purples
That liberal shepherds give a grosser name,   170
But our cold maids do dead men's fingers call them.
There on the pendent boughs her coronet weeds
Clambering to hang, an envious sliver broke,
When down her weedy trophies and herself
Fell in the weeping brook. Her clothes spread wide;
And, mermaid-like, awhile they bore her up,
Which time she chanted snatches of old tunes,
As one incapable of her own distress,
Or like a creature native and indued
Unto that element. But long it could not be   180
Till that her garments, heavy with their drink,
Pull'd the poor wretch from her melodious lay
To muddy death.
LAERTES   Alas, then, she is drown'd?
QUEEN   Drown'd, drown'd.
LAERTES   Too much of water hast thou, poor Ophelia,
And therefore I forbid my tears. But yet
It is our trick; nature her custom holds,
Let shame say what it will. When these are gone
The woman will be out. Adieu my lord.
I have a speech of fire, that fain would blaze,   190
But that this folly douts it.   *Exit*
KING   Let's follow, Gertrude.
How much I had to do to calm his rage!
Now fear I this will give it start again.
Therefore let's follow.

Exeunt

ACT V, SCENE 1

A churchyard

Enter two Clowns (a Grave-digger and a Second Man)
FIRST CLOWN   Is she to be buried in Christian burial that
wilfully seeks her own salvation?
SECOND CLOWN   I tell thee she is, and therefore make her
grave straight; the crowner hath sat on her, and finds it
Christian burial.
FIRST CLOWN   How can that be, unless she drown'd herself
in her own defence?
SECOND CLOWN   Why, 'tis found so.
FIRST CLOWN   It must be *se offendendo*; it cannot be else. For
here lies the point. If I drown myself wittingly, it argues an act,   10
and an act hath three branches: it is, to act, to do, to perform.
Argal, she drown'd herself wittingly.
SECOND CLOWN   Nay, but hear you, goodman delver –
FIRST CLOWN   Give me leave. Here lies the water – good. Here
stands the man – good. If the man go to this water and drown
himself, it is, will he, nill he, he goes. Mark you that. But if the
water come to him and drown him, he drowns not himself. Argal,
he that is not guilty of his own death shortens not his own life.
SECOND CLOWN   But is this law?
FIRST CLOWN   Ay, marry is't, crowner's quest law.   20
SECOND CLOWN   Will you ha' the truth on't? If this had not
been a gentlewoman, she should have been buried out o'Christian
burial.
FIRST CLOWN   Why, there thou say'st; and the more pity that
great folk should have countenance in this world to drown or
hang themselves, more than their even-Christen. Come, my
spade. There is no ancient gentleman but gardeners, ditchers,
and grave-makers. They hold up Adam's profession.
SECOND CLOWN   Was he a gentleman?
FIRST CLOWN   He was the first that ever bore arms.   30
SECOND CLOWN   Why, he had none.
FIRST CLOWN   What, art a heathen? How dost thou understand
the Scripture? The Scripture says 'Adam digg'd'; could he dig

without arms? I'll put another question to thee: if thou answerest
me not to the purpose, confess thyself.
SECOND CLOWN   Go to.
FIRST CLOWN   What is he that builds stronger than either the
mason, the shipwright, or the carpenter?
SECOND CLOWN   The gallows-maker, for that frame outlives a
thousand tenants.   40
FIRST CLOWN   I like thy wit well, in good faith; the gallows
does well. But how does it well? It does well to those that do ill.
Now thou dost ill to say the gallows is built stronger than the
church: argal, the gallows may do well to thee. To't again, come.
SECOND CLOWN   'Who builds stronger than a mason, a
shipwright, or a carpenter?'
FIRST CLOWN   Ay, tell me that, and unyoke.
SECOND CLOWN   Marry, now I can tell.
FIRST CLOWN   To't.
SECOND CLOWN   Mass, I cannot tell.   50

Enter HAMLET and HORATIO at a distance

FIRST CLOWN   Cudgel thy brains no more about it, for your
dull ass will not mend his pace with beating; and, when you are
ask'd this question next, say a grave-maker. The houses that he
makes last till doomsday. Go, get thee to Yaughan; fetch me a
stoup of liquor.

Exit SECOND CLOWN.   FIRST CLOWN digs and sings

In youth, when I did love, did love,
  Methought it was very sweet,
To contract-a the time for-a my behove,
  O methought there was nothing meet.
HAMLET   Has this fellow no feeling of his business, that he   60
sings at grave-making?
HORATIO   Custom hath made it in him a property of easiness.
HAMLET   'Tis e'en so. The hand of little employment hath the
daintier sense.
FIRST CLOWN   *(sings)*
But age with his stealing steps
  Hath claw'd me in his clutch,

And hath shippèd me intil the land,
  As if I had never been such.   (*Throws up a skull*)
HAMLET   That skull had a tongue in it, and could sing once;
how the knave jowls it to the ground, as if it were Cain's   70
jaw-bone, that did the first murder! It might be the pate of a
politician, which this ass now o'er-reaches; one that would
circumvent God, might it not?
HORATIO   It might, my lord.
HAMLET   Or of a courtier; which could say 'Good morrow,
sweet lord! How dost thou, good lord?' This might be my Lord
Such-a-One, that praised my Lord Such-a-One's horse, when he
meant to beg it, might it not?
HORATIO   Ay, my lord.
HAMLET   Why, e'en so. And now my Lady Worm's – chapless,   80
and knocked about the mazzard with a sexton's spade: here's fine
revolution, an we had the trick to see't. Did these bones cost no
more the breeding, but to play at loggets with 'em? mine ache
to think on't.
FIRST CLOWN   (*sings*)
A pick-axe, and a spade, a spade,
  For and a shrouding sheet,
O, a pit of clay for to be made
  For such a guest is meet.   (*Throws up another skull*)
HAMLET   There's another! Why, may not that be the skull of a
lawyer? Where be his quiddities now, his quillets, his cases, his   90
tenures and his tricks? Why does he suffer this rude knave now
to knock him about the sconce with a dirty shovel, and will not
tell him of his action of battery? Hum! This fellow might be in's
time a great buyer of land, with his statutes, his recognizances,
his fines, his double vouchers, his recoveries. Is this the fine of
his fines, and the recovery of his recoveries, to have his fine pate
full of fine dirt? Will his vouchers vouch him no more of his
purchases, and double ones too, than the length and breadth of
a pair of indentures? The very conveyances of his lands will
hardly lie in this box; and must the inheritor himself have   100
no more, ha?
HORATIO   Not a jot more, my lord.
HAMLET   Is not parchment made of sheepskins?

HORATIO   Ay, my lord, and of calves' skins too.

HAMLET   They are sheep and calves which seek out assurance
in that. I will speak to this fellow. Whose grave's this, sirrah?

FIRST CLOWN   Mine, sir.   (sings)
O, a pit of clay for to be made
   For such a guest is meet.

HAMLET   I think it be thine, indeed; for thou liest in't.   110

FIRST CLOWN   You lie out on't, sir, and therefore it is not yours:
for my part, I do not lie in't, and yet it is mine.

HAMLET   Thou dost lie in't, to be in't and say it is thine: 'tis for
the dead, not for the quick; therefore thou liest.

FIRST CLOWN   'Tis a quick lie, sir; 'twill away again from me
to you.

HAMLET   What man dost thou dig it for?

FIRST CLOWN   For no man, sir.

HAMLET   What woman, then?

FIRST CLOWN   For none, neither.   120

HAMLET   Who is to be buried in't?

FIRST CLOWN   One that was a woman, sir; but rest her soul,
she's dead.

HAMLET   How absolute the knave is! we must speak by the card,
or equivocation will undo us. By the Lord, Horatio, these three
years I have taken a note of it: the age is grown so pick'd that the
toe of the peasant comes so near the heel of the courtier, he galls
his kibe. How long hast thou been a grave-maker?

FIRST CLOWN   Of all the days i'the year, I came to't that day
that our last King Hamlet overcame Fortinbras.   130

HAMLET   How long is that since?

FIRST CLOWN   Cannot you tell that? Every fool can tell that: it
was the very day that young Hamlet was born; he that is mad and
sent into England.

HAMLET   Ay, marry, why was he sent into England?

FIRST CLOWN   Why, because he was mad. He shall recover his
wits there; or if he do not, it's no great matter there.

HAMLET   Why?

FIRST CLOWN   'Twill not be seen in him there; there the men
are as mad as he.   140

HAMLET   How came he mad?

FIRST CLOWN   Very strangely, they say.

HAMLET   How strangely?

FIRST CLOWN   'Faith, e'en with losing his wits.

HAMLET   Upon what ground?

FIRST CLOWN   Why, here in Denmark. I have been sexton here, man and boy, thirty years.

HAMLET   How long will a man lie i'the earth ere he rot?

FIRST CLOWN   I'faith, if he be not rotten before he die – as we have many pocky corses nowadays, that will scarce hold the   150
laying in – he will last you some eight year or nine year. A tanner will last you nine year.

HAMLET   Why he more than another?

FIRST CLOWN   Why, sir, his hide is so tanned with his trade, that he will keep out water a great while; and your water is a sore decayer of your whoreson dead body. Here's a skull now; this skull has lain in the earth three and twenty years.

HAMLET   Whose was it?

FIRST CLOWN   A whoreson mad fellow's it was. Whose do you think it was?   160

HAMLET   Nay, I know not.

FIRST CLOWN   A pestilence on him for a mad rogue! 'A poured a flagon of Rhenish on my head once. This same skull, sir, was Yorick's skull, the king's jester.

HAMLET   This?

FIRST CLOWN   E'en that.

HAMLET   Let me see.   *takes the skull*
Alas, poor Yorick! I knew him, Horatio, a fellow of infinite jest, of most excellent fancy. He hath borne me on his back a thousand times; and now, how abhorrèd in my imagination it is!   170
my gorge rises at it. Here hung those lips that I have kiss'd I know not how oft. Where be your gibes now? your gambols? your songs? your flashes of merriment that were wont to set the table on a roar? Not one now, to mock your own grinning? quite chapfallen? Now get you to my lady's chamber, and tell her, let her paint an inch thick, to this favour she must come; make her laugh at that. Prithee, Horatio, tell me one thing.

HORATIO   What's that, my lord?

HAMLET   Dost thou think Alexander looked o'this fashion i'the
earth?   180
HORATIO   E'en so.
HAMLET   And smelt so? pah!   *puts down the skull*
HORATIO   E'en so, my lord.
HAMLET   To what base uses we may return, Horatio! Why may
not imagination trace the noble dust of Alexander, till he find it
stopping a bung-hole?
HORATIO   'Twere to consider too curiously, to consider so.
HAMLET   No, 'faith, not a jot. But to follow him thither with
modesty enough, and likelihood to lead it, as thus: Alexander
died, Alexander was buried, Alexander returneth into dust, the   190
dust is earth, of earth we make loam; and why of that loam,
whereto he was converted, might they not stop a beer-barrel?
Imperious Caesar, dead and turn'd to clay,
Might stop a hole to keep the wind away.
O, that that earth, which kept the world in awe,
Should patch a wall to expel the winter's flaw! –
But soft, but soft awhile, here comes the king,

Enter PRIEST & c. in procession; the Corpse of OPHELIA, LAERTES and
Mourners following; KING, QUEEN, their trains & c.

The queen, the courtiers. Who is this they follow?
And with such maimèd rites? This doth betoken
The corse they follow did with desperate hand   200
Fordo its own life; 'twas of some estate.
Couch we awhile and mark.   *retiring with HORATIO*
LAERTES   What ceremony else?
HAMLET   That is Laertes,
A very noble youth: mark.
LAERTES   What ceremony else?
PRIEST   Her obsequies have been as far enlarg'd
As we have warrantise. Her death was doubtful;
And but that great command o'ersways the order,
She should in ground unsanctified have lodg'd
Till the last trumpet. For charitable prayers,   210
Shards, flints and pebbles should be thrown on her;
Yet here she is allow'd her virgin crants,

Her maiden strewments, and the bringing home
Of bell and burial.
LAERTES   Must there no more be done?
PRIEST No more be done.
We should profane the service of the dead
To sing a requiem and such rest to her
As to peace-parted souls.
LAERTES   Lay her i'the earth,
And from her fair and unpolluted flesh
May violets spring! I tell thee, churlish priest,   220
A ministering angel shall my sister be
When thou liest howling.
HAMLET   What, the fair Ophelia!
QUEEN Sweets to the sweet. Farewell.   *scattering flowers*
I hop'd thou shouldst have been my Hamlet's wife.
I thought thy bride-bed to have deck'd, sweet maid,
And not have strew'd thy grave.
LAERTES   O, treble woe
Fall ten times treble on that cursèd head,
Whose wicked deed thy most ingenious sense
Depriv'd thee of! Hold off the earth awhile
Till I have caught her once more in mine arms.   230
Leaps into the grave
Now pile your dust upon the quick and dead
Till of this flat a mountain you have made,
To o'ertop old Pelion or the skyish head
Of blue Olympus.
HAMLET *advancing* What is he whose grief
Bears such an emphasis? whose phrase of sorrow
Conjures the wandering stars, and makes them stand
Like wonder-wounded hearers? This is I,
Hamlet the Dane.   *leaps into the grave*
LAERTES   The devil take thy soul! *grappling with him*
HAMLET Thou pray'st not well.
I prithee, take thy fingers from my throat;   240
For though I am not splenetive and rash,
Yet have I in me something dangerous,
Which let thy wiseness fear. Away thy hand!

KING   Pluck them asunder.
QUEEN   Hamlet, Hamlet!
ALL   Gentlemen!
HORATIO   Good my lord, be quiet.

The Attendants part them, and they come out of the grave

HAMLET   Why, I will fight with him upon this theme
Until my eyelids will no longer wag.
QUEEN   O my son, what theme?   250
HAMLET   I lov'd Ophelia. Forty thousand brothers
Could not, with all their quantity of love,
Make up my sum. What wilt thou do for her?
KING   O, he is mad, Laertes.
QUEEN   For love of God, forbear him.
HAMLET   'Swounds, show me what thou'lt do –
Woo't weep? woo't fight? woo't fast? woo't tear thyself?
Woo't drink up eisel? eat a crocodile?
I'll do't. Dost come here to whine?
To outface me with leaping in her grave?   260
Be buried quick with her, and so will I.
And if thou prate of mountains, let them throw
Millions of acres on us, till our ground,
Singeing his pate against the burning zone,
Make Ossa like a wart! Nay, an thou'lt mouth,
I'll rant as well as thou.
QUEEN   This is mere madness;
And thus awhile the fit will work on him.
Anon, as patient as the female dove
When that her golden couplets are disclos'd,
His silence will sit drooping.
HAMLET   Hear you, sir,   270
What is the reason that you use me thus?
I lov'd you ever; but it is no matter.
Let Hercules himself do what he may,
The cat will mew and dog will have his day.   *Exit*
KING   I pray you, good Horatio, wait upon him.

Exit HORATIO

to LAERTES
Strengthen your patience in our last night's speech;
We'll put the matter to the present push.
Good Gertrude, set some watch over your son.
This grave shall have a living monument.
An hour of quiet shortly shall we see;   280
Till then, in patience our proceeding be.

Exeunt

ACT V, SCENE 2

A hall in the castle

Enter HAMLET and HORATIO

HAMLET   So much for this, sir; now shall you see the other.
You do remember all the circumstance?
HORATIO   Remember it, my lord?
HAMLET   Sir, in my heart there was a kind of fighting
That would not let me sleep; methought I lay
Worse than the mutines in the bilboes. Rashly –
And praised be rashness for it; let us know
Our indiscretion sometimes serves us well
When our deep plots do pall: and that should teach us
There's a divinity that shapes our ends,   10
Rough-hew them how we will.
HORATIO   That is most certain.
HAMLET   Up from my cabin,
My sea-gown scarf'd about me, in the dark
Grop'd I to find out them; had my desire,
Finger'd their packet, and in fine withdrew
To mine own room again; making so bold,
My fears forgetting manners, to unseal
Their grand commission; where I found, Horatio –
O royal knavery! – an exact command,
Larded with many several sorts of reasons   20
Importing Denmark's health and England's too,
With ho! such bugs and goblins in my life,
That, on the supervise, no leisure bated,
No, not to stay the grinding of the axe,
My head should be struck off.
HORATIO   Is't possible?
HAMLET   Here's the commission; read it at more leisure.
But wilt thou hear me how I did proceed?
HORATIO   I beseech you.
HAMLET   Being thus be-netted round with villainies,
Ere I could make a prologue to my brains   30
They had begun the play. I sat me down,

Devis'd a new commission, wrote it fair –
I once did hold it, as our statists do,
A baseness to write fair and labour'd much
How to forget that learning, but, sir, now
It did me yeoman's service. Wilt thou know
The effect of what I wrote?
HORATIO   Ay, good my lord.
HAMLET   An earnest conjuration from the king,
As England was his faithful tributary,
As love between them like the palm might flourish,   40
As peace should still her wheaten garland wear
And stand a comma 'tween their amities,
And many such-like 'As's of great charge –
That on the view and knowing of these contents,
Without debatement further, more or less,
He should the bearers put to sudden death,
Not shriving-time allow'd.
HORATIO   How was this seal'd?
HAMLET   Why, even in that was heaven ordinant.
I had my father's signet in my purse,
Which was the model of that Danish seal;   50
Folded the writ up in form of the other,
Subscrib'd it, gave't the impression, plac'd it safely,
The changeling never known. Now the next day
Was our sea-fight; and what to this was sequent
Thou know'st already.
HORATIO   So Guildenstern and Rosencrantz go to't.
HAMLET   Why, man, they did make love to this employment.
They are not near my conscience; their defeat
Does by their own insinuation grow.
'Tis dangerous when the baser nature comes   60
Between the pass and fell incensèd points
Of mighty opposites.
HORATIO   Why, what a king is this!
HAMLET   Does it not, think'st thee, stand me now upon –
He that hath kill'd my king and whor'd my mother,
Popp'd in between the election and my hopes,
Thrown out his angle for my proper life,

And with such cozenage – is't not perfect conscience
To quit him with this arm? and is't not to be damn'd
To let this canker of our nature come
In further evil?   70
HORATIO   It must be shortly known to him from England
What is the issue of the business there.
HAMLET   It will be short. The interim is mine,
And a man's life's no more than to say 'One.'
But I am very sorry, good Horatio,
That to Laertes I forgot myself;
For by the image of my cause I see
The portraiture of his. I'll court his favours.
But sure, the bravery of his grief did put me
Into a towering passion.
HORATIO   Peace! who comes here?   80

Enter OSRIC

OSRIC   Your lordship is right welcome back to Denmark.
HAMLET   I humbly thank you, sir.
                    aside   Dost know this water-fly?
HORATIO   No, my good lord.
HAMLET   *aside*   Thy state is the more gracious; for 'tis a vice
to know him. He hath much land, and fertile; let a beast be
lord of beasts, and his crib shall stand at the king's mess.
'Tis a chough; but, as I say, spacious in the possession of dirt.
OSRIC   Sweet lord, if your lordship were at leisure, I
should impart a thing to you from his majesty.
HAMLET   I will receive it, sir, with all diligence of spirit. Put   90
your bonnet to his right use; 'tis for the head.
OSRIC   I thank your lordship; it is very hot.
HAMLET   No, believe me, 'tis very cold; the wind is
northerly.
OSRIC   It is indifferent cold, my lord, indeed.
HAMLET   But yet methinks it is very sultry and hot for my
complexion.
OSRIC   Exceedingly, my lord; it is very sultry, as 'twere, I cannot
tell how. But my lord, his majesty bade me signify to you that he
has laid a great wager on your head. Sir, this is the matter –   100

HAMLET I beseech you, remember –

HAMLET moves him to put on his hat

OSRIC Nay, good my lord; for mine ease, in good faith. Sir, here is newly come to court Laertes; believe me, an absolute gentleman, full of most excellent differences, of very soft society and great showing. Indeed, to speak feelingly of him, he is the card or calendar of gentry, for you shall find in him the continent of what part a gentleman would see.

HAMLET Sir, his definement suffers no perdition in you; though I know to divide him inventorially would dizzy the arithmetic of memory, and yet but yaw neither, in respect of his   110 quick sail. But in the verity of extolment, I take him to be a soul of great article; and his infusion of such dearth and rareness, as to make true diction of him, his semblable is his mirror; and who else would trace him, his umbrage, nothing more.

OSRIC Your lordship speaks most infallibly of him.

HAMLET The concernancy, sir? why do we wrap the gentleman in our more rawer breath?

OSRIC Sir?

HORATIO Is't not possible to understand in another tongue? You will do't, sir, really.   120

HAMLET What imports the nomination of this gentleman?

OSRIC Of Laertes?

HORATIO His purse is empty already; all's golden words are spent.

HAMLET Of him, sir.

OSRIC I know you are not ignorant –

HAMLET I would you did, sir; yet in faith, if you did, it would not much approve me. Well, sir?

OSRIC You are not ignorant of what excellence Laertes is –

HAMLET I dare not confess that, lest I should compare with   130 him in excellence; but to know a man well, were to know himself.

OSRIC I mean, sir, for his weapon; but in the imputation laid on him by them, in his meed he's unfellow'd.

HAMLET What's his weapon?

OSRIC Rapier and dagger.

HAMLET That's two of his weapons – but, well.

OSRIC The king, sir, hath wager'd with him six Barbary horses: against the which he has impon'd, as I take it, six French rapiers and poniards, with their assigns, as girdle, hangers and so. Three of the carriages, in faith, are very dear to fancy, very responsive   140
to the hilts, most delicate carriages, and of very liberal conceit.
HAMLET What call you the carriages?
HORATIO I knew you must be edified by the margin ere you had done.
OSRIC The carriages, sir, are the hangers.
HAMLET The phrase would be more germane to the matter if we could carry cannon by our sides; I would it might be hangers till then. But on: six Barbary horses against six French swords, their assigns, and three liberal-conceited carriages; that's the French bet against the Danish. Why is this 'impon'd', as you call it?   150
OSRIC The king, sir, hath laid, that in a dozen passes between yourself and him, he shall not exceed you three hits. He hath laid on twelve for nine; and it would come to immediate trial if your lordship would vouchsafe the answer.
HAMLET How if I answer no?
OSRIC I mean, my lord, the opposition of your person in trial.
HAMLET Sir, I will walk here in the hall. If it please his majesty, 'tis the breathing time of day with me. Let the foils be brought, the gentleman willing, and the king hold his purpose – I will win for him an I can. If not, I will gain nothing but my   160
shame and the odd hits.
OSRIC Shall I re-deliver you e'en so?
HAMLET To this effect, sir; after what flourish your nature will.
OSRIC I commend my duty to your lordship.
HAMLET Yours, yours.   *Exit OSRIC*
He does well to commend it himself; there are no tongues else for's turn.
HORATIO This lapwing runs away with the shell on his head.
HAMLET He did comply with his dug before he suck'd it. Thus has he, and many more of the same bevy that I know the drossy   170
age dotes on, only got the tune of the time and outward habit of encounter; a kind of yesty collection, which carries them through and through the most fann'd and winnow'd opinions; and do but blow them to their trial, the bubbles are out. *Enter a LORD*

LORD My lord, his majesty commended him to you by young
Osric, who brings back to him that you attend him in the hall.
He sends to know if your pleasure hold to play with Laertes, or
that you will take longer time.

HAMLET I am constant to my purposes; they follow the king's
pleasure. If his fitness speaks, mine is ready, now or whensoever,   180
provided I be so able as now.

LORD The king and queen and all are coming down.

HAMLET In happy time.

LORD The queen desires you to use some gentle entertainment
to Laertes before you fall to play.

HAMLET She well instructs me.   *Exit LORD*

HORATIO You will lose this wager, my lord.

HAMLET I do not think so. Since he went into France I have
been in continual practice; I shall win at the odds. But thou
wouldst not think how ill all's here about my heart; but it is   190
no matter.

HORATIO Nay, good my lord –

HAMLET It is but foolery; but it is such a kind of gain-giving
as would perhaps trouble a woman.

HORATIO If your mind dislike anything, obey it. I will
forestall their repair hither and say you are not fit.

HAMLET Not a whit, we defy augury; there's a special
providence in the fall of a sparrow. If it be now, 'tis not to come;
if it be not to come, it will be now; if it be not now, yet it will
come: the readiness is all. Since no man has aught of what he   200
leaves, what is't to leave betimes? Let be.

*Enter KING CLAUDIUS, QUEEN GERTRUDE, LAERTES, Lords,
OSRIC and Attendants with foils, & c.*

KING Come, Hamlet, come, and take this hand from me.

KING puts LAERTES' hand into HAMLET's

HAMLET Give me your pardon, sir; I've done you wrong,
But pardon't, as you are a gentleman.
This presence knows,
And you must needs have heard, how I am punish'd
With sore distraction. What I have done

That might your nature, honour and exception
Roughly awake, I here proclaim was madness.
Was't Hamlet wrong'd Laertes? Never Hamlet. 210
If Hamlet from himself be ta'en away,
And when he's not himself does wrong Laertes,
Then Hamlet does it not, Hamlet denies it.
Who does it then? His madness. If't be so,
Hamlet is of the faction that is wrong'd;
His madness is poor Hamlet's enemy.
Sir, in this audience,
Let my disclaiming from a purpos'd evil
Free me so far in your most generous thoughts,
That I have shot mine arrow o'er the house 220
And hurt my brother.
LAERTES   I am satisfied in nature,
Whose motive, in this case, should stir me most
To my revenge; but in my terms of honour
I stand aloof, and will no reconcilement,
Till by some elder masters, of known honour,
I have a voice and precedent of peace,
To keep my name ungor'd. But till that time
I do receive your offer'd love like love,
And will not wrong it.
HAMLET   I embrace it freely,
And will this brother's wager frankly play. 230
Give us the foils. Come on.
LAERTES   Come, one for me.
HAMLET   I'll be your foil, Laertes; in mine ignorance
Your skill shall, like a star i'the darkest night,
Stick fiery off indeed.
LAERTES   You mock me, sir.
HAMLET   No, by this hand.
KING   Give them the foils, young Osric. Cousin Hamlet,
You know the wager?
HAMLET   Very well, my lord;
Your grace hath laid the odds o'the weaker side.
KING   I do not fear it. I have seen you both;
But since he is better'd we have therefore odds. 240

LAERTES   This is too heavy; let me see another.

HAMLET   This likes me well. These foils have all a length?

OSRIC   Ay, my good lord.

They prepare to play

KING   Set me the stoups of wine upon that table.
If Hamlet give the first or second hit,
Or quit in answer of the third exchange,
Let all the battlements their ordnance fire.
The king shall drink to Hamlet's better breath;
And in the cup an union shall he throw
Richer than that which four successive kings   250
In Denmark's crown have worn. Give me the cups;
And let the kettle to the trumpet speak,
The trumpet to the cannoneer without,
The cannons to the heavens, the heavens to earth.

Trumpets the while

Now the king drinks to Hamlet! Come, begin;
And you, the judges, bear a wary eye.

HAMLET   Come on, sir.

LAERTES   Come, my lord.   *They play*

HAMLET   One.

LAERTES   No.

HAMLET   Judgment.

OSRIC   A hit, a very palpable hit.

LAERTES   Well; again.

KING   Stay, give me drink. Hamlet, this pearl is thine.
Here's to thy health!

Trumpets sound, and cannon shot off within

                        Give him the cup.   260

HAMLET   I'll play this bout first; set it by awhile.
Come.

They play

Another hit; what say you?

LAERTES   A touch, a touch, I do confess.

KING   Our son shall win.

QUEEN He's fat, and scant of breath.
Here, Hamlet, take my napkin, rub thy brows;
The queen carouses to thy fortune, Hamlet.
HAMLET Good madam!
KING Gertrude, do not drink.
QUEEN I will, my lord; I pray you, pardon me.
KING *aside* It is the poison'd cup! it is too late. 270
HAMLET I dare not drink yet, madam; by and by.
QUEEN Come, let me wipe thy face.
LAERTES My lord, I'll hit him now.
KING I do not think't.
LAERTES *aside* And yet 'tis almost 'gainst my conscience.
HAMLET Come for the third, Laertes; you but dally.
I pray you, pass with your best violence;
I am afear'd you make a wanton of me.
LAERTES Say you so? come on. *They play*
OSRIC Nothing, neither way.
LAERTES Have at you now! 280

LAERTES wounds HAMLET; then in scuffling, they change rapiers, and
HAMLET wounds LAERTES

KING Part them! They are incens'd.
HAMLET Nay, come, again. *QUEEN falls*
OSRIC Look to the queen there, ho!
HORATIO They bleed on both sides. How is it, my lord?
OSRIC How is't, Laertes?
LAERTES Why, as a woodcock to mine own springe, Osric;
I am justly kill'd with mine own treachery.
HAMLET How does the queen?
KING She swounds to see them bleed.
QUEEN No, no, the drink, the drink – O my dear Hamlet!
The drink, the drink! I am poison'd. *Dies*
HAMLET O villainy, ho! Let the door be lock'd! 290
Treachery! Seek it out.
LAERTES It is here, Hamlet. Hamlet, thou art slain.
No medicine in the world can do thee good;
In thee there is not half an hour of life.
The treacherous instrument is in thy hand,

Unbated and envenom'd; the foul practice
Hath turn'd itself on me. Lo, here I lie,
Never to rise again. Thy mother's poison'd –
I can no more – the king, the king's to blame.
HAMLET The point envenom'd too!   300
Then, venom, to thy work.   *Stabs KING*
ALL   Treason! treason!
KING   O yet defend me, friends, I am but hurt.
HAMLET   Here, thou damn'd, incestuous, murd'rous Dane,
Drink off this potion! Is thy union here?
Follow my mother.   *KING dies*
LAERTES   He is justly serv'd;
It is a poison temper'd by himself.
Exchange forgiveness with me, noble Hamlet;
Mine and my father's death come not upon thee,
Nor thine on me.   *Dies*
HAMLET   Heaven make thee free of it! I follow thee.   310
I am dead, Horatio. Wretched queen, adieu!
You that look pale and tremble at this chance,
That are but mutes or audience to this act,
Had I but time – as this fell sergeant, death
Is strict in his arrest – O, I could tell you –
But let it be. Horatio, I am dead;
Thou livest; report me and my cause aright
To the unsatisfied.
HORATIO   Never believe it.
I am more an antique Roman than a Dane –
Here's yet some liquor left.
HAMLET   As thou'rt a man,   320
Give me the cup: let go; by heaven, I'll have't!
O good Horatio, what a wounded name,
Things standing thus unknown, shall live behind me!
If thou didst ever hold me in thy heart,
Absent thee from felicity awhile,
And in this harsh world draw thy breath in pain
To tell my story.

March afar off, and shot within

What warlike noise is this?

OSRIC   Young Fortinbras, with conquest come from Poland,
To the ambassadors of England gives
This warlike volley.
HAMLET   O, I die, Horatio;   330
The potent poison quite o'er-crows my spirit.
I cannot live to hear the news from England;
But I do prophesy the election lights
On Fortinbras: he has my dying voice.
So tell him, with the occurrents, more and less,
Which have solicited – the rest is silence.   *Dies*
HORATIO   Now cracks a noble heart. Good night sweet prince,
And flights of angels sing thee to thy rest.
Why does the drum come hither?   *March within*

Enter FORTINBRAS, the English Ambassadors, and others

FORTINBRAS   Where is this sight?
HORATIO   What is it ye would see?   340
If aught of woe or wonder, cease your search.
FORTINBRAS   This quarry cries on havoc. O proud death,
What feast is toward in thine eternal cell,
That thou so many princes at a shot
So bloodily hast struck?
FIRST AMBASSADOR   The sight is dismal;
And our affairs from England come too late.
The ears are senseless that should give us hearing,
To tell him his commandment is fulfill'd,
That Rosencrantz and Guildenstern are dead.
Where should we have our thanks?
HORATIO   Not from his mouth,   350
Had it the ability of life to thank you;
He never gave commandment for their death.
But since, so jump upon this bloody question,
You from the Polack wars – and you from England –
Are here arriv'd, give order that these bodies
High on a stage be placèd to the view;

And let me speak to the yet unknowing world
How these things came about. So shall you hear
Of carnal, bloody and unnatural acts,
Of accidental judgments, casual slaughters,   360
Of deaths put on by cunning and forc'd cause,
And, in this upshot, purposes mistook
Fall'n on the inventors' heads. All this can I
Truly deliver.
FORTINBRAS   Let us haste to hear it,
And call the noblest to the audience.
For me, with sorrow I embrace my fortune.
I have some rights of memory in this kingdom,
Which now to claim my vantage doth invite me.
HORATIO   Of that I shall have also cause to speak,
And from his mouth whose voice will draw on more.   370
But let this same be presently perform'd,
Even while men's minds are wild; lest more mischance
On plots and errors happen.
FORTINBRAS   Let four captains
Bear Hamlet, like a soldier, to the stage;
For he was likely, had he been put on,
To have prov'd most royally; and, for his passage,
The soldiers' music and the rites of war
Speak loudly for him.
Take up the bodies. Such a sight as this
Becomes the field, but here shows much amiss.   380
Go, bid the soldiers shoot.

A dead march. Exeunt, bearing off the dead bodies;
after which a peal of ordnance is shot off.

Commentary and Cross-References to the Play for Each Scene

I, 1

Deep night. As one guard relieves another a note of alarm and uncertainty is sounded, and something more. 'Who's there?' 'Nay, answer me: stand, and unfold yourself.' An innocent opening breathes the hint of a metaphor for the play: one of indistinct vision, and the discovery or unfolding of a character. Here Barnardo and Francisco are at once at ease with each other, and with Marcellus and Horatio as they arrive. But under the surface a signal is set, with a number to come. Francisco's comment as he prepares to leave is blunt enough: 'For this relief much thanks: 'tis bitter cold, / And I am sick at heart.' At the same time it may be poetically telling. A felt implication can stretch to Denmark itself. While the idea of a stricken nation in dire need of relief occupies no dramatic space at all in the here-and-now, there is always a part of the spectator's mind open to what may be termed a gestural reference. On first hearing it is as nothing; later on the words may or may not be recalled; and a deeper acquaintance with the play can trigger a further resonance. By such signals a certain groundwork is laid, allowing for a deeper experience overall. It appears to be created half accidentally, the characters' words at times reflecting preoccupations – nothing so strong as themes – in the author's mind. The ambiguities of poetry are present also on stage: every play-script is a poem to an extent, the boards reverberating now and then to a rarer frequency. The direct charge and force imparted by the deployment of a poetic form to drama – in English the blank-verse pentameter – is another matter, to be alluded to later.

The play's the thing. We are primarily concerned with what happens on stage that can be heard and seen. The present enterprise is no more than a subjective attempt to realise and re-present what it is, in the main, that in *Hamlet* we hear and see.

'Thou art a scholar; speak to it, Horatio.' The line takes us out of our own time and back to Shakespeare's. It seems we are to see Horatio (to be revealed as a fellow-student of Hamlet's at Wittenburg) as something of an outsider. While he appears well-known to the guards, and is able to sum up the current situation in Denmark, later Hamlet has to tell him who Laertes is; and it may be that Shakespeare is deliberately unclear as to his background. He remembers the old king's armour from one occasion, his frown from another; though in the next scene he seems to indicate he saw him once only. Horatio is both within the audience's reach and out of it, an enigmatic being whose part is in a sense overtaken by another's. Before we see him with the prince (as always later), we meet a perceptive and learned figure, who with a passionate bravery challenges the Ghost to speak (128f). After this, still and always a vivid character, and of a constant interest in its own right, his part is cast within Hamlet's shadow.

After the nervy staccato dialogue of the opening has more or less settled into a discourse of even pentameter, the Ghost's entry sets the pulse racing. Horatio's name is used almost as a talisman by the guards as they call on him to speak to it, mark it, question it. His challenge rings out; it is gone. At its re-entry Horatio offers up a prayer of startling power, the short end-stopped phrases hammering home the central request; but the cock crows and again it is gone. The nerve-jangling moments of verse that precede and twice interrupt a discursive flow testify to the vulnerable state of the three humans, who await and are visited by an otherworldly presence. It may be malign: Horatio instinctively names it an 'illusion'; yet once it is gone, the group is quickly enough at ease. A Shakespearean audience would have been less removed from the situation than a modern one. One may take Horatio's description of Rome before the death of Julius Caesar as breathing the aura of factual truth, following his hard-headed sketch of the current Danish national crisis; and similarly his acceptance of the supernatural power of the cock-crow ('I . . . do in part believe it') would encourage the theatrical events to be taken at face value. But the men are soon enough comfortable together; and after the reassuring appearance of early morning in its innocence ('But look, the morn in russet mantle clad / Walks o'er the dew of yon high eastern hill'), the responsibility for further action is to be passed to 'young Hamlet'. So the first scene invites the audience to an emerging imaginative world.

Other lines and phrases signal a thematic intent beyond the immediate effect; each student of the text will have his or her own list. The intent may be said to be of the authorial hand, though in no more than a half-deliberate way; and indeed the full intent of such a hand belongs as much to the notional sum of readings in time, as to the single hand that drove the quill. 'It harrows me with fear and wonder', shivers Horatio on first seeing the Ghost, a riveting instant in itself, with a ripple effect such as to intimate something of the play's atmosphere. Fleetingly the mind may be aware of a complex weather-front of emotions, perhaps to strike again and again with a thunderbolt immediacy. 'Is not this something more than fantasy?' asks Barnardo, the words foreshadowing a battle of the mind on the part both of a number of the characters, and of the audience, to distinguish between what is and what is not. 'This bodes some strange eruption to our state,' surmises Horatio, little knowing his friend is to be the instrument of the nation's unmaking and re-creation. 'It is as the air, invulnerable,' gasps Marcellus of the Ghost, and it could be Hamlet crying out against the aura that seems to shield the King. Every scene has a handful of such references, that may look before or after, to add a quickening of their own.

The night itself is almost a character at the play's opening. In the final two scenes of the first Act a similar hour holds sway but it is in the first that its shade is felt. The word itself comes up several times (not so later), as something of its substance is sketched in. (Certain stars and superstitious beliefs; a war-industry that 'Doth make the night joint-labourer with the day'; a touch of 'this dead hour' till the crowing of the cock.) Scenes 4 and 5 confirm a presence that has been made known.

I, 2

The King makes a wonderfully telling first impact. Carrying all before him, he declares he has taken his brother's queen to wife, sums up a fraught situation on the international front and takes a precise step to deal with it, graciously hears Laertes' request to return to France and grants it with a tender bonhomie, takes his nephew to task for skulking in an 'unprevailing woe' and himself prevails, through the Queen, in his wish to have Hamlet stay on awhile at court; and with a splendid celebratory peroration, makes his exit. One imagines that in the general view he is the rightful monarch (whatever Hamlet's technical claim may have been); and that the young prince, popular as he no doubt is, is little more than a shadowy wisp beside him. In the eyes of the many the new order is established, under way, the country can go forward. In the person of the King Denmark prospers. The Queen is happy. For those who may have some sympathy with the prince, Claudius would seem to have won the personality game with ease.

At this stage – it is easy to forget – one does not know the truth of the matter. The King's phrases of convenience, 'wisest sorrow', 'defeated joy' and so on, can seem more politic than oxymoronic. A speedy regal marriage is not in itself an earth-shaking event, in this case rather the reverse; and Hamlet's refusal to emerge from the doldrums and so to speak enter his country's new age is apt to smack of an adolescent tiresomeness. And yet – such is the charge that animates the prince – a few words from him are all it takes to recast the hidden balance of forces, and give an entirely different shape to the stately scene before us.

From his first uttered words the character is an electric one. The wordplay in his first two remarks is arresting, the nerve they exhibit exhilarating (whether voiced as an aside or aimed directly at the King): there is another force on stage. He continues the tactic with his mother, answering her platitude, 'Thou knowst 'tis common, all that lives must die . . . ' with, 'Ay, madam, it is common.' Both parties at the top of the new order have been challenged, if not quite directly or to the general ear; and now we find something out about the challenger. And what we learn defines the character as unique, both among those on stage, and – at a remove – in the way that every member of the audience is unique.

Hamlet's lines on his melancholy tap at the root of individuality, a hidden essence. ' . . . All forms, moods, shapes of grief' do not 'denote me truly', he tells his mother, or tries to tell her, 'For they are actions that a man might play' (82–4). He is something an actor cannot act. 'But I have that within which passeth show; / These but the trappings and the suits of woe.' We are in the presence of someone who can switch effortlessly from a bitter wit to being open with the detail of his being. Without unlocking something for which there is no key, he is able, almost in passing, to reveal the private aspect, the ineluctable core.

At the same time we appreciate the King's panache and the prince's rapier-quick intelligence, tipped with the poison of enmity. Again and again the final scene is foreshadowed. Meanwhile, even as the protagonist of the drama sets out towards his destined future, the man of flesh and blood is left to languish in the present. The audience already is aware of a clash of 'mighty opposites' (V,2,62); but there is no set path to the contest to follow, as they witness the action on all sides against a cataract of words forever pinning them to the "stage-time" spot. They too are subject to the present, to the way a drama works. Whatever hints there may be, whatever one's knowledge of the entire script, nothing is to be taken for granted. A spectator is of the stage if not on it. All things are possible.

Of a sudden a suppressed spirit, for a moment no longer an undercurrent to the tide of events, is in full flow (129f). The royal couple and attendant throng are swept to the back of the mind as Hamlet's sadness extends the stage so as virtually to include the spectator, such is the power of soliloquy. It is the despair of paralysis: he has nowhere to go. He can do no more than stay, observe, and wish to die. Inexpressibly hurt, he is reduced to childish hyperbole to describe the devastating betrayal by his mother in the re-shaping of his family. There is no way forward.

With a feverish clarity he sees the world as a disused garden, over-taken by the grotesque: 'things rank and gross in nature / Possess it merely' (136–7). By contrast his late father's attentiveness towards his mother, remembered in a loving detail, is Edenic in its simplicity. We cannot say he intends a hint of the original garden, or that Shakespeare intends it. Such intent as there may be lies in the words themselves, to be taken as any mind may wish to take them.

In the prince's disappointed outlook, with its heightened opposites, a longing for good underlies a defeated vision. His first soliloquy movingly reveals a mind out of step with itself and the world; and a man of savage energies, altogether frustrated, who is beginning to consider using them against himself.

His vivacious greeting of Horatio (and courteous acknowledgement of Marcellus and Barnardo) bears witness to a chameleon-like disposition, and a quick and free sociability. Unutterably alone one instant, a gregarious animal the next, he personifies a certain type of immaturity, that of a nature so packed with potential it can never be quite at ease. To come to terms with itself it may be required to meet an intense and transformative challenge, a kind of ordeal by fire. It seems not impossible that at a subsidiary level Shakespeare was visiting the process, quite simply, of growing up; and taking as his base a character with all the natural gifts in the world.

A snippet of a few lines shows the range of the man, and the cavorting paths of the intellect and the psyche he is subject to. 'Thrift, thrift, Horatio! the funeral bak'd meats / Did coldly furnish forth the marriage tables. / Would I had met my dearest foe in heaven / Or ever I had seen that day, Horatio! / My father, methinks I see my father' (181–5). The magical glimpse leads into a shift from stasis to the beginnings of action, on the prince's part; and we are taken up with a new phase. But the stamp of the mind that is scarcely at one with itself, already sporadically developed, is by now imprinted on our own minds; it is part of how we know him. The stage is set for the play's inner direction to find its extraordinary route.

For the remainder of the scene we observe Hamlet at once getting to grips with whatever of substance he can find in the new situation. A series of questions establishes what it can; and with quick instructions to the other men, the prince falls into the leadership role as if born to it. We do not know yet that 'it is an honest ghost', as the prince is later to tell Horatio; but we have a firm sense of the old Hamlet as a capable king, and his son does not lack decisiveness in this first instance. 'I'll speak to it, though hell itself should gape', he promises, as indeed he does, tearing himself free from his companions who fear for his safety. A link both filial and royal is established at some level at the start of the action.

At the outset of the first soliloquy lies a much-debated word: is it 'solid' or 'sullied' or 'sallied' ('assailed')? Textual readings are inconclusive. 'Solid' is adopted here on the basis of its many contrasts (intensified by 'too too') with 'melt, / Thaw and resolve itself into a dew', and the frustration so shown, making for a better poetry. The tenor of the following lines, an exclamation from the wilds of despair, tells us more of 'that within which passeth show' (85). They intensify the sense of a hidden self, the more so with the final cry, 'But break, my heart, for I must hold my tongue!' In its very next words the voice recovers its poise to greet a close friend with a telling phrase: 'I am glad to see you well, / Horatio, or I do forget myself.' Who is Hamlet? It is a question no words (but only a deed) will answer. But we begin to gather a sense of the man. As he mulls over what the visitation may mean, it is as if an intimation of foul play is brought to the surface. 'Foul deeds will rise, / Though all the earth o'erwhelm them, to men's eyes.' Everything in him is on the alert. The hidden self has a direction to follow.

I, 3

Outside the court we meet the play's second family in a tender scene that turns a little troubling. One imagines the young aristocrat Laertes as a courtier, soldier, scholar in the mould of the prince, if not at his level; and the rift between them, beginning here, is to mirror and in some way define Hamlet's departure from himself. There is a wonderful opportunity for a director to show the son as just beginning to turn into the father, with the two speeches each with its blend of pious exhortation and urgent concern; and further room for humour in the way the sister may respond to the brother and the brother endure the father. But more to the fore is the family bond that appears to embrace all three (despite Polonius's sharpness with his daughter), and that contrasts with Hamlet's torn loneliness. It is the only time we see the three of them together, and the memory of their closeness will add a haunting touch to the wilderness to come.

The homilies of son and father are absorbing. A display of moral argument seems to stretch a little beyond the needs of the immediate situation. Laertes breathes innocence, Polonius experience. Perhaps Shakespeare is developing a theme of hierarchical male authority. The brother talks down to the sister, the father to the son. What little the sister says in return delightfully makes his own point back to the brother with a deft humour and no fuss at all. What the daughter says to the father after his tirade, on the other hand, is burdened with a terrible acceptance of the loss of her free will and freedom. The hint of the youth turning, in time, into someone who – with the best of motives – may wreck the life of a wife or daughter, lies there, like a seed.

If Polonius is overbearing towards his son, he is more paternal than patronising. However the acting is directed, his speech is a marvel of succinct advice. One wonders if the playwright did not originally intend a somewhat different role for him, but let the sententious busybody take over as the plot evolved. There are other instances in the play of a slight inconsistency as to character detail and development. Here we have a compelling blend of impatience, affection and finely-considered 'precepts'; but when the father questions the daughter the same elements at core, caught up in the current of his irritation, turn to something very different.

We come to Ophelia and a portrait of sorrow. Here she is loving and playful with Laertes, dutiful towards her father; but already, by the time Polonius has finished with her, one senses a woman divided from herself. The casual cruelty of her father's dismissiveness ('You speak like a green girl . . . think yourself a baby . . . '), and of his unequivocal instruction not 'to give words or talk with the Lord Hamlet', is explosively renewed in Hamlet's own verbal assault later. There is a great deal of accidental cruelty in the play. Many are affected and no-one more than Ophelia, who after her father's death has no words but a madwoman's for her feelings. A pure character tipped into its opposite by the hand of fate, she is innocence knocked flying in a grotesque world.

Time and again the state is given a presence backstage. Apart from the sight and sound of the royal couple (and retinue), reference abounds to Denmark's sensitivities and anxieties as a nation. Here Laertes informs his sister that on the prince's choice 'depends / The safety and the health of this whole state', and that it will require 'the main voice of Denmark'. Polonius tells her, ' . . . with a larger tether may he walk / Than may be given you.' The background reality of many thousands of lives, and the exalted status and significance of the throne, are constant reminders to the audience that this is also a play about a country. Though it is a truism to say so, it was written at a time when national continuity was not something to be taken for granted. To an extent, perhaps, one should keep in mind a sense of the possible effect of a play's first performance.

I, 4

'Who is't that can inform me?' asks Marcellus on the battlements in Scene 1, to be authoritatively answered by Horatio, who knows all about the rumours of frantic preparation for war and why they are likely to be right. His character is subtly recast now. Hamlet's "straight man" is to become an intriguing figure in his own right, but the sheer energy and independence of spirit shown early on are no more on display. One feels they are not so much withdrawn as overshadowed; nevertheless, there would appear to be an authorial switch of intent that is slightly carelessly covered over. It does not matter, such is the riveting force of the action. Now the character begins in an uncertainty as to the hour, continues with an almost wide-eyed question ('Is it a custom?'), shows a certain vigour in a vain attempt to stop Hamlet following the Ghost, and resorts to platitude, however apt, at the scene's end ('Heaven will direct it'). It is left to Marcellus to take a decision ('Nay, let's follow him').

Meanwhile the prince's part is driven on from a wan excitable shadow to something approaching a fiery brilliance. Commenting on the decline of the country's reputation as a result of its 'heavy-headed revel' he finds a parallel in a 'vicious mole of nature', the single fault that so often can bring down an individual. There is a thematic point to this, taking the play as a study of the dark side of morality, a note to which the audience is already half-attuned; but of more immediate interest is the scything power of the speaker's mind. He finds three sources of personal error: an inherited trait; an unaccountable development of a certain disposition ('complexion', 27) to the point of irrationality; and a more deliberate tendency to exaggerate a habit of behaviour, that in moderation is commendable ('plausive', 30) but in excess the opposite. Almost by accident it seems we are offered a glimpse of a moral philosopher in full flow, even (in embryonic form) of a philosopher king . . . at which point the Ghost enters, the drama continues. But what we must already have half suspected now we know: prince or not, this is no ordinary student before us but a genius.

If Horatio's address to the Ghost in the first scene was electrifying, at least to the audience, Hamlet's now is intimate and profound. He is engaged with the world of good and evil as is no other member of the cast – already perhaps we sense this – and in some respect carries the audience's own experience to its felt limit. If and when we venture upon the unknown, in existential terms, it is with 'thoughts beyond the reaches of our souls'. And his engagement is no mere theoretical exercise. 'I do not set my life at a pin's fee; / And for my soul, what can it do to that, / Being a thing immortal as itself? / It waves me forth again: I'll follow it.' At the outset of what is to become the most tortuous of quests, we see someone daring and forthright in word and deed.

'The air bites shrewdly; it is very cold.' 'It is a nipping and an eager air.' At the scene's start Hamlet and Horatio exchange words that in the lightest way reflect an internal weather also. At its end Marcellus' comment, 'Something is rotten in the state of Denmark', could not more tellingly sum up a sense of underlying corruption and evil. Following the Ghost's re-appearance and virtual abduction of Hamlet, the murky vapours of the first Act are momentarily crystallised in the sentinel's brooding remark. The language (in particular the prince's musings on suicide and his 'mole of nature' speech) has tended to blacken the heavens; the source of pollution is now lodged at the core of the state itself. This is more or less identical with the throne, whose present occupant, by his reported revelry off-stage, is already in line, so to speak, for such a charge in the mind of the audience. Yet his outwardly impressive royal nature may still for a short time keep it at bay. The sudden trenchant intimation of decay on the part of a minor character, a half-knowing apprehension, seems to speak for other characters as well, and directly to the audience. The latter know (even the first audience, if they know it is a revenge tragedy) but suspend full knowledge. Further moments of such crystallisation are to occur, not all of them dark or louring in aspect. So by fits and starts the drama does its work.

I, 5

The Ghost is very human. After waving to Hamlet to retire with it with 'courteous action', it addresses him not only with every appearance of an urgent and vital need to "open up", but employs the art of emotional blackmail as directly and bluntly as ever parent has done, laying a burden on a child. After hints of appalling purgatorial torment, 'If thou didst ever thy dear father love – ' is near excruciating in its naked appeal. The Ghost's concern for son and wife confirms a spirit of natural human tendencies: 'Taint not thy mind, nor let thy soul contrive / Against thy mother aught . . .'; and its sub-stage capers betray a restless anxiety for the secrecy the mission will need. 'It is an honest ghost', the prince tells his companions, and not a soul in the audience is in any mood to doubt it.

At the outset of the single most important conversation of his life Hamlet retains a certain independence: 'Where wilt thou lead me? Speak! I'll go no further.' The Ghost accepts this, and sets about imposing its claim for family honour and justice on a desperately lonely and impressionable mind. What follows is life-altering. It is arguable that the major theme of the play is not revenge but change. To say it is about "growing up" can appear to trivialise it; but certainly the maturing process of a gifted individual is on hand, as if on a seemingly endless loop beneath the immediate threshold. Such a change does not take place overnight. Quite deliberately the author leaves a sign of a self-delaying mechanism, the notebook-writer unable to become at once the doer, in the business with the 'table of my memory' and 'my tables'. The frustration and shame leading on from the delay are to be all-consuming; yet in the balance of things, in a notional overall picture that is denied to the present character on stage, they can also be seen to be natural, perhaps even necessary. One may wonder if the character behind the character on stage, the author, may be more directly involved with his play than it is customary to imagine.

How many gifted young people lose their spark, feel the flame grow dull at the core of their being? How many young artists of genius, in whatever medium, are caught in the headwind of fashion, to make more or less of a name for themselves, but little or no enriching progress? Can it be that an unfathomably great writer wrote *Hamlet* in part to re-live and in some way to record the struggle? Such a question, while unanswerable, may not be entirely illegitimate, if it leads to a greater understanding of the magnificent tangle that this drama amasses and unwinds.

There is to be a focus on the inner man. The theme of procrastination, the eager son who 'with wings as swift / As meditation or the thoughts of love / May sweep to my revenge' only, in his own eyes (if the Ghost's words), to become 'duller . . . than the fat weed / That rots itself in ease on Lethe wharf', is to feature almost obsessively in what is to come. And yet that is action and never its opposite. One senses the playwright has laid down a challenge to himself, to net the unobtainable, to capture the thing of contradictions, without visible borders, the charged personal matter where nothing is still. No two views of it are ever the same.

As his companions catch up with him, the Ghost gone, the prince seals up the entrance to his inner self. He offers a medley of glimpses of an exterior, from the 'wild and whirling words' Horatio lays at his door, to courteous exchange and the promise of 'love and friending', from a flamboyant evasiveness to a deadly seriousness at the oath of secrecy. Finally he leaves in a chastened quietness ('Nay, come, let's go together'). It is an inconstant passage that seems to mark out a pattern of being for him, a surface that it appears he can hardly help, and yet one assumed to divert attention from an inchoate determination within. He is not one thing or the other, not consistent, not whole; nor can he be till the deed is done. It is interesting that his later opening up to Horatio about the Ghost's revelation (III,2,68–69: 'the circumstance / Which I have told thee of my father's death') does not take place on stage. Horatio is the absolute friend. One imagines without him Hamlet may have not managed at all. But the central character himself is to be perceived, as the dramatist so presents him, as a hellishly corked-up bottle, all but exploding. The shock that has entered his system, and that is to reveal itself in a number of outbursts of one sort and another, is for the time being almost like a wild animal inside him which he has to contain.

In any discussion of a fictitious character the question looms of authorial intent: did Shakespeare see it like that, and so on. While it is naturally a question of considerable interest, and one the holder of an opinion would probably like to be answered in the affirmative, it cannot be answered at all. One can have no more than a rough idea of the mind behind the creation, a situation which applies also to one's own artistic efforts; and so the matter is best left abandoned. A work of art is not in the charge of the artist. In general the concept of intentionality amounts to not much more than a distraction.

' . . . How strange or odd soe'er I bear myself, / As I perchance hereafter shall think meet / To put an antic disposition on . . . ' (169–71). If the adoption of such a personality is both voluntary and involuntary, as such it reflects what is almost a principle of the invisible dynamic of the world behind the eyes. A causal ambivalence is at play in any mind that is making its way in the world. We sense it in Hamlet, we know of it at first hand; and despite its extravagant story-line, the drama is to offer a kind of shifting pictorial expression of the dithering maze. Its primary purpose is to entertain, but the root of its success may lie to some small extent in the recognition, on the spectator's part, of an inner blindness. Meanwhile the changed character in front of us knows all too well the fate of Denmark rests on him alone. The burden of Atlas on his shoulders, he utters (what feels like) an aside that reflects a sense of having entered a world of his own, a space where hyperbole is no more than cold fact. 'The time is out of joint: O cursèd spite, / That ever I was born to set it right!' Picking up, ironically enough, on the King's comment on how young Fortinbras of Norway perceives the country (' . . . thinking by our late dear brother's death / Our state to be disjoint and out of frame . . . ', I,2,19-20), the image reminds of a central unseen player: Denmark itself.

II, 1

The second family is visited by a deepening shadow. In itself the 'bait of falsehood' to take the 'carp of truth' (63) would scarcely have been found offensive, in an era when information-gathering as to illicit activity was rife, and the idea of personal liberty less developed than now. For an aristocrat to check on his son's behaviour to many would seem more advisable than not; and the careful detail Polonius goes into with Reynaldo, including a batch of phrases to use in conversation, commends itself as a model of statecraft. Reynaldo is to go so far and no further, and let Laertes 'ply his music' (continue undisturbed). In the implication of dishonourable activity Shakespeare is ahead of his time; and yet such a hint one may detect, not only in the language the father is driven to in his enthusiasm, but also by an inclusive comparison with later and more intrusive scenes of spying. At this moment the son is to be presented as under the influence of 'a savageness in unreclaimèd [wild, unsettled] blood' (34), as 'a thing a little soil'd i'the working' (40); and one feels a subtle point being made with regard to the parental proprieties, a hint that is not yet pressed home.

A door is opened and a room never entered. No more is to be heard of Laertes in Paris. It is as if the matter is there for reasons beyond itself, to signal an unfortunate tendency in the character of Polonius, and to introduce a theme of personal trespass. But there is more to it than that. At some level a gradual recognition may be said to operate over the play of a secondary role for Laertes, beyond the striking figure that he cuts: by echo and by contrast more deeply to define the central character. At this point the carefree student prefigures the spied-upon prince with his unspeakable burden. The dramatist uses his licence in an unexpected fashion; and (again) the pace of the action absorbs what may have been a slight hiatus in the line of events. The room is bypassed.

With Ophelia's entrance the absent prince is quick to dominate the stage. Her report of his shocking appearance and piteously intense behaviour, at once meaningful and meaningless, occupies the imagination: the question of Hamlet's madness fills the air, even as the two alarmed individuals before us play out the scene. Is this the 'antic disposition' he warned Horatio he might 'put on', or more? An unbearable suffering is indicated – is it an act? Possibly we know already that we do not know, that we will not know and neither will Hamlet himself. Meanwhile we may suppose he has been reflecting on the Ghost's torments. Unwittingly Ophelia has hit the mark: ' . . . with a look . . . As if he had been loosèd out of hell / To speak of horrors . . .' (83–4). With that he will be tormented himself by his own hesitancy (some time appears to have passed). We may sense he is driven to the woman he loves for succour – but can tell her nothing – as to the woman he hates (after she has cut him off), to tantalise and terrify her. All is true, all is supposition, nothing is true. In place of a more or less clearly delineated individual, a state of non-fixity is established, to hold virtually till the end.

Meanwhile Ophelia and Polonius, their lives now caught up (as all are to be) in the slipstream of an unpredictable trajectory, offer an impeccable example of an accepted power-structure. It is no accident that almost every time in the play Ophelia addresses her father it is with the words 'my lord'. Polonius has her in a vice; and yet he is well-intentioned, she accepts his concerned if summary bidding, all is "as it should be". The iconoclast playwright, even as he creates a perfect storm around the major character, makes unambiguous use of a set of social mores. Not a few of the first audience will have left the theatre more aware of the destructive element it may harbour.

The old man himself is charmingly rendered. He means to do no wrong but only good. His moment of agitated forgetfulness with Reynaldo – a picture of innocence if ever there was one – still does not hide the interfering despot: we sense he is an unwitting danger to others, if not yet to himself. His patriarchal authority is one thing, his excessive enthusiasm another. It is touching that he is aware of the latter fault, even putting it on a level, on one reading, with his daughter's credulity. 'By heaven,'

he says to her, 'it is as proper [natural] to our age / To cast beyond ourselves in our opinions, / As it is common for the younger sort / To lack discretion' (114–17). He is not aware of falling prey to the habit even as he speaks. As we know, it is not 'the very ecstasy [madness] of love' that bedevils the prince; the officious old stager is too eager both to seize on a solution to Hamlet's antics, and to rush it to the King. He is a creature of hidden ironies, of pathos and purpose both, a fond oppressor, and finally his own victim, a casualty of the way things are.

At the start of the scene an innocent phrase opens up a line of activity in the play later to be centred on Hamlet, an underworld of spying and prowling round and almost of stalking a person's identity. While the King has every reason to try and find out what is in his nephew's mind, the atmosphere surrounding his efforts, together with those of his busy-body counsellor, suffuses a part of the drama. Such is its claustrophobic effect that Shakespeare could be said (now some way ahead of his time) to be discussing an issue of personal privacy. The innocent-sounding activity proposed in 'You shall do marvellous wisely, good Reynaldo, / Before you visit him, to make inquiry / Of his behaviour' (3-5) is to gather an unnerving force as it travels from Laertes to Hamlet. Of more immediate resonance is Ophelia's description of the prince's sigh, ' . . . so piteous and profound / As it did seem to shatter all his bulk / And end his being' (94-6). One is left in no doubt that he is brought to the point of an utter and despairing exhaustion – and at the same time one suspects the young man of exaggerating his condition in part as a kind of accusation to a former girl-friend. There is much in the play that partakes of an "either-and-both" syndrome: contradictions rule, little is to be pinned down.

II, 2

'Something have you heard / Of Hamlet's transformation', says the King to Rosencrantz and Guildenstern; the Queen refers to 'my too much changèd son'; Polonius speaks of a gradual declension 'into the madness wherein now he raves'. Time has passed and one imagines the prince's state of mind as not merely a disturbing issue at court but something of a cause célèbre in Denmark. It is slightly strange that Hamlet's two old friends enjoy what in its manner is a perfectly normal conversation with him, that Polonius witnesses him, in the company of the Players, at home with himself and others and in the full possession of his faculties; and that no-one blinks an eye, so to speak. It seems the audience is invited to take on the idea of a sporadically alarming state of unrest in the prince's behaviour, for which the episode of his silent aping with Ophelia has set a precedent. A director can encourage a constant sense of simmering volatility in the persona; but what she or he cannot do is solve the question for the audience of the limits of Hamlet's self-control. The image of a wild animal within has been used to suggest an after-effect of the Ghost's revelation: but one may take the idea in a slightly different direction. There is a wild animal in the human psyche. Are we not all prey to moods that visit us with an unexpected, silent, irrational outburst? The veneer of civilisation is peeled back a little in Hamlet's case but he mirrors an element us all, if at a far remove. In its very uncertainty the character reminds of a universal in our ordered lives, the inconstant self.

Rosencrantz and Guildenstern are no doubt overwhelmed by the warm confidence in them the King and Queen express. That they are readily able to betray their old comrade's trust seems a natural consequence of smooth statecraft. The actions of both the King and Polonius epitomise a certain erosion of humanity in the name of good politics; in passing the play identifies a taint at the heart of public life. It takes a leader of greatness to rise above it; such is the implication at the play's end. Hamlet 'was likely . . . to have prov'd most royally', says Fortinbras, after entering the final body-strewn stage; and we know he is right, though how we know is something of a mystery (and how he knows a greater one). This is at the level of the state: the play has a far sharper implication to do with the common basis of individuality, and the distinction between true and a kind of accidental evil. Of the last, the King embodies the one and Hamlet and an array of lesser characters the other.

The ambassadors from Norway bring good news. Everything has worked like a charm. The danger young Fortinbras has posed, that has occasioned such a 'sweaty haste' in Denmark's night-and-day preparations for war, has been averted. The sure-footed King is gracious towards Voltemand and Cornelius (as he was earlier to Laertes), and there is no reason not to think he is perfectly genuine in his good manners, that deal with and respond to the outward form of things. Indeed one senses there is good in him; but (as his soliloquy shows later) he does not know how to shed his monstrous ego, which his personality has evolved to protect. Everything about him is considered, careful. Whereas Hamlet can forget himself in his delight at the company of friends.

Polonius's part blooms in the royal presence. As an 'assistant for a state' who still hunts 'the trail of policy' with an infallible nose, he is overjoyed to be able to put the new king on the right path. He savours the moment, revelling in a word-play that has a touch of senility drifting beneath it – one recalls his "senior moment" with Reynaldo – and delivers his diag- nosis. The words are spoken, one feels, as if they possessed a talismanic quality. Denmark's servant is keeping the ship of state afloat, as in his mind he always has. Condition: "madness"; cause: "unrequited love for my daughter" – the truth about a person is hardly to be captured in such abrupt terms. It is however a common failing to try and do so, and Shakespeare may be tapping into an audience sense of this. The audience knows the cause is off the mark; and in the condition too, it seems fair to say, they distance themselves from the old man's judgement. Always (after the farewell to his son) he is less right than wrong.

No doubt to a contemporary audience there was less offence than now in his appropriating and reading out to the King a private letter of his daughter's, but it is yet another example of the sullying of the personal that the play is full of. The letter itself says a great deal. Initially fulsome, self-parodic, almost its own addressee, by means of a metaphysical conceit it cuts through to plain speech – the fourth line of the quatrain – till at the last, after the ditching of all frills, in the final phrase it finds the conviction of true poetry. A journey of art in miniature, it carries a suggestion both of Hamlet's outer layer and his core; but of course there is no way to unpick one to come at the other. Ophelia is helpless, Hamlet too; while the audience is paradoxically refreshed by the revelatory glimpse of a soulless truth. Meanwhile the King reserves his judgement, defers to Polonius as to the next step, and – as we later discern – carefully adds to his own picture of the man-boy who has cast a shadow over his horizon, the shadow of a whirlwind.

Polonius's decisiveness in going 'round to work' illustrates Hamlet's hesitancy by contrast, as the First Player's 'rugged Pyrrhus' speech is to do differently and powerfully later. The sense gathers of the prince having come to a stop. 'What might you . . . think / If I had played the desk or table-book . . . ?' the counsellor asks, the last word recalling Hamlet's rejection of and reaching for the same. And yet the idle particle has a hive of activity at its centre, a buzzing nucleus. The prince's disdainful toying with Polonius in their meeting leaves the impression of one merely biding his time, in the greater scheme of things. He takes the initiative and keeps it, swiftly criss-crossing paths in conversation, presenting this face or that to the dogged seeker after truth – who may as well have been a dog for all his understanding of what is going on. The dying note plucked at the end of the encounter, ' . . . except my life, except my life, except my life', is replaced by a snort: 'These tedious old fools!' – once the speaker is on his own. A 'machine' to himself, indeed; but energised by those around him, anything but listless, and as sarcastic and exasperated as you like; this is no mind at the end of its tether. And even as one writes one sees the exhausted, spent spirit seeking out Ophelia, as if 'loosèd out of hell / to speak of horrors,' unable to speak at all. Certainly there are two Hamlets. In a sense it is the level and manner of their disengagement that make up the inner drama.

After his dismissive comment on Polonius the young man's eager greeting of two friends brims with a sudden warmth. Their laddish banter, that seems almost to invite retribution from the divine figure of

Fortune, is the tomfoolery of young men the world over and world-long. But of course all is not as innocent as it seems. 'Denmark's a prison' leads to the incomparable "nutshell" image, with the suggestion in 'bad dreams' of otherworldly horrors; and finally Hamlet puts his old childhood friends on the spot. Guildenstern's admission, 'My lord, we were sent for,' brings on an admission of Hamlet's own, a mental torment, the despairing vision of a magnificent futility. He sees everything, it means nothing. At the one point where everything matters there is nothing worth the name. It is all a 'quintessence of dust'. His inner eye is shut.

We come to the Players, and to an astonishing warmth and identity of interest at once established between one of the noblest blood and members of an unsalubrious profession. Many of the first audience will have been taken aback by the departure from their own familiar mores; it may well be that the writer is making a point. Some of that audience, together (one may hazard) with the bystander Polonius, may have discovered evidence of both sanity and madness in the prince's behaviour with the troupe, and not known what to make of it. But to us now – and surely to Shakespeare as he wrote – what could be more sane? Hamlet has the First Player recall a speech that seems a remarkable and not entirely convincing choice for a man in his state – in a sense a choice too far. What he himself recites of it perfectly suits his hidden side, so to speak, the picture of an implacable hero striding forth to avenge a father's death. One sees him appreciating the hyperbole along with the intent. It is what the Player comes to next that is slightly baffling. Ilium here is the central structure of Troy, its castle or citadel; with the thunder of its fall Pyrrhus is frozen at the very point of striking the blow. The sword 'seem'd i'the air to stick' – the warrior is almost abstracted from the scene, standing 'as a painted tyrant' who ' . . . like a neutral to his will and matter / Did nothing' (450–3). After an eternal moment of paralysis he regains himself and rains blow on blow. This part of the speech seems to endanger the immediate dramatic context – would the prince really have been so unruffled, listening to it, even if he had forgotten it was coming? – and to be written more for the benefit of the audience, hinting as it does at the main action in miniature. Of course it can be argued the other way; and in any case it is a kind of incongruity that Shakespeare gets away with time and again, in the interest of a compelling passage. The prince dismisses the Players with a reference to their business ('they are the abstracts and brief chronicles of the time') that invests the character for an instant with the passing shadow of an authorial presence – and now altogether as himself, makes sure both they and Polonius are to be looked after ('Look you mock him not'). Much latterly in this long scene has had to do with the outward personality of the main part – he is becoming increasingly visible – and now he is alone, the inner situation again comes to the fore. But only as much of it as the character himself can see and only in the way that he sees it. His musings themselves are blind, a character within, and no less part of the action.

Hamlet's first soliloquy ('O that this too too solid flesh would melt . . .' I,2,129) has the young man at his most hapless. Later, trying to come to terms with the Ghost's shocking revelation, he is distraught ('O all you host of heaven! O earth! what else?' I,5,92), but determined, if bewilderedly, on a plan of action. Now he sneers at himself, strikes attitudes, hardly knows which way to face, and finds a temporary settling of the nerves in an artifice already in the making (as we know from his words to the First Player), for which it might be said there is both good reason and no need at all. 'The spirit that I have seen / May be the devil' he muses, though if he casts his mind back he will surely again be in no doubt that 'it is an honest ghost', as he vouchsafed to Horatio. But no-one can truly cast their mind back; and in any case in his present mood to 'have grounds / More relative than this' can seem to make a deal of sense. In his emotional state he knows he is vulnerable. Beneath all such argument lies the sickening self-accusation of its being a mere pretence at action; and beneath that lies an active intent that is never still. But its means of operation runs counter to what he can see of what he is doing. He has taken a vow of immediate vengeance and cannot forgive his own delay. Yet delay is a part of the modus operandi by which his being is carrying out the Ghost's command.

From his first words in the play his behaviour towards the King has been such as to catch him off guard, to take him by surprise. If primarily out of disgust at the situation as he finds it, even then his attitude may be influenced by a presentiment of foul play ('O my prophetic soul! My uncle!'). On the ghostly confirmation of his uncle's guilt, an intensification of the same pattern of elusive unpredictability, at times merely within range of the King and at times more or less directly laying down a challenge, indicates a continuity in the prince's approach that takes him right through to the final episode. If not a strategy as such it has a strategic element. His deepest aim is to bring the King into the open. The journey of a full vengeance demands a self-committing response from the quarry, whereby its guilt will be known to all. The 'antic disposition' Hamlet summons up as protective colouring may have a sense of such a drawn-out process at heart; but such awareness of a "long-game" approach would seem to be minimal. Indeed to be blind to his own deeper intent, the watching audience blindfold with him, is at the root of the character's evolution as it is of the play's. Such a layered set of purpose, unclear to the mind it lives in, lacerating in its contradictions, probably lacked any such diagrammatic crudeness to its creator. One imagines the writer operated with a subtle set of interchanging imperatives but with a single end in view. He may not have reasoned it out coldly but let his instinct carry him along. The effect has been to provide what may be an unparalleled example in theatrical use of a character's unconscious at work.

While in this Act the sense of what we might now term the unconscious has begun to claim its hidden space, at the same time Hamlet has become a more real person, more accessible to the audience. His deep interest in the theatre, and in those who make it what it is (even writing for them), can make us feel at times as if the author is close by – but Shakespeare takes care to give the character full scope. Nevertheless he may have enjoyed the hint of a hint, so to speak, of a personal stake in the creation. Others too naturally come more to life. Polonius's prating verbal connoisseurship adds a certain zest to his personality, what with his 'effect defective', his 'tragical-comical-historical-pastoral', his disdain for 'beautified' and his glee at 'mobl'd'. We are reminded of his patriarchal inhumanity in the full force of a single word. 'At such a time I'll loose my daughter to him,' he confides to the King and Queen, indeed as if to be 'assistant for a state' were to 'keep a farm' (160–5). The Queen can have an amusing moment (director permitting) as she appears to mix up

'Guildenstern and gentle Rosencrantz', but the revelation of an independent stage character is still to come, after which she again is little more than an acquiescent subsidiary being. Yet her occasional interjections and comments create a personable role of not a little intricacy and depth. The King is a precisely nuanced character. 'Well, we shall sift him,' he says of Hamlet, secure in his ability to catch what is of most consequence in his nephew's mind. He is sharply perceptive, noting of him (at the scene's beginning) that 'nor the exterior nor the inward man / Resembles that it was', and in no doubt that something 'hath put him . . . from th'understanding of himself'. So the two independent and gifted characters track each other. With the forceful couplet at the scene's end, as the prince rouses himself to take a drastic step – 'The play's the thing / Wherein I'll catch the conscience of the king' – the hunt is on in full cry. But in which direction?

Talking with Rosencrantz and Guildenstern twice Hamlet lets his mind stray to the family scene that haunts him. 'It is not very strange,' he comments on the fashion for boy actors, 'an aery of children', taking over the stage; 'for mine uncle is King of Denmark . . . '. Again, he tells the two men they are welcome; 'but my uncle-father and aunt-mother are deceiv'd'. His next remark suggests an awareness of a slight instability in his mental self-control. 'I am but mad north-north-west: when the wind is southerly I know a hawk from a hernshaw [heron].' (The emendation from 'handsaw' in the last word is a suggestion of old that tends to be ignored.) The passage feeds the current already surging through the play, the question of Hamlet's madness, never quite answered: here the subject's own words add momentum. Yet to a degree it is an unreal debate, a superfluous, even diversionary discussion the playwright allows to develop for reasons of his own, as we shall see. Another moment of self-awareness comes in the soliloquy that ends the scene, 'Yet I, / A dull and muddy-mettl'd rascal, peak / Like John-a-dreams, unpregnant of my cause . . . ' (534–6). A superb phrase, the last four words sum up the utter emptiness the prince feels he is possessed by, with regard to the act of revenge. Perhaps they also hint at an unknowing state, whereby a plan has been conceived and has begun to take a shape. The living body knows it but not yet the mind. Nor will the mind fully comprehend the process later. All too conscious of what "should be", at no point in the gestation can it admit to itself the path it has taken. Yet the result cannot exactly be called an unplanned outcome.

A rhapsody of words. It may be a good moment to turn to another matter entirely, an element in all plays of old, and one that commentators naturally tend to take for granted. The play is a poem. The use by the dramatist of blank verse has its own effect, and if – as this study does – one takes a particular play in isolation, it may be worth enquiring into it at a few places. Little of note may emerge and yet it seems a relevant exercise, as a part of the dramatist's art in writing and the audience's in listening. Certainly it has its own intrinsic interest. Here one may mention a humdrum use of the iambic pentameter as a narrative instrument merely to impart information. Voltemand reporting back from his trip to Norway (60f) says what he has to say (after a formal line conveying courtesies) in two clear sentences, of eleven and eight-and-a-half lines respectively. There is no attempt to heighten the tone with colourful description or to portray tension within a staccato punctuation usage; the whole is a model of "civil service mandarin", the even tenor reflecting (at most) the quiet satisfaction of a job well done. And yet the two extended sentences have their own beauty. The clauses interconnect and continue with an unbroken lucidity, as if nothing could have prevented the desired outcome, or the clearer state of affairs now obtaining. The verse engages with the audience, on stage or beyond, in the least demanding way; and yet the rhythm has hold of the mind. The switch from past to historic present draws us in further: it is an everyday poetry that does its job perfectly. Undramatic in the casual sense, it is as apt to the drama of the moment as any number of more memorable and striking passages.

To take a single line by contrast from elsewhere in the scene (166), the pentameter can take on an altogether different personality. 'But look, where sadly the poor wretch comes reading,' says the Queen of her son. In part the lilt of the line, almost suggesting a slow step, in part the fore-

most aspect of the spectacle lent by the early adverb, in part a light allit-
erative weighting as the book comes more into view – none of these parts
or others, however added, can meet the sum of the whole. Not only does
the Queen speak the words, but heart and mind they carry an inner presence. At that moment the audience could not know her more.

When together Hamlet, Rosencrantz and Guildenstern speak in prose.
That is to say, the pauses are entirely the product of sentence usage and
not additionally informed by poetic metre (or rhyme). Crucial for poetry
in the traditional sense, the early line-break by no means controls the
poetic effect. Its use without true depth, often very acceptable when that
is deliberate, results in verse. Conversely poetry can leap out in the
absence of a metrical pattern, when the economy and richness of what is
said forms and sets as it is spoken (heard, read) in a perfect mould. Artists
of prose have snatches of poetry in their work. This is an area in which
everything is subjective; but one may note in Shakespeare any number
of instances in which it has happened, or at least is accepted to have done
so. The impulse of the dramatic action that launches such thrusts in his
plays seems to leave each of these moments in a clarity of its own. A naked
spontaneity, by contrast with the traditional clothing of the poetic
surround, offers a refreshing touch. Hamlet to Rosencrantz (of Denmark,
241f): 'Why, then, 'tis none to you; for there is nothing either good or
bad, but thinking makes it so. To me it is a prison.' Rosencrantz: 'Why
then, your ambition makes it one; 'tis too narrow for your mind.'
Hamlet: 'O God, I could be bounded in a nutshell and count myself a
king of infinite space, were it not that I have bad dreams.' So in the
prince's merest conversation there is poetry to be celebrated.

And the more so as his inner world comes into view. Later in the same
conversation (286f) Shakespeare has his word-magician speak miracles.
A glimpse of the heaven and hell of Earth and human existence rivets the
spectator: once experienced, it is never quite gone. As he takes the first
significant step on his stumbling journey, one is aware of the quite
extraordinary potential of this young creature. And in that he is as all of

us. It is over-fanciful but one can imagine the character, at times, to embody the distilled essence of the human species in its genius and error and journey of a nigh impossible striving. Yet at the same time he could scarcely be more different from anyone we know or have known.

III, 1

The King is on the hunt, anxious to determine the cause of Hamlet's erratic behaviour. Such is the emphasis on his 'lunacy' that we assume he has been hard at it, though as always we are unsure whether he is the master of his 'antic disposition' or it of him. On the look-out for any sign of a deliberate threat, the King may suspect knavery in his use of 'puts on' (2), indicating both a sharp eye on his part and a sharpened sense of danger. Guildenstern's careful observation of 'a crafty madness' (8) is apt to feed the latter. There is a tremor to the sovereign confidence but the King shows little of it, no doubt relieved at the distraction the Players are sure to provide for his nephew. The atmosphere remains one of intense pursuit: all are there who can assist in the chase, Rosencrantz and Guildenstern unreservedly dutiful, Polonius as eager as the King; and the two obedient women caught up in a convergent interest in Hamlet's recovery and happiness. Set against the intent and somehow hollow male personalities of the moment, they offer a telling contrast, beings animated by love, even though all we hear from Ophelia is a polite five words.

Polonius's dramatically convenient comment on the frequent hypocrisy of 'pious action' (47-50), after positioning his daughter with a holy book, draws an immediate reward in the King's aside. One would have thought the old man to be too excited to indulge in sententious musing. The vigour of his closing image makes his words at once acceptable to the audience (as poetry can sometimes close a probability gap on stage), even as it stings the King into a wildly unexpected admission. Suddenly we see the vulnerable side of the man. He has a conscience; and more, in reacting to the words 'the devil himself', for a moment he is lost, *in extremis*. If the Ghost is in Purgatory a part of the brother is in Hell.

The tone of Hamlet's deep drift of thought, as he comes up close to an irrevocable option (57f), is almost that of a man at peace with himself. The froth of the first lines of his first soliloquy is no more (I,2,129-32); the question is met lucidly and as if with relief. One feels it is a meeting he has been waiting for. It is now not so much the sin of suicide that deters him as the unknown, 'the undiscover'd country', a dread afterlife. It is a matter of practical considerations he has to deal with, rather than an injunction from on high. If still from within a religious standpoint, the resource of a thinking mind is brought to bear. It ranges impersonally over the human condition, exploring the case of an individual laid low by 'outrageous fortune', 'a sea of troubles' that bids fair to overwhelm us all; at which the fateful being is seen in close-up, in the midst of the ills of society, brutally and piercingly listed. Yet the tone remains even. Nothing flamboyant or egoistic is here. The philosopher speaks, his own case that of Everyman. His particular suffering is too much known to be aimlessly rehearsed, and so to disturb the visionary sweep of his mind. The singular personal pronoun is absent till he sees Ophelia.

On his own it is clear Hamlet is not mad. The faculty for intellectual (as opposed to instinctive) thought, the 'discourse of reason' that distinguishes the species (I,2,150), marvellously present in the 'To be or not to be' discussion, bespeaks a capable, indeed crystalline mind. It is also one of deep human sympathies. But when he is with others the matter is not so clear. Excitement can take him close to an affective disorder; at the very least, anyone with him can be in for a bumpy ride. Each of the main characters is to endure this in one way or another. Here he sees his ability to reason, his greatest asset, as his greatest liability. 'Conscience' in the sense of 'awareness' puts the brakes on action; all is prey to 'the pale cast of thought'; so far from being assisted by his capacity for 'discourse' it has led him off course. So he perceives himself and so, in the grip of this confusion, he is to proceed. The very fact he cannot lose his mind brings him close to losing it. At the same time he cannot admit to his reliance on it. He is twisted up, so to speak, in its folds; in a torment of delay, he cannot see what it is doing for him.

Did Shakespeare himself reason all this out, or something like it? Hardly in this way. A hallmark of his dramas is a crackling acceleration of narrative pace that can occur at any moment and especially once the narrative is launched. From the Ghost's first appearance a series of episodes hurtles the plot on; and yet each has all the stage time it needs. (The playwright appears particularly generous to the Players.) One sees a quill driven by a sense of what is absolutely possible, by which is meant not only what works there and then, but in the wider scheme of things. The author has set up a momentum towards a given end. He has his tangle; it will tighten, but so as at the last to unravel. Trusting to his dramatic instinct he brings characters on and off in situations that chime with the state of play and the pull of the ending. To an extent the drama is allowed to create itself (mirroring life); the author's role is to hit the right note with each development. It is surely fulfilled. Each conversation, each episode, each character at every point, if one makes allowance here and there for a slight dramatic hiatus, in *Hamlet* is absolutely possible.

Whether or not the prince suspects or notices Polonius or the King (so-called 'lawful espials', 33) at any time in the conversation with Ophelia is up to the director. Perhaps he turns his head and raises his voice at 'all but one' for the King to hear (145); yet if the sentence in which it appears is taken less consequentially, it can suggest a moment of reason sent sprawling by anger, with as much or more dramatic potential. Not that the "conversation", which it scarcely is, needs such a boost: it is more like a bolt of lightning, scorching Ophelia where she stands, book forgotten, than any kind of an exchange. When one reads it one half-directs it in mind, imagining (for example) a wild, somewhat unco-ordinated physical accompaniment to the prince's torrent of words – alarming gestures, a striding, whirling around, towering over the woman – such as to confirm her apprehension of his madness. And of course this can be played as only in part 'put on'. She is a focus for his frustrations, which carry his mind away, up to and beyond the line of its own self-control.

The dramatic matter of Hamlet's madness is a thing of wonder. Constantly re-emerging it engages the audience as much as it does some of the cast, if differently and without requiring a definitive answer, as if to a question. After the first Act it inhabits the play. It is a fact, an enigma, an illusion, a charade. The evolving state of mind that envelops the prince is to be comprehended by the audience but not to be pinned down. Several times he goes beyond the pale. His behaviour is careless or aggressive to the point of impossibility, were he in charge of his actions in the accepted sense. He is in charge, but he is not in a normal world.

The implication of his situation – in short, the presence within him of the Ghost, its story, its suffering, its being – is that different rules may apply if he is to find the strength to do what he must. As audience we lack the time to spell this out to ourselves except for a sense we may have of his being in control whilst not in control. There is no form or formula of words for a state of mind: one may feel that to make this very point is a part of the play's agenda, if one wholly interpreted within the need to grip and entertain. Shakespeare is not didactic. In the exploration of this theme he has brought off what may be an unparalleled balance between a play's visible and dark matter, a character's foreground and background. So we follow Hamlet's journey, aware of who he is, a complex being we know the better for there being no word to mechanise the knowledge.

His excoriating treatment of Ophelia seems to crash, like water breaking through a dam, out of a wall of silence. He has visited her and said nothing; he has written to her and received no reply. Now he speaks. Whatever the motives behind the verbal assault two stand out, a need to hurt her and a need to hurt himself. The vicious repeated stab of 'Get thee to a nunnery' is calculated against her in particular; while his exasperated rant at the female of the species (140f) no doubt arises as much from his feelings about his mother ('Frailty, thy name is woman!' I,2,146). All this is also a kind of attack on his own better nature, which again and again in the play sweeps the clouds aside to spring into being, but which here he is intent to disown (121f). It is not only Ophelia, not only women who cannot be trusted. 'We are arrant knaves, all; believe none of us' (126–7). In a fallen world he strips himself bare.

The picture Ophelia draws of Hamlet after his stormy exit, as well as revealing her own overwhelming love, signals something of the princely image at large. It is no surprise to us that in happier times all eyes were on him, 'the observ'd of all observers', nor that they still are. 'He's lov'd of the distracted multitude', the King says of him later; and one has the impression of a young man not only of legendary talent but with a flair for living that is bound to rivet the gaze. Ophelia's sorrow at the collapse of one so gifted comes before her words of sadness for herself. It is a tribute to her love for him and at the same time a reminder of her lack of ego. She is unable to put herself first.

The King ignores the weeping woman entirely, her father all but does the same; they are caught up in the chase, each sharing the next step (or something of it) with the other. The difference in their assessment of what they have overheard is striking. Polonius sees no more than he has already decided on. But the King is far more astute; indeed, his incisive intelligence sets him apart from all except his enemy. 'There's something in his soul / O'er which his melancholy sits on brood;' he judges of Hamlet's volatile and depressed state, 'And I do doubt the hatch and the disclose / Will be some danger' (161f). The image stayed in Shakespeare's mind, to be used later by the Queen (V,1,266f). Finely adjusted for the speaker in the later example, there emerging as an intuitive loving insight, it is surely an accurate vision of the intangible, describing what can only be described by metaphor. Of course in the Queen's case it carries a certain irony; while here the King is alert to what the 'disclose' may bring. A few lines on he is again able to catch at the elusive aspect, noting 'This something-settl'd matter in his heart, / Whereon his brains still beating puts him thus / From fashion of himself' (170f). The incubatory image took him nearer the truth.

A phrase of Ophelia's catches the eye. 'And I, of ladies most deject and wretched, / That suck'd the honey of his music vows . . .'. A director might be tempted to have Ophelia briefly place her hand on her stomach at the second line. With the implication of a sexual relationship (or of her wish for one), the dismissal to a nunnery in retrospect is more cutting by far, and her mad song later ('Young men will do't, if they come to't . . . ', IV,5,59) is searing with what is unsaid. The hint of a responsive yet repressed personality harbouring a greedy body is there in any case with the song; such a stage direction at this point gives the character a stronger contour. But it may be too much; as so often in the play, Shakespeare leaves things open.

The haunting melody of one of the world's great passages of poetry fills the mind. This reader finds it impossible to leave the scene without some sort of ragged attempt to recognise the musician's art. In the 'To be or not to be' soliloquy the pattern of the pentameter lends its harmony to the bleakest of outlooks. One may wonder how the gap is bridged in a multitude of cases between a singularity of feeling and a regular poetic form. To something wild, sporadic, inconsistent or in any other way uneven, a broadly symmetrical impetus is added such as to contribute a further sense to that of the words. Perhaps it is a sense of the emotions: whatever is being said is based in an emotional reality, a pressure with its own inchoate existence. It is this very existence, it may be, that is acknowledged in the continuity that attaches to a poetical form.

It does not matter if it was short-lived; that it was, is all. A song of the unseen is given its tangible force in a music of words. The song may be a howl but in itself (if it is not fake) it has a living wholeness, an integrity. Whatever it was, the vitality of a non-verbal or semi-verbal current is re-adopted in the music. It is explored further and given a final and communicable sense, the words and ways of the mind at its service, even as it is spun out into a poem or passage of poetry.

Fortunately any such passage will render a critic's ramblings instantly forgettable. Intricacies of mechanical detail, when the reader returns to Hamlet's lucid vision, will be beside the point. The author's mastery of blank verse, perhaps nowhere more apparent, may be felt to reside in the depth and clarity of the current that informs the 'discourse of reason', and in a poignancy for which there are no words. One may discover a quiet nobility in the lines such as to reflect the true stature of the speaker. And there will be a musical element to be appreciated as one will.

III, 2

If a playwright with a number of masterpieces behind him and an actor himself wanted to pass on a few tips on stage delivery, one wonders if he could do better than the opening episode of this scene. In some forty lines we have an actor's handbook. An irrepressible directorial zest fires the moment; this is someone with a depth of experience and 'a kind of joy' in the pastime (to take Rosencrantz's words on Hamlet's alertness to the Players' visit). If the author has invested deeply in the character it is for the character's benefit. We see a new side to the prince. As his stage interest and knowhow draw on a kind of ranging acuity a different man stands before us, altogether active: for an instant it seems there is nothing he cannot do. A creative spark is in the air. The author does not hide the overlap, which is after all a superficial one. It is almost as if he invites the audience to entertain the idea of a tenuous link that can lead nowhere. It is all conjecture; and yet an interesting one.

Another question presents itself, also without answer, but more capable of discussion. Just as the First Player's declamation of the non-event of Pyrrhus' pause (II,2,448f) seems also to operate in an unofficial capacity, a kind of chance reminder to the prince, so now Hamlet's words appear to reflect on his own situation. This is not to take away from the present effect: the need in acting is wonderfully stated, to 'use all gently; for in the very torrent, tempest, and, as I may say, the whirlwind of passion, you must acquire and beget a temperance . . . '. 'O'erstep not the modesty of nature', he insists. The stage enthusiast has the courage of his conviction to carry all before him. Are we to suppose he reflects, as he speaks, on his own lapses and lack of stability, his own harlequinades? Almost certainly not. But the passage may remind us – if not himself – of the speaker's own position at some level, and also perhaps of its helplessness, its impossibility. What room is there in his world now for 'the modesty of nature'? Where is the temperance in killing a king?

One sees two different worlds, the stage and unstaged life. The cruel demands of the latter are ever-present. Even as Hamlet so finely elucidates 'the purpose of playing', concluding 'to show . . . the very age and body of the time his form and pressure', one may recall his despairing cry, 'The time is out of joint: O cursèd spite, / That ever I was born to set it right!' (I,5,188–9). Hamlet utters his advice to the Players in a full-hearted confidence; but a different kind of self-belief is needed for what he must do.

An aspect of the author's time passes across the surface of his play, a sickly abuse of privilege and its imitation, a deadly invasiveness. What the prince is to root out on stage, the play is 'to hold as 'twere the mirror up to' in the world beyond the Globe. We watch it to undergo a theatrical experience; but we are reminded of the rot in the world around us, now as much as then.

Warm to his boyhood friends when they turned up before (though even then they had been primed by the King), we may suppose Hamlet picks up something from their brief appearance now. At any rate at their next meeting he is far more abrupt; and here he turns to Horatio in pure relief. We learn much of the loyal friend from this speech, and all we learn increases his mystery. Hamlet clearly is acquainted with the details of his background; we need not be, to understand Hamlet. But what of the man himself? Shakespeare makes an interesting decision: there is nothing more we need know. Goodness is. It may not understand everything ('There are more things in heaven and earth, Horatio . . , ', I,5,165–6), and yet it can have an inner momentum that requires us to take note. Horatio's role has a latent power. As an anchor for Hamlet in a capsized world his is a fully responsible character; as an example of the human personality in a better world, where 'blood and judgment are so well commingl'd, / That they are not a pipe for fortune's finger / To sound what stop she please' (61-3), it is a beacon. The part of the fellow-student is a quiet one to play, the more endearing for the mystery, in its own way a chronicle of love.

Hamlet's manner with him is a touch unsettling, mirroring in small a tendency to impulsive, sometimes wildly unpredictable behaviour on his part. Virtually everyone is thrown off course by it. Here it is as nothing. One infers a momentary unease on the listener's part in the effusive lines ending, 'Something too much of this' (66). The speaker checks himself and gets down to brass tacks. The self-admonition is telling. A couple of times the prince admits to excess after the event; only here does he catch himself as a certain balance begins to go. Because he is with someone he

would not offend for the world, and the situation is of no external consequence, he can afford to look at himself and apply a brake. Elsewhere he
seems to trust to an underlying instinct to propel him into action and
take him where it will. Such is the only way.

'I must be idle,' he says, changing mood again like an actor clamping on
a new mask. Dallying in words with the King, Queen and Polonius, he
switches to a highly suggestive badinage with Ophelia, momentarily
dispelling (by its opposite in tone and content) any lingering disturbance
from the 'nunnery' outburst. His status as tolerated madman no doubt
helps in all this; but we do have a hint, in the swift ease with which he
leaps into a situation (the later moment with Laertes in the grave comes
to mind), of a remarkable actor in potential, and not only on-stage. One
can almost sense the world of human affairs waiting for him, even if at
present it is a distant prospect. In the antechamber, so to speak, for all
his sense of inertia, he has a bent for the initiative. His innuendoes to
Ophelia are cleverly charged and yet beyond the pale, a royal banter that
must have startled a first audience. (It may be recalled when we next see
her, stark mad.) One can experience – and forget – a touch of disappoint-
ment in the development of Ophelia's character: the quick-witted
rejoinder to her brother before he leaves for France (I,3,46f) is a far cry
from her childlike questions and comments following the dumb-show
and prologue. Perhaps the playwright is adding a touch, a little too
openly, to prepare for a casting-adrift of the mind.

At the flip of a switch Hamlet re-visits an internal world, briefly to
confront his devils. It is something that happens to him, or that he lets
happen; it has none of the deliberateness of 'I must be idle' about it. In
response to 'You are merry, my lord,' an unbearable frustration speaks
out. 'O God, your only jig-maker,' a hell in five words, hangs in the air.
He reverts to a rehearsed complaint, ' . . . my father died within's two
hours,' follows it up with a sardonic originality; and finally settles down
for the dumb-show.

With the all-too-familiar sequence of events acted out in silence of a king dying asleep in a garden and his widow accepting a new love, one would have expected someone as alert and resourceful as Claudius to have managed things better, simply cancelling the play on the grounds of an unfortunate choice. The business of poison and poisoner would be seen as adding insult to injury and quite intolerable. But time and again drama gets away with the unlikely in favour of a pulsating plot (as too in the later genre of prose fiction); and one can picture a frozen Claudius, transfixed by the enactment of what he thought was wholly hidden, and shrugging off an interrogative glance from his wife into the bargain. This episode may be deemed to run counter to the sense of the drama as "absolutely possible" that has been advanced for its every manifestation of personality (see note on III,1, paragraph 5); but skilled direction should carry it off well enough. So too with Ophelia's subdued state of mind. In general it may be said that the "play within the play", even while veering near the bounds of probability here and there, has the impact of a thunderclap as a declaration of war; and given the fluid and uncertain state of play between the two opponents, that the slow insidious build-up is very acceptable.

Another question presents itself: where is the 'speech of some dozen or sixteen lines' which Hamlet wrote and inserted into the original play? With his (presumably) additional alteration of a Duke and Duchess into a King and Queen, and the sly presentation of a king's nephew as a king's poisoner, *The Murder of Gonzago* becomes *The Mousetrap* – so named at least for Claudius's benefit. The extra lines may not of course have been reached before the play's premature ending. Otherwise they could lie in the long speech of the Player King, in which a common failing is reiterated many times over. 'Purpose is but the slave to memory . . . Whe'r love lead fortune, or else fortune love' (172–87) could drop out with little difficulty. However, there is no need to identify the passage Hamlet wrote and supplied. Is it a 'necessary question of the play' (36)? It is not: but merely another riddle the playwright leaves for the playgoer, seemingly ensuring the complete lack of an answer. Despite oneself one plays along with the charade, unable to resist a stab in the dark.

Meanwhile – whether or not Hamlet is supposed to have written (some of) the Player King's diatribe of doubt – is there not a moment of agony in it for himself, to have to listen to a repeated echo of what we know is hammering at his brain? Is not the speech a reflection of the Ghost's silent observation of his own faltering purpose? Has he written it, or asked for the play, in part to remind himself, or punish himself? All the wrong question. Again the playwright finesses a minor conundrum, to go with the major one of Hamlet's mental state. Nevertheless, in respect of the Player's speech there is an answer of a kind. Whatever Hamlet's secondary response, so to speak, and again there may well be none at all, we are made the more aware. His is the wound; but all we can say for sure, as to the present effect of the actor's words, is that (however lightly) we are the one wounded.

It is marvellously poised. Just as when Hamlet earlier listens to the First Player picturing Pyrrhus inert in mid-revenge, or when he himself offers the Player inspirational advice as to the need for a fit restraint in acting, here again we assume he is wholly taken up with the externals – but we do not know. Does he reflect at all on the content of the Player's words (or his own) as it reflects on him? By the very question the edge of the play is sharpened.

Such a moment has an aspect of the play's method in little. We are conscious, in some way, of what is happening to Hamlet; but it resists cross-section, defies static analysis. It is change itself. In the general case of irony on stage the audience can be clear as to whom the further effect of the words is for (if for anyone beyond the audience itself). Here there is a strong suggestion of irony and nothing to be concise about at all, with regard to its application, apart from the fact that we are made to feel a vulnerability in the situation a little more keenly. So the play defines itself, in unusual part, by an indefinable increase in audience engagement.

We do not have to like Hamlet for this to be so. Rather he exists by our side; and probably as someone towards whom we have mixed feelings, if any. It is time to put the business of establishing a character into perspective. What happens with Hamlet happens with every fictional role in whatever medium. The difference lies in the extent to which we perceive the character as something with a more or less fixed identity, an outline that even as it shifts stays safely within the mind's focus. It is as if Shakespeare decided, perhaps in the first place as an experiment in character invention, to lessen one kind of impact, the strength of the outer casing, in favour of another, that might be allowed to develop and work itself out.

It would explain a "chancy" feel to the play, to the whirlwind that leaves a trail of havoc from Elsinore to England. One might also mention a whirlwind of dramatic commentary down the years. What stance is one to adopt to Hamlet or *Hamlet*? It is a character, or a play, to be given its head and let run.

The prince may well have his eyes on his mother as *Gonzago* is performed, as well as his uncle. 'Madam, how like you this play?' he asks her. Even after witnessing the unfortunate change of heart in the dumb-show of a Queen whose situation is not unlike her own, she appears not upset in the slightest, offering a neutral comment, 'The lady doth protest too much, methinks'. Possibilities flash across the mind. Could Gertrude be a consummate actress herself? Could the King's amenable consort be more self-possessed, of steelier resolve even than he? It seems more likely that her response betokens an innocent mind. But one does not know. The question of her guilt must surely have leapt out at Hamlet, if not during the meeting with the Ghost, then once the horror started to sink in. It is remarkable that Shakespeare does not make the son's concern over the mother's involvement more of an overt issue; except that not to do so is in keeping with a kind of instrumental ambiguity the play depends on. Later when he meets her in her chamber the matter is raised but not pursued. There is of course no fact to the matter. Yet the question is to be kept alive, as the larger play proceeds.

The Player Queen exits, her return foreshadowed in the dumb-show. The prince as master of ceremonies is in his element. He conducts a variety of conversations almost at the same time, finely tantalising Claudius, continuing his suggestive banter with Ophelia, and urging on the stage poisoner with great good cheer. No-one can match him in this mood. At once the show is over. Recoiling on himself, he is at a loose end. In a state of minor agitation the "unstricken deer" (see 251–2, also 224–5) does no more than 'play', quoting a ballad (possibly) and making up a poor rhyme of his own. It is a pivotal moment. The King has lost his composure in public, one imagines for the first time. He is alarmed and has life-and-death forces at his disposal. Yet as if tapping his foot Hamlet merely passes the time, commenting, 'For if the king likes not the comedy, / Why then, belike he likes it not, perdy' (271–2), and calling for music. But he has moved the game on a little. Beneath a veneer of idle frivolity he awaits a response, with no idea in the world of what form it will take. It is not a game he intends to lose.

At the re-entry of his two old friends he stays in 'antic' character, or rather, he allows its mantle to remain, now more as a cloak. When he tells Guildenstern 'My wit's diseased' (296) one is inclined to feel he means it, that he cannot deal with a germ of feyness his mind seems infected by. But once the recorders are brought in he is lethally direct. With a clinical precision he argues Guildenstern into an indefensible position, and proceeds to flay him and Rosencrantz for their gross efforts to sound him out. It is not so much the trespass on the ground of their friendship that seems to enrage him as the sheer presumption behind the intent. A ruthlessness has begun to form. When he has a clear target, as here, there is nothing of the 'antic disposition' about him. He knows exactly what he is doing; and even as he excoriates his old companions, we feel they merit it. But such a target is a rarity. Later we are to see him stumble into savage action at certain moments. He is to lose his equilibrium (as he has begun to do once or twice already), to regain it with a little difficulty. The lack of balance in the state of affairs, from his point of view, is to be reflected in his state of mind.

Polonius now comes in for a withering treatment, a light bruising no doubt more effective to the onlookers for its being unfelt. Horatio and the chastened spies provide the showman's audience. The old man departs believing that by humouring the prince – fine statesman that he is – he has obtained his agreement to see his mother. But it is all too clear who has been humoured. Finally on his own the prince turns his attention to a more urgent confrontation. He has had enough of sparring. He appears spontaneously to echo the Ghost's warning, ' . . . nor let thy soul contrive / Against thy mother aught . . . ' (I.5.85–6), in context a sign he knows he can commit murder. It is a reminder of the anger he must feel, and of his awareness of the liability it can be. The end-couplet (369-70), too, surely conveys a trace of filial affection. So prepared, at one with himself, he departs the stage in a deadly composure.

' . . . The croaking raven doth bellow for revenge' (234–5). This is a take-off of a passage in an anonymous contemporary play and of overblown melodramatic blank verse in general, a popular style as we see from the 'Pyrrhus' speech. The prince is in gloriously high spirits as Lucianus overdoes the stage villain role – 'Begin, murderer; pox, leave thy damnable faces, and begin.' As an example of a pentameter that fails in its (ostensible) poetic purpose, the "raven" line could not be bettered. For its opposite we may take a line from the scene's concluding speech, 'I will speak daggers to her but use none' (367). A deal could be said of the business of poetry by calling on this line alone; but it would lead the reader nowhere except off the track. The two lines are not of course juxtaposed in the play; they are so here merely for the interest as to what can be lost or gained in a line.

A phrase that scythes the air as the prince turns on Guildenstern itself speaks volumes. 'You would play upon me; you would seem to know my stops; you would pluck out the heart of my mystery . . . ' (336–7). The final image says all there is to be said against the activity that dominates the first half of the play. Within an Elizabethan revenge tragedy a voice speaks out beyond genre and era against all the prying forces that peer into and label a person. *Hamlet* is an existentialist play. Through its lead character it resists, as it seems, any supposition that we are there to be defined by others. To 'pluck out the heart of my mystery' is to kill it. In its way the play defends the notion of individuality according to which we all get by – and, it may be said, come to treasure the world.

Just as the Trojan war episode recited at the prince's request on the first appearance of the Players illustrates a fairly tame use of blank verse, tending always to sensationalism, so the rhyming couplets of *Gonzago/Mousetrap* require little mental effort on the part of their audience. In either case the contrast with the general run of Shakespearean verse is marked. Yet to listen to a Shakespearean play is not hard work in itself, just as to be alert is not hard work. There have been better extended uses of the couplet on stage, including whole play-scripts. But the form is intrinsically non-dramatic, too tidied-up for the dynamic of theatre that ignites the air. One cannot impose a pattern on a flame. It is useful at moments, notably in Shakespeare's case to sign off a scene (as here). One should add however that some of the greatest poetry in English is in couplets. In narrative or meditative mode the form can carry all before it. In "the play within the play" an immediacy is lost, quite appositely in context; but by the contrast of that thin fare with what is everywhere around, one may notice, for a moment, a richer array. The tumble of poetry, interlaced with poetic prose; and everywhere, like a struck match, the fire of existence.

III, 3

Having broken cover the King is intent to clear the other from the land. Before, with Polonius, he was relaxed enough to find an excuse: the trip was to be for the other's sake (III,I,168f). Now he can think only of his own safety. The shadow-play of the hunter and the hunted, that the other characters do not see, is more pronounced; while still for the audience, who catch it from the start, the roles of the two figures flickeringly interchange. It is a kind of side-show, eventually to merge with the main one, that we follow and do not follow, another aspect of the principle of uncertainty that appears to have taken over the stage. Quick but never hurried, quiescent for long patches, it has the spectacle of the chase in epitome.

The parts of Rosencrantz and Guildenstern have flattened out a little. Hamlet's 'excellent good friends' as he called them on re-meeting his co-students, and with whom he swapped puns on the Goddess of Fortune's body, have lost their colour. Now no more than pawns, they remind the audience of the sovereign power, the 'divinity' that 'doth hedge a king', as Claudius is later to refer to his mystic status. One accepts their awe before him, and a natural anxiety not to offend; but the fawning creatures we see here are a far cry from the rollicking lads who with a kind of shame-faced grace admitted their mission earlier to their friend. Yet Hamlet has hardened too: he has little room now for sympathy. The difference is that in the minor characters a certain subtlety seems to have been drained from their make-up (as in the case of Ophelia, though one's perception is to change). The alteration is a little disappointing; and yet people do sometimes narrow, gaining access to high places. Perhaps, too, one should allow for the effects of the prince's shock treatment. Dramatically speaking, the figures we encounter now are all too easily acceptable – and still (as with Ophelia) one misses a friend or two oneself.

We come to the King as king, to the man behind the public face; and to a soliloquy as remarkable as any in the play. His response to his ever-eager counsellor (who reports ready and correct for the next spell of eavesdropping) is an affectionate one. 'Thanks, dear my lord,' has nothing duplicitous to it, rather sounding a vulnerable note. With such a light touch are we attuned to that most clamorous of conversations, the outer and the inner self, the person torn between.

Hell is close for Claudius. The Cain and Abel story was less of a story then. His honesty is devastating. Unlike Hamlet, there is nothing he does not see of his situation. Born of hard experience, his soliloquy speaks with the clarity of an inner light fighting the darkness. In a last desperate chance to prevail, such a capacity for good seems to lie at its heart, such gentleness; as he kneels, all is not lost. At this moment of poise the power not of prayer but the need for it fills and transforms the silence. The all-consuming battle continues even as Hamlet's lines echo out from his part of the stage. Finally, in a simple factual couplet, the King admits defeat. On one level the scene is almost a theological enquiry: the right to true prayer is to be earned. But with the soul-devouring conflict played out before us, the innocence in the monster unable to gain a hold, it is no theoretical issue. The scene in its way is as compelling as any.

Side by side as the speeches are, and as their speakers virtually are for the second one, the contrast reveals more of the inner character of the older and the younger man. Hamlet's logic is clear, convincing, correct (in the Christian tradition). He becomes more conscious of the proper way to gain revenge, to 'trip him, that his heels may kick at heaven'. If his father (even as he speaks) must suffer the purgatorial flame then his murderer cannot be allowed to die in a state of grace. His soul must be 'as damn'd and black / As hell, whereto it goes.' The prince is right; we are with him; and yet the character itself (for once) is the less compelling one. His reasoning is flawless as the logic of a student may be flawless. Perhaps this is the real contrast: Hamlet does not know sin. He errs, and is to err grievously; he does everything but sin; but at this point at least, he is more the man of theory. His uncle's cry is born of experience. Almost as in a diptych, the scene offers a portrait of the generations. (One recalls the speeches of father and son to Ophelia in I,3.)

A trace of church dogma also finds its way into Hamlet's musings. To die free of mortal sin is to go to heaven. Shakespeare cannot have been quite indifferent to the ins and outs of theological debate; but the second speech does not so much explore a certain tenet as employ it. In more than one way perhaps the prince's words to himself are less compelling than those of the older man. And yet, within the terms of the dramatic situation and Hamlet's evolving personality, the speech is a splendidly striking one. Sword in hand, he is poised (we remember Pyrrhus) – and it is sheathed for good reason. One may note the two bristling short lines that seem to come with a deep breath of impatience or resolution. It is a moment of clarification for the speaker, however he may later picture it to himself. By contrast, the view the older man reaches is flat fact, a part of his make-up, which he is not about to forget. While he may have won our sympathy for an instant, he knows he is unable to surrender 'those effects for which I did the murder' (54), but is bound to 'retain the offence' (56). For all his long-ing he cannot change; he is resigned to the dying of the light. Whereas Hamlet looks forward. The scene is a powerfully balanced one, with the closing irony of the situation a final constructional touch. Age against youth, warmth against coldness, a sense of arrest and the need for action differently informing either side, the scene is less lauded than a number in the play; but it is finely devised.

'By my fay, I cannot reason,' says Hamlet to his two friends earlier (II,2,256), in his unsettled state of mind suddenly tiring of their word-play (after he has as it were won a trick at it). While the playwright loves to indulge in it, sometimes with quite unlikely characters, here it seems the natural repartee of students, which one imagines as deriving in part from an intensive study of grammar, rhetoric and logic. Certainly Rosencrantz in more serious mood can reason well. His extended metaphor on the consequences of 'the cease of majesty' (15f) is startlingly vivid, the 'massy wheel . . .' descending with 'each small annexment' an ineradicable image. 'For we will fetters put upon this fear / Which now goes too free-footed', determines the King (25–6), the alliteration seeming to yield a wonderful adjective out of thin air. 'Free-footed' for 'fear' in its inventiveness and directness is authentically Shakespearean. Once alone he allows his guilt, together with a vision of its absolution, to well up. 'What if this cursèd hand / Were thicker than itself with brother's blood, / Is there not rain enough in the sweet heavens / To wash it white as snow?' (43–6) The plea is of such eloquence it is almost a sin to comment on it. Merely to refer to the ease of the lines will do, recalling as they do the pure flow of Hamlet's thought in the 'To be or not to be' soliloquy, but here encamped somehow in a sensual knowledge of life's richness. 'Even to the teeth and forehead of our faults' (63), again typi-cally direct of the writer, also has his fondness for a couplet of nouns. The climax of the speech, an almost unbearable appeal to his own better nature, leaves nothing to be said but prayer, or thoughts of prayer, which we cannot hear: ' . . . and heart with strings of steel, / Be soft as sinews of the new-born babe. / All may be well.' Again a sensual image, and a hope for a miracle. When he rises, at the end, the tone is flat, as his thoughts have proved to be. In the previous imagery we may discern a trace of something exalted, as though a great step were indeed possible. But the practicalities of his life rule against it.

Hamlet's description of his father's unpreparedness for death, in religious terms, at one point carries a kind of counter-imagery. 'He took my father grossly, full of bread [a term for being in a state of sin], / With all his crimes broad blown [blooming], as flush as May' (80-1). Whether it is deliberate on the author's part or not, the words seem to turn a metaphorical richness, also sensual, against the kneeling figure, whose thoughts now are not inspired at all. Poetry can use the mind in ways the mind does not sometimes fully realise. Of course the author might have intended this effect and much more; or he might have been surprised at the suggestion. It does not really matter. A poem exists apart from its maker; and in *Hamlet*, a poem of the greatest magnitude, any number of effects will continue to announce themselves. If it were not so it would be cause for a certain alarm.

III, 4

The presumed backstory is that Hamlet came from Wittenburg at his father's death to find his mother already entangled with his uncle, the wedding taking place not long before we first see the three of them (I,2). One takes the present scene as the first time mother and son have been alone together since his return, at least for a conversation of any length. As such it is a meeting that has been waiting to happen, regardless of the Ghost's appearance and dread news. The question that is to dominate now has been long on his mind.

His shock at her entering a new conjugal life within four months (according to Ophelia) of his father's funeral is deep, wellnigh ineradicable. While he is disgusted at her new choice one tends to feel any replacement would have been unacceptable. His disillusionment – 'Frailty, thy name is woman!' – seems never to leave him. With this twist and what we are to see of Ophelia's preoccupation below the cover of sanity, Shakespeare makes a telling departure in the dramatic use of sex. He does not overplay it with either character, and productions (and theories) that do so, one way or another, run the risk of losing a subtle thread.

Only Hamlet and the Ghost condemn the marriage as a union of in-laws. An interesting historical question is raised as to any lingering sense of shock that may be felt by an Elizabethan or Jacobean audience at

Henry VIII's extraordinarily bullish way with the Catholic Church. After all this began with his acquiring a special dispensation to marry his brother's widow, Catherine of Aragon. There may be an echo of his personality in Claudius: in both one sees the effrontery that carries all before it. One may fleetingly wonder if the author expects his audience to make the connection. But since the play is a fiction set in another country and another time, one probably does better to take the accusations of incest merely as personal reactions to uncle and brother.

Instinctively the prince suspects Claudius ('O my prophetic soul!' I,5,40). He loathes the man, as is clear when we first see them. The Ghost's words bring that loathing to boiling-point; the perturbation of the King at the murder-play adds to their power: as the son sets off for his mother's room, one pictures him in a towering rage. But also as curiously relaxed, still shielded by uncertainty, waiting for things to unfold. He passes by a perfect opportunity to deliver an (apparently) inadequate revenge. Yet as always, when engaged in some more or less circuitous way upon fulfilling his mission, he appears (if not later to himself) to be acting without a thought as to his own safety. He carries on towards his mother and to a moment of reckoning. He has warned himself to 'be cruel, not unnatural . . . [to] speak daggers to her but use none' (III,2,366–7). Something is to change. In a sense it is all he knows.

The opening dialogue between mother and son resembles nothing so much as a modern cameo of stern reproving parent and angry overbearing teenager. Hamlet certainly seems younger than the thirty years he is to be assigned in Act V, in Shakespeare's day verging on middle age. Here and there in his plays the writer is a tad loose with time detail, a natural law coming in for a touch of deft stage-management; and even within this scene there is a sense of a shifting-forward. But it stops short of a mature acceptance of what may be called the paraphernalia of being. That cannot be his as yet.

Ten lines in and he lays hands on her (it appears), forcibly preventing her leaving and sitting her down. A few seconds more and his sword is out and someone is dead. It is almost as if the lunge he did not make at the King some moments earlier has taken place now, blindly and wrongly. He may do no more than shout and tower over the Queen, but however directed, there is a brute physicality to his behaviour that is frightening, to her at least ('thou wilt not murder me?'). He is wearing a callousness now, as if to signify there is no going back. The lightning-bolt through the arras sears the same impression into the story's surface. One senses Hamlet is at first as frightened as the Queen by what he has done – at least, it could be so directed. ('Nay, I know not: is it the King?') Her horror at the 'rash and bloody deed' enables him to regain the advantage, turning her words back on herself. ('A bloody deed! almost as bad, good mother, / As kill a king and marry with his brother. / . . . Ay, lady, 'twas my word.') He does not follow through with the accusation and we hear no more of it. He may remember that while the Ghost was aware the Queen's conscience would trouble her, it hardly seemed a matter of aiding and abetting murder: ' . . . Leave her to heaven, / And to those thorns that in her bosom lodge / To prick and sting her' (I,5,86-8).' If Hamlet has doubts on the matter the Queen's lack of reaction at the Players' play will surely have reduced them. Here his attention switches to what is clearly a more urgent concern.

One may wonder why it has not turned more to the body he has discovered of the 'intruding fool'; and even more perhaps, why the Queen allows it to lie there as though it does not matter. The reason is that it does not. The playwright plunges son and mother into a life-and-death matter of the soul itself that cannot be delayed. At first one may suppose the Queen is too frightened to do anything but follow Hamlet's lead; but very soon she is as involved as he is, if not more.

'Look here, upon this picture, and on this' (53). Possibly a locket miniature of his father worn by Hamlet set by a larger painting of Claudius, the two portraits could hardly fail to focus the Queen's thoughts on past and present, the abrupt change in her life. Intent to press home the advantage, to make her re-assess her situation, Hamlet compares the two pictures in wildly bombastic terms. He longs for her to come to her senses, or at least to gain a perspective on what she has done. But it is his own perspective he insists on. If earlier one is prompted to wonder if Hamlet and Ophelia (may be supposed to have) slept together, one is now as likely to see a distinctly virginal figure, all too easily preoccupied with the sexual act and knowing next to nothing about it. The playwright may well deliberately have sprung the trap of such a "double take"; it would be in keeping with an ambivalent stance towards actuality the play often adopts. At this point one of his aims seems to be to underline the prince's immaturity in a particular area at the same time as his more general disgust. The area is no doubt less to do with the sexual act than with the nature of love that goes beyond a loving friendship; nevertheless, the former is taken as the key point in the son's advice to his mother, to the extent that he seems virtually obsessed by it.

Again and again Hamlet impresses upon his mother's mind his abhorrence of her physical involvement with Claudius. 'Damnèd custom', 'Could you on this fair mountain leave to feed / And batten on this moor?', 'When the compulsive ardour gives the charge / . . . and reason pardons will,' 'In the rank sweat of an enseamèd bed / . . . honeying and making love / Over the nasty sty – '. The direction of his thoughts could not be clearer. Before leaving he urges her to 'Refrain tonight, / And that shall lend a kind of easiness / To the next abstinence'; and finally, still determined to make her see the same horror movie as the one that defies his belief, he plays it out for her: 'Let the bloat king tempt you again to bed; / Pinch wanton on your cheeks; call you his mouse; / And let him, for a pair of reechy kisses, / Or paddling in your neck with his damn'd fingers . . . '. If in a state of shock, and for a time uncertain as to what she feels, the Queen must nevertheless see her son with a part of her mind as possessed of a kind of demented intrusiveness.

A sword darts out against an unseen voice; a volley of words sharp as arrows storms the air, to fall, as we are to see, uselessly to the ground. In one way or another the prince is blind to the consequences of his actions. Yet in spite of all he remains in the chase. As he makes things happen more happens. Without seeing his way, with an implacable force bearing down on him, he still is able to retain some element of control, simply by keeping things moving.

Capping his triumphant comparison of the portraits he tells his mother her 'matron's bones' are too old for love's passion. His proprietorial docketing of her inner life is not only absurd, and wrong (since it is as clear as can be that she is in love with Claudius, and he has been around long enough to know it) – but ironic too. He is every bit as invasive as those who would 'sound me from my lowest note to the top of my compass' (III,2,338). From a distance he is still a negotiator of an unseen path that is somehow drawing him on, acting in blind faith, taking each step as it appears. Not to do so is to surrender all. Up close he is a blundering tenderfoot. This situation has the latter aspect at its height; and yet the former is not absent.

The Queen is shaken – understandably after the death of Polonius, Hamlet's fire turned on her, and the shameful reminder of the memory of her first husband. Whether in the appalling self-realisation she now comes to, she is thinking of anything more than the giddy haste of the second marriage, we cannot know; nor, perhaps, can she. It is a dramatic situation we are by now not unfamiliar with. Was she complicit in the murder? Probably not. Has she at any time suspected or half-suspected her new husband? Who can say? Nothing is certain. Why has she not explored Hamlet's view of his father's death? One can imagine a sequence leading to her questioning Horatio about the Ghost's appearance, for example. Is her distress due to the most natural of reasons, simply seeing old Hamlet's likeness again? With the portrait in front of her, the sheer pressure from his son might bring to the surface a buried guilt in her forgetting him so soon. So we go round in circles, no doubt as the dramatist intends.

What is certain is that she is struggling to cope. As Hamlet mounts his attack, pitching the sexual act in the crudest of terms, blasting Claudius with a torrent of belittling abuse, the Ghost enters. Perhaps it is the concern for a late wife that gives the apparition its solidity, so to speak, the remnant of a living affection. 'O, step between her and her fighting soul', it tells the 'tardy son', as the son so sees himself. He at once guesses at the reason for the visitation, which is 'but to whet thy almost blunted purpose,' as the Ghost confirms. But it isn't, unless we are to propose an almost supernatural coincidence; it is at least also to rescue the Queen. As with the import of the 'black and grainèd spots' she has seen within herself, little is sure when looked into further. Even the presence of the Ghost is now limited on stage to the prince's mind. In a performance there is no time to discuss questions such as these, barely to notice them; yet they are woven into the backcloth of the play.

The dramatic reality nevertheless is stark. The Queen is convinced her son is clean mad. For a moment, in her eyes, he is the one who needs rescuing from a precipice of existence, a wordless and terrible danger. With the Ghost's departure a sense of relative safety is restored. Hamlet fends off an accusation of 'ecstasy' ('madness') and renews his attack. But it is now more of a plea, with correspondingly gentler language. 'For love of grace . . . Forgive me this my virtue . . . ' and thrice 'good night', the second followed by a beautiful avowal of filial respect and affection, and something more. 'Once more, good night; / And when thou art desirous to be bless'd, / I'll blessing ask of you.' For a moment they are two fallen creatures, and who knows, the audience with them. And then the savage peroration, sneeringly showing her he knows how likely she is to scurry back to Claudius's bed, and tell him all about her frenzied son into the bargain. Yet the coarser Hamlet does not oust the other. Since the opening exchanges Gertrude has shown no anger, calling upon 'sweet Hamlet' even as he twists the knife so compulsively the Ghost has to step in (on a "natural" reading). She appears submissive now; but promises merely not to pass Hamlet's words on to Claudius.

Rather surprisingly the prince knows he is to be sent to England; even more surprisingly, he lets his mother know he suspects knavery and intends to reverse its direction, revelling in the clash to come. With some thoroughly tasteless word-play he sets about the removal of Polonius's body – one presumes Gertrude is beyond shock – and dragging it along, bids his mother good-night a fifth time. One feels he means it, that he wishes her no harm, that there is good in him, though much is awry. A bizarre picture to end the Act on, it perfectly catches the discontinuity in the prince's character. The first Act ended, after his first encounter with the Ghost, a scene of almost impossible tensions, with a few companionable words to Horatio and Marcellus, 'Nay, come, let's go together.' So the final good-night here, after a stormy scene and Act with its horrific addition, allows a closing note to linger of a submissive quiet. Here is the dilemma of his being, a man of cataclysmic intent and action, who would be at one with his fellow-creatures, despite all.

It is impossible to escape a certain constriction in the position of a commentator on *Hamlet*. One talks of the prince as of a visible entity, in the sense that any living person is visible to other people. In the interests of understanding that person the onlooker has a licence to hypothesise, to assess, to diagnose; in the case of a fictitious character an author often encourages a reader's or spectator's speculative involvement, which itself becomes a part of the literary dynamic. So far so good: but with this character Shakespeare has changed the rules of the game a little. No-one has a clear view of him till the end; nor he of himself, perhaps, at any time. Because he is reacting in large part to an inner situation he is directed to a degree by the unconscious. To put it simply: Shakespeare lets things happen to him, providing him with a compulsion to meet those events and adapt to them as he will. It is a kind of incoming tide that we see, as much as a shaped personality. While the author must more or less consciously himself have plotted the various collisions that take place and their effects, yet because he also planned and plotted something of an undirected charge, the commentator is swamped by that even as he or she engages in any part of the task of clarification. The intentionalist argument by which one can hope, if not to keep abreast of the creator as one mulls the creation, at least at times to be on a wavelength, so to speak, is more than usually obstructed by this. It tends to be an argument, however, that is both self-deceptive and unnecessary. It is probably only in a matter of degree rather than kind that this particular character confounds the commentator. In any case one may trust to the reverse of the intentionalist approach, to what might be termed the hardy perennial outlook, by which the meaning of an artistic creation is never exhausted and may itself forever change a little, to see one through.

Poetic effects, while subject to the same general caveats as the purely dramatic, shed a shaded illumination of their own. An arresting image, or merely a deft and precise use of words or a word, can alert the receptive mind to a certain further significance. Within the current of a gently insistent poetic form, a felicitous effect can do more than delight. In its own passing moment a step is taken – and sometimes a giant stride – towards transcending the artifice of an art-form. When Hamlet accuses the Queen of a falsity that makes of 'sweet religion . . . a rhapsody of words' (47–8) a senseless jumble is suggested. The use of 'rhapsody' offers an example of a sudden clarification of a state of mind: we are one with the speaker's disillusion. The range of meaning of the word has now changed a little and with that in mind the phrase has been borrowed to suggest the whole of the poem of *Hamlet* (see Introduction). Thrilling and loose-knit now, the sequence that is suggested still has a wild touch to it. Therein too lies the poem's dramatic power.

'Such an act / That blurs the grace and blush of modesty, / Calls virtue hypocrite, takes off the rose / From the fair forehead of an innocent love / And sets a blister there . . . ' (40–4). One almost feels the penultimate word invade the Queen's mind. (To brand the brow had been a mooted punishment for a prostitute.) With the 'vicious mole of nature' Hamlet notes in particular men (I,4,24), the 'black and grainèd spots' in her 'very soul' that appal the Queen (89–90), that 'ulcerous place' the prince so energetically brings to life (146f), and any number of suggestions of rot and corruption that crop up, almost like an infection, in the language of the play, this latest pustule adds to a lurking sense of virulent decay that includes the nation itself. Certainly it is a potent vein of metaphor the poet mines; but there is another, more lightly touched upon, to do with blind consequence, to tell us as much, if not more.

Meanwhile, almost in the same breath as the 'blister' and the 'rhapsody of words', with an all-suffusing hyperbole Hamlet has 'heaven's face' and 'this solidity and compound mass' of the earth differently reflecting their shame and sadness at the new marriage. This is the same clear-eyed iconoclast who everywhere sees through cant and catchwords, brilliantly mocking Osric's verbiage for example. Without doubt over the scene he makes a melodrama of his outrage for the Queen's benefit; without doubt, too, he is governed by a simplistic vision of the new departure in his mother's life: one feels he cannot help it. There is a moment when his inspired sensationalism rivets the listener to the spot: 'Eyes without feeling, feeling without sight, / Ears without hands or eyes, smelling sans all . . . ' (78–9). One is alone in a cold blankness. But the Queen is the one listening. It is a memorable instance of the service poetry can render to dramatic empathy.

'For at your age / The heyday in the blood is tame, it's humble, / And waits upon the judgment . . . ' (68-70). One recalls Hamlet's words of praise for Horatio, ' . . . and bless'd are those / Whose blood and judgment are so well commingl'd, / That they are not a pipe for fortune's finger / To sound what stop she please' (III,2,60-3). One wonders if the author may have had in mind the balance of the two vital powers, passion and reason, as a motif of a sort, with Horatio the unassuming model in the background. He may have begun to explore the idea through the repeated use of 'blood' with 'judgment' and found it too pointed to do so. These are the only two occasions in the play when the words come together. (One should note, however, the same division of powers in the phrase, 'Excitements of my reason and my blood,' IV,4,58, though in this case their relation is left implicit.)

Another speculative foray into authorial intent concerns the final phrase of the speech, ' . . . and reason pardons will' (88). One reading, which some editors follow, is 'panders' for 'pardons'. 'Acts as a pander to' is foully apposite, especially when it is remembered that 'will' had a secondary meaning of 'sexual organ' (male or female). And yet 'pardons' has its own force, can also profit from the secondary meaning, and perhaps concludes the passage more effectively. The Queen's reply would seem to follow on more naturally from the less explicit suggestion.

A little later the prince snarls at his mother not to do 'this . . . that I bid you do,' which, after succumbing to the King's advances, is 'to ravel all this matter out, / That I essentially am not in madness, / But mad in craft.' In other words (she is not) to say he is merely pretending to be mad. One wonders if – as part of the complex situation – this can be seen as a near-admission on his part. But he needed have no fears if so; for at the start of the next scene Gertrude, while breaking her solemn promise to tell Claudius nothing of their conversation, confides a very different view of her son's state of mind. It is a fairly thorough example of Hamlet's misjudgement of his mother.

Finally, to conclude the commentary on this most absorbing of scenes, there is the story of the 'famous ape' (196f). No-one now knows what it is. The general import is clear enough: it serves as a warning to Gertrude that to blab may be dangerous. The ape does not know what it is doing in imitating the birds. And yet one can see the prince himself on the roof and preparing to hurl himself from the basket. If anyone is intent to 'try conclusions' it is he.

IV, 1

The first three scenes run straight on from the last, with a handful of indefinite pauses thereafter. Time in Shakespeare is measured by events. At once we see the Queen turn to the King and breathlessly confide her view of her son as 'Mad as the sea and wind . . . '. She shares her husband's alarm as to what may happen next and is at one with his determination to 'ship him hence'. She has a brief word of regret for the passing of the 'good old man', no more; just as when it happened she spoke of a 'rash and bloody deed' and was then compelled to think of other things. The King has no time for anything but himself. A gust of urgency sweeps the stage now, almost amusingly resisted by Hamlet himself, who knows the hunt is up ('Hide fox, and all after', IV,2,28) and revels in passively driving it on. One may internally upbraid the royal couple for sparing so little thought for the life of their old counsellor, and even more the prince for his gross jokes over the corpse; but one knows at the same time that they are all variously caught up in the situation as it sweeps them into the unknown. One also knows they are at the mercy of a kind of heightened current of the self.

Only Horatio, of the main characters, is not. Part of the claim the play makes upon us surely derives from the spectacle it presents of a wild internal force in a number of lives. (When her own being is invaded by such an impulse Ophelia is scarcely equipped to accommodate it.) It can be argued we are all more or less blindly driven. Hamlet's moments of self-recollection after error are the more memorable for their rarity and depth. There are only two that go beyond a throwaway remark; and while his apology to Laertes at the end is decisive and all-encompassing, his weeping now over the body of Polonius, as reported by the Queen, is as telling in its way. We know the Queen may be making it up, to attenuate her son's fault; but unexpected as it is, once said we also know it is "absolutely possible". The polar opposite of the scene at the end, when the prince finally is able to come to terms in public with his wrongheadedness, this is a passing wordless recognition, alone, off-stage, no more than affirmed by an observer – and for all these reasons, poignant itself beyond words.

The simile of 'some ore / Among a mineral of metals base' (25–6) to suggest a richer vein in a mine ('mineral'), the whole excavation a look into Hamlet's mind as it were, creates a remarkable picture. ('Some ore' may have suggested 'or' to Shakespeare, gold, though it may merely indicate a particular seam that 'shows itself pure'.) One has the sensation of Hamlet crying helplessly. For the textural journey from a mine and rock-streak to a mind and tears it must stand as one of the more daring images in the poetry of its time. So far as the Queen's veracity is concerned, it is tempting to take the intricacy of the word-picture as evidence for, though some may take it against. The idea of a torrent of tears when alone with the corpse, in among the prince's coarse and brutal references to it when with others, does not seem far-fetched. But yet again the author has left a little conundrum.

IV, 2

'Safely stow'd', murmurs the recalcitrant, ready again to face the world. As it appears in the form of Rosencrantz and Guildenstern his dismissive bluster turns to an angry challenge. He knows they are to 'bear the mandate' on the ship (III,4,206), no doubt the 'letters seal'd' with the King's orders; and vents his spleen this time on Rosencrantz. In their short exchange he continually wrong-foots him; but also himself, as if half in play, admitting his rather splendid picture of a chewing ape is 'a knavish speech'. He is soon ready with another barb however. It is as if he is already in the field, set for a new round of the chase, practising his moves. 'The king is a thing . . . of nothing', he declares. 'Bring me to him.' As he advances he knows he is to circle further away. He is to set sail, no less – and still the hunter and the hunted are drawn closer together; and still the roles interchange. The long stalking manoeuvre, the narrowing range, the identity of the fox itself, all is up in the air.

Something is happening. Things are moving on. He delights in the King's disturbance, and does what he can do: a pitiful effort if viewed from the outside, merely to rattle the monarch whenever he can. But as if on an inner plane, a deadly encounter is in the making. Physical distance is as nothing. The world is reduced to an arena of two forces. Without a second thought the prince lays himself open to a murderous offensive, even if one conducted by proxy. His opponent is breaking cover.

Were they at length to be employed in sovereign leadership, one fancies the prince's quick wit and word-mastery might be such as to gain friends at home, consolidate alliances, lift a nation at peace or war. As it is they tend to emerge in a kind of biting humour. There are moments with his three fellow-students early on where his jesting has more of the innocent student about it; and near the end, with Horatio, he guys Osric wonderfully yet without disturbing the courtier's sublime equanimity. In the idle battle of wits with the Grave-digger for once he meets his match. But very often he uses a mordant inventiveness to supply a tongue-lashing commentary or riposte – which can be shocking and almost indecently funny at the same time. 'Indeed this counsellor / Is now most still, most secret and most grave, / Who was in life a foolish prating knave. / Come, sir, to draw toward an end with you' (III, 4, 215–18). Here the body is 'Compounded . . . with dust, whereto 'tis kin'; and a little later, the great statesman is to provide the agenda for 'a certain convocation of politic worms'. The voice, dripping with sarcasm, that tells Rosencrantz what goes on in the ape's jaw (17f), has found a narrow métier. It is still riveting. This image incidentally manages a compound life with a fine aplomb, the officers becoming nut-like foodstuffs and reverting to sponges squeezed dry by the hand, without a hitch in the understanding. It is partly the force of its separate components that makes the curious trope acceptable, partly its impromptu nature, that seems to allow for a slight disjointedness. The speaker is thinking on his feet. And he can (be directed to) make wild facial and hand movements to illustrate the transmogrification. But one can explain only so far. A true poet seems to get away with anything.

Including, with this character, a certain incoherence. 'The body is with the king, but the king is not with the body' (25-6) could mean a number of things. No more than a kind of impertinent flourish, it hints much but says little. The audience on and off-stage are flummoxed for a second as the very embodiment of a non sequitur moves on.

IV, 3

Claudius is all too aware of Hamlet's popularity in the country ('He's loved of the distracted multitude', 4). We remember Ophelia's 'The observ'd of all observers' (III,1,151) and find it easy to visualise a still magnetic figure. To Ophelia's list one might well add an irrepressible sense of humour, before all soured. Still there is a gaiety in his air. The King is a prince in the Machiavellian ideal, observant, quick on his feet, decisive, without compunction. The more disturbed he is the more intriguing is the duel to the spectator, the detached onlooker at some level present in every member of the audience. However caught up, inevitably we also stand back and to a degree assess the antagonists. The King's agitation is a sign of weakness that leads him to take a sudden pre-emptive action (which Hamlet already plans to adapt in some chilling way, as he has told the Queen, III,4,207f); or to overplay his hand, as eventually happens. But this is looking ahead. The difference between the two is perhaps the more pronounced now, as the King's swift ruthlessness stands out against the prince's more gradual and chancy approach, beset as it is with scruples and self-remorse. Yet as a more murderous intent establishes itself in the behaviour of the latter, for all their distance they are closer together.

Hamlet's patter on (what I should not call) the diet of worms, arising from a last gibe at Polonius and a new opportunity to belittle the King, casually embraces the human species. 'We fat ourselves for maggots' (22–3) encapsulates the cynic's philosophy. Of course he has good reason for his disillusionment; but at the same time we can hear a clever student speaking, showing off a little, enjoying a freedom of vision that dares subvert the established order. In the world of words he is king. 'This mad young man', as the King calls him (IV,1,19), has an everyday side to his extravagance, not that the King at that point sees him as one of a class of callow intellectuals. Yet there is more than a touch of that particular kind of immaturity in his behaviour. Life has not yet caught up with his teeming mind, even if it is working at the speed of light to do so.

Given that Ophelia laments 'That unmatch'd form and feature of blown youth / Blasted with ecstasy' (III,1,156–7), one must suppose Hamlet's appearance to encourage the general idea of his madness, at least some of the time. There may well also be a considerable degree of pantomime to go with much of his speech. Nevertheless the King must surely sense by now he has a cold-eyed enemy at his heels. His 'Alas, alas!' at the disquisition on the worm-feast is for the attendant onlookers, one feels: the idea of the prince's insanity is to be promoted far and wide. We see later from a remark of the Grave-digger that it is so. Yet the King may well judge the prince is not quite sane either. How he is perceived by all, except perhaps Horatio, is something of a mystery; but it is a mystery that reflects an essential privacy of life. We live in the mist of *Hamlet* more than it is generally convenient to admit. From the start the King has surely felt an insult in the prince's words that is partially displaced by their riddling character. One can visualise a grinning head, cocked to one side, delivering the next words, a simple and brilliant demolition of society's hierarchies. Is the King bemused? He may be. Does he feel the insult? Almost certainly yes. But no-one knows quite what they feel, including ourselves as we watch; and that too is a part of our everyday turmoil.

'A man may fish with the worm that hath eat of a king, and eat of the fish that hath fed of that worm' (27-8). Twenty-four monosyllabic clipped words (none of more than four letters) make play with a devilish exactitude. Out of the confines of the iambic pentameter the poet drops into prose to make it poetry too. Within the said confines he can work a conversational episode into a metrical line. '[K.] . . . for England. [H.] For England? [K.] Ay, Hamlet. [H.] Good' (45). Five feet, two iambs, two spondees, an iamb, as Hamlet stresses the two syllables of his 'England' in such a way as to cause the King further alarm. Poetry in prose, prose in poetry; of course there can be no absolute dividing-line. Poetry springs from prose and prose can spring to receive it. The latter happens naturally enough in the context of a poetic play, when a great poet flexes his fingers, so to speak, to let his language speak with a renewed freshness.

Under a veil of nonsense, which the King both does and does not see through, Hamlet launches a continuous barrage of abuse. There is a deal of room for variation in its delivery. 'Nothing, but to show you how a king may go a progress through the guts of a beggar' might be off-hand or shouted into the face. A mixture of sophistry and startling cheap rudeness, it is all a form of challenge to the sovereign power. He cannot afford this. There is only one answer and he has devised what seems a fine method for it. But the prince's manic behaviour in the past hour or so, since the Players came to the stage at his direction, has taken the more guileful opponent out of himself. He has been forced into a direct (if covert) action. 'Do it, England; / For like the hectic in my blood he rages, / And thou must cure me' (63–5). If the nephew is ill the uncle is ill too. A deft piece of theatre, to separate the two at the moment when either is almost shaking with a kind of aggressive anxiety, yet neither is able to dispatch the other cleanly. It seems the court is not big enough to hold them both, nor even the country.

IV, 4

All we see of Fortinbras before the very end is here, as he issues a level-headed instruction to his army captain to claim a promised right of way over Danish territory to fight the Pole. He seems to have taken his uncle's rebuke to heart – and, simply, grown up. There is no suggestion of the wayward personality Horatio describes, 'of unimprovèd mettle hot and full' (I,1,97); and Hamlet's reference to him later in this scene, as a 'delicate and tender prince . . . with divine ambition puff'd' (48–9), seems lodged in the past. The Norwegian prince we see now (as Hamlet does not) is self-contained, no apparent egoist; and his brief step onto the stage at this point is, remarkably, all that is needed by way of preparation for his second and final appearance, when with a due sense of the profundity and sadness of the occasion, he enters to take over the Danish reins. The symmetry of his and Hamlet's royal position, the reversal of power from Denmark to Norway, his personal journey from young hothead to authentic candidate for the crown, all add a certain depth and shade to Hamlet's own portrait; as, somewhat differently, does Laertes' familial and personal role. The figure of Fortinbras aside, it is a not unwelcome diversion from the embroilments of the Danish court merely to glimpse the affairs of other countries for a moment. The author knows when to unroll a dramatic map, instinctively on the watch against spectator fatigue in any shape or form.

Indeed this scene and the churchyard episodes to come breathe the open air and the clear sky. The play opened with a good deal of activity on the castle ramparts at night: otherwise within hall and chamber it has tightened the strings of a psychological Gordian knot. Hamlet's account of his adventures on board ship, and differently, Gertrude's flowery portrayal of Ophelia's last moments, also remind us of a more open world, if one no less perilous or cruel. Just as the playwright will surprise us with a comic scene, and sometimes at a grimly tense moment, so (perhaps less obviously) he will work the changes on the simple physical fact of a changing environment. Or rather, instinctively unfolding a narrative with an eye to holding his audience, he will let the changes work themselves.

With the Captain the Danish prince is a model of quiet courtesy. On his own, as he ponders the almost thunderous example he has just seen of passionate commitment to a cause, an army 'of such mass and charge' on the march, he is more excited (32f). But he does not tempestuously rave against himself as he did following the 'Pyrrhus' speech, when the First Player seemed to transform his own being with a display of feeling, 'and all for nothing!' (II,2,524). Here are no sudden rhythm-sundering pauses, no rapid volley of self-piercing questions, no floundering in a morass of guilt that is at times suspiciously close to a wallowing in it. Given his situation at the time we can hardly blame the earlier Hamlet for a tendency to indulge himself in his shame; and in that soliloquy the practical, forward-thinking side of his mind finally comes to his rescue and he pulls himself clear. In fact he develops an idea which is to set in motion a chain of events leading to the markedly more composed individual we see before us now. In his thoughts on suicide ('To be or not to be . . . ', III,1,57f), shortly before the Players' performance in the royal presence, he is in a state less of despair than of an acceptance of failure too deep to despair at. In the present (and final) soliloquy he is by no means free of a penchant for self-dramatisation, nor would he be Hamlet if he were; but a stronger man speaks, more assured, and closer to self-belief. He has put himself in harm's way (he is going to the ship); and seems able to act with a confidence that win or lose, a plan is working.

Of course, even to call it a plan is to label it with too much intent. It is a way of not standing still. As he leaves the court behind him, the prince may be walking to his doom. But a deep calculus within him offers it as the way to take. To come back to the metaphor of the chase, he knows the King is no longer in unchallenged territory. As treasured sovereign (especially after his swift response to the alarming Norwegian threat), and as husband to a restored and treasured Queen, he was untouchable. But he has been lured from his thicket, and with racing blood, on unfamiliar ground, is more apt to make an error. It is painful to write such a sentence, and one dare not think what it must be like to read it. The picture it suggests is nowhere near the front of Hamlet's mind, as we see from the wave of dissatisfaction with himself, that passes through him as he sees 'The imminent death of twenty thousand men, / That for a fantasy and trick of fame / Go to their graves like beds . . . '. But at some half-realised level, below even the defining level of unvoiced words in thought, perhaps it may be suggested as an acceptable trope for what is taking the prince on and forward.

This is all by way of making sense of what we see before us, arising from the bare boards of a stage. It is in the dynamic that Shakespeare has created. Here his protagonist speaks to himself and the world of a personal situation. He has it wrong, of course, at least partially, in that he does not admit his reason, argued so lucidly at the time, for sparing the King's life when he was at prayer. He appears unable to put any kind of gloss at all on the Ghost's words that must surely haunt him, 'thy almost blunted purpose'. But no-one has accurate inner vision. Like any one of us he knows of the hollow in the skull and finds a way forward, in his case manfully and with conviction. The overt presentation of his situation, irresistibly offered by the chance encounter, imposes itself and he cannot help but lay a searing charge against himself. 'Bestial oblivion', cowardice, a too-busy mental focus, all jostle to convict him of the worst of crimes. Dishonour fills his being. Even so he is able to trust to his instinct.

He speaks of more than his own situation. In the faintest of sketches, and behind his own failure, the prince seems to convey something of the privileged position of humankind. Early on he takes note of it, only to let it pass him by. 'What a piece of work is a man! How noble in reason! how infinite in faculty!' he exclaims to Rosencrantz and Guildenstern (II,2,292–3); but in his morbid state of mind 'the paragon of animals' has reduced itself to 'this quintessence of dust'. In a small but significant change of outlook, now (despite all) a frail thread of hope can be felt to run down the present speech, unifying it in its structure and core determination. After remarking on the divine gift of thought to the human species (36–9), the speaker does not at once disassociate himself from the good of it, as it were shutting the door on himself. Rather he admits his inadequacy. The tone is thoughtful rather than dismissive. All through the speech the lines are steady, with a kind of underlying drive to them. On the one side the observations throughout (till the end) are self-lacerating; on the other there is a spirit animating the whole from which the conclusion seems naturally to derive and take strength.

The man carries the belittling judgement of the Ghost about with him. Though an appeal against it may be evident to the playgoer the player cannot make it. Yet within the net the dramatist has cast over his character's understanding, the beginnings of a resolution to the situation, at once internal and external, can be sensed. Despite his suggestion of 'some craven scruple / Of thinking too precisely upon the event,' the steps he has taken are starting to tell. Other characters are to claim our immediate attention, yet as we leave him behind us, perhaps a stronger being lingers in our minds, on his way to the shore.

There is an interesting rhythmical departure in half-lines in the first exchanges between Hamlet and the Captain. Five lines of three beats broaden into the customary five. '[H.] Good sir, whose powers are these? [C.] They are of Norway, sir. [H.] How purpos'd, sir, I pray you? [C.] Against some part of Poland. [H.] Who commands them, sir? [C.] The nephew to old Norway, Fortinbras.' The symmetry lightly underpins a casual courtesy on meeting, following which the two men chat more expansively. It is one of a number of examples of variation on the use of the pentameter, for a certain effect to derive itself from the direct speech of the moment, to be found here and there in the play.

'This is th'impostume [abscess] of much wealth and peace / That inward breaks . . . ' (27–8). Another violent image of 'rank corruption', to recall the 'ulcerous place' the prince kindly let the Queen know he saw as her soul (III,4,149–50), the idea here also links with the excuse he makes to her a second later for speaking like that. 'Forgive me this my virtue; / For in the fatness of these pursy [swollen] times, / Virtue itself of vice must pardon beg . . . ', he informs her high-handedly. Here a luxury of 'wealth and peace' has led invisibly to the rot. Earlier too, condemning 'this heavy-headed revel east and west' in his country under the new régime (I,4,17), he makes the same point, if not quite so vividly. Now he finds the same fault in Norway as in Denmark. In part the criticism seems to come from a love of being critical, and a fondness for the sweeping generalisation, that goes more with the youthful student than with whatever the student is to become. In part, too, he has a point: war and the swagger of its preparation surely often stem from a degenerate section of society whose wealth is turned to ambition for more. But his inconsistency reminds of the former. Here a straw is reviled (26); in no time at all it is a banner to be followed (55). Nevertheless one feels that on a personal level he is less dismissive, less high-handed now.

The imagery of taint and corruption, generally of another or others when seized upon by the prince, also attaches to himself, it goes without saying. As he admits, 'my wit's diseas'd' (III,2,296). Others use it also, both the Queen (who sees within her 'very soul / . . . such black and grainèd spots . . . ' III,4,89–90), and the King, helplessly flailing ('O limèd soul, that struggling to be free, / Art more engag'd!' III.3.68–9). Theirs is a more direct self-knowledge than Hamlet's; but he has the philosopher's eye to see the disease and decay of a virus at large. The abhorrent infection at loose in Denmark is the underside of the play, at the last to be eradicated at maximum cost. Within the metaphor of the chase, good and evil too circle and track each other, represented not by the two adversaries alone, but by the movement of each individual, whatever his or her complexities.

'Sure, he that made us with such large discourse, / Looking before and after, gave us not / That capability and god-like reason / To fust in us unus'd' (36–9). Despite his wearied self-disgust Hamlet does not renounce his humanity, as in the 'quintessence of dust' passage, or somehow stand outside it, as in 'To be or not to be.' His acceptance of certain Christian doctrines (most visibly Purgatory and 'the dread of something after death', III,1,79) is one thing; but here he is in God's hands. A character more at one with itself, but no less vulnerable, holds forth for the last time alone. Its progress is as to be as irregular as ever; but even as we observe it (and we see more in retrospect), for all the gaping lack of substance in terms of achievement, we may sense a steadier commitment to a cause.

'What a piece of work is a man!' exclaimed the prince earlier. Do we not now have before us an apt description of the distinguishing mark of the species? Its 'large discourse' (36) is surely the gift of thought, speech, language, and vitally, of 'looking before and after'. To be able to have the past and future as concepts in the mind is the cornerstone of all we have built with mind and hand. 'That capability and god-like reason', which has led to so much and has so far to go, is both apparent and inexplicable in great works of art, and not least in this play.

We come to 'the invisible event' (50), another term this commentary has put to extracurricular use. Here it means whatever the future may bring. Hamlet envies Fortinbras his insouciant defiance of fate. But it seems that Shakespeare has worked into his play something less to do with attitude and more with a permanent actuality of our living and being. By bringing us close up to it he has magnified the gap between present and future, one thing and the next. We are blundering travellers down a path of intent that continually reshapes itself. A great deal we see clearly enough; at the same time we are steeped in a half-seeing, at times in blindness, prone always to error. (One thinks of the ape in the basket.) There is a wealth of allusion to a kind of unsightedness. Images recur of a missed or unintended target: for the former, the King's announced hope (in sending Hamlet away) that ' . . . slander, / Whose whisper o'er the world's diameter / As level as the cannon to his blank / Transports his poison'd shot, may miss our name / And hit the woundless air' (IV,1,40-4). For the latter, Hamlet's all-significant apology to Laertes at the start of the fatal fencing match (V,2,217–21): 'Sir, in this audience, / Let my disclaiming from a purpos'd evil / Free me so far in your most generous thoughts, / That I have shot mine arrow o'er the house / And hurt my brother.' Another pair of images springs from a shared root to branch different ways. Each tells of the same withheld event. First the King (III,1,161–4), 'There's something in his soul / O'er which his melancholy sits on brood; / And I do doubt the hatch and the disclose / Will be some danger'; and later the Queen (V,1,268–70), 'Anon, as patient as the female dove / When that her golden couplets are disclos'd, / His silence will sit drooping.' The similarity within either metaphorical pair, together with the uncertainty linking them all, suggests a narrative tendency that a host of other reference supports. It is a direction in the author's mind, no more. But it may be an element in his thinking, working to an extent unseen even by him, that allowed the play to find its unifying procedure, and to realise its distinctive effect.

IV, 5

The death of Polonius lies at the back of proceedings, in the play's terms a real figure behind its figurative language of uncertain targets. It is an unresolved issue, waiting, like the body itself, to receive due attention. Though Hamlet told the Queen, 'I . . . will answer well / The death I gave him,' we are not aware he has done so. Beyond his tears of remorse, themselves no more than reported, from its very occurrence the deed has lingered unregarded and unexpiated; nor is it possible to see how reparation may be made, given the business on hand. We see from the Danish mob's later backing of Laertes for the crown that the family was of the highest rank; and we learn of the old man's 'obscure funeral' (204). The King has tried to hush up the affair. But in an unseen dynamic of cause and effect the atrocity sits lodged like a time bomb.

'I will not speak with her.' What a marvellous opening line. There is only one 'her' it can be; but our first impression is of a disturbance within the Queen herself. It is confirmed by her haunted reflection on sin and guilt a moment later (17–20). Is this an admission of more than a betrayal of her first husband's memory? All of a sudden the question re-presents itself: did she turn a blind eye to Claudius's crime? Did she aid and abet it? Could these few lines indicate a more shocking involvement, together with an ability to mask it, than we may have suspected? The character is deliberately left open-ended; but it does seem the 'black and grainèd spots' her inner sight was transfixed by in the interview with Hamlet, so far from swiftly vanishing as at first appeared, have proved indelible. Later Gertrude is quick to defend the King, to the point of catching hold of the raging Laertes as he threatens him. As Claudius she is trapped by her situation, unable to give up what he termed the 'effects' of old Hamlet's death –in her case her new husband – yet it seems knowing she should. Perhaps her son's use of the word "murder" has lingered in her, turning acceptance to a diabolical doubt. Perhaps remorse at an 'o'er-hasty marriage' has been made to feel like the dread weight of a sin by the displacement of recent events, as if precipitating a minor landslip in the mind. So we come full circle on the question of her prior involve-ment; and instead we look at the present, and see before us, brimming below the surface, a near-uncontainable anxiety, as of one caught up in an insoluble crisis.

'Let her come in.' The Queen is persuaded to admit her; but she – and we – are hardly prepared by the Gentleman's words for the shock of her entrance. The name stays; but in both inner substance and (presumably) outer appearance the life it depicts is savagely other. Such is true, helpless madness. For all the depth of response to be evoked by the death of a character in a tragedy, perhaps the most tragic moment of the play is here.

The last we heard from Ophelia was during the Players' play, when she appeared to discover a trace of her lost spiritedness in response to the prince: '[H.] I could interpret between you and your love, if I could see the puppets dallying. [O.] You are keen, my lord, you are keen. [H.] It would cost you a groaning to take off my edge. [O.] Still better, and worse.' (III, 2, 228–32. 'Puppets' probably had a slang sexual meaning.) While the main cause of her disintegration is naturally taken as her father's death at the hand of the man she loved, the shock of Hamlet's double-edged and contradictory assault on her sexuality has surely added to the confusion. The icy coldness of 'Get thee to a nunnery', followed by the charged warmth of his later innuendoes, may well have wrought a kind of havoc in her, even if she managed to field it all at the time.

Now, beginning with the 'beauteous majesty' of the Queen, it is not clear that Ophelia recognises anyone. Two things are on her mind, the death of her father and sexual betrayal. It seems unlikely that one is based on fact and the other on a kind of victim's fantasy. Hamlet has cared nothing for her no doubt protected sensibilities in his sexual chatter of either kind; and one could argue for the mind's compulsive development of the implications therein, after a rude verbal awakening. But the sheer accuracy in the pretty song of the ways of young men, who 'will do't, if they come to't,' argues otherwise; as do her own words, that seem to ascribe her state to seduction. After the King describes her mind-wanderings as 'conceit upon her father' she is quite direct. 'Pray you, let's have no words of this; but when they ask you what it means, say you this': and then the song. But of course there is no need for such an argument. It is another false trail laid by the dramatist, who in this play delights to turn the mind of his audience one way and another on the same issue. There is a purpose of sorts: with each conundrum the existential maze down which so many of his characters are lost more nearly includes the spectator. Meanwhile (as with the Queen) we look at the character before us now. It is difficult to imagine a single playgoer unable to respond to the pathos of the situation.

The Queen may start at Ophelia's first lines of song and wonder if they are addressed to her, though the singer may recognise her only fleetingly at the most. 'How should I your true love know / From another one?' She will then stand by perhaps with thoughts of her own as a medley of lyrical snatches romanticise death and unromanticise mating. Ophelia appears to comprehend and not to comprehend at the same time, treating all alike with a plaintive sing-song finality. Of course a director may require a different tone of voice at different moments; and there is scope for dancing, clumsy or delicate, likewise unexpected bodily movement or a dallying with clothes. Her former restraint could be quite thrown to the winds; though to have her grace turn ugly may lessen the impact. However she is presented, the shock to the onlookers of a lady of her station using the language she does is tangible. All at once she is something holy, distributing flowers, like blessings most apposite . . . after which again she recalls her father's journey to the grave. Her last words tell us she is at one with the ideal world, however lost to the harsh one about her. Surely in a state of grace, suddenly she is brushed with a trace of compassion for all. *'God ha' mercy on his soul!'* And on all Christian souls, I pray God.' She leaves with an ordinary 'God be wi'ye' that seems to linger, unforgettable in its innocence.

The contrast with the King, who never ceases to plot and plan in his own interest, is marked. Instinctively he addresses the child in Ophelia, 'How do you, pretty lady?', presenting himself as a friend, even in the midst of her ditty about the loss of virginity – 'Pretty Ophelia!' He knows how to handle her, as later he does Laertes, and everyone and every situation he encounters except for the one eclipsing them all. He has made a deft and decisive effort to deal with that, but clearly is not at ease: there is much on his mind. Images of warfare trouble him. 'When sorrows come, they come not single spies, / But in battalions' (74–5); all too effectively as it seems: 'O my dear Gertrude, this, / Like to a murdering-piece [a multi-shot cannon], in many places / Gives me superfluous death' (90–2). He leads a disturbed country: ' . . . the people muddied, / Thick and unwhole-some in their thoughts and whispers . . . ' (77–8); and foresees Laertes, whom he knows to be back under cover in Denmark, feeding off their 'pestilent speeches'. Polonius's death has borne a terrible fruit in his daughter's outlook; what will it do to his son's? Despite all, in the crisis that suddenly bursts in on him, he is at once able to assume the initiative, as sure-footed as ever.

The court invasion is gross and terrifying. A bloody coup is all but fact: the doors are broken, the Swiss guards overborne, Laertes is ready to kill. The King needs no protection. His complete confidence in the blameless part he has played, as in the virtue of his sovereign role, is enough to give the younger man pause. An aura of power Claudius is able to adopt at will is never more tellingly employed. It is no retreat behind a formality; Laertes finds himself with a patient and reasonable man with every sympathy for his position. On Ophelia's second entrance Claudius makes no attempt to intervene in the meeting (such as it is) between brother and sister; and one can imagine that when she has gone and Laertes turns back to him, the shaken youngster is ready to repose a certain trust in the person who wants only to share in ('commune with') his grief. It is a masterpiece of management. In his own way the King has a genius to match Hamlet's. For all his fears, with the nephew out of the way, the uncle is in his element.

Laertes erupts onto the scene, his Danish supporters at his heels. They seek the throne for him while he seeks only revenge for his father; but initially it seems the one could lead to the other. It is a far cry from the polite youth who begs his father's and his king's permission to return to Paris after the coronation, and the slightly pompous brother who warns his sister not to pay too much attention to a prince's protestations of love. This is a hardened animal driven by a passion of the blood. Finally – as he dies – the balance between the blood and the judgement is discovered; and all the journey of immaturity, with its terrible cost, is a thing of the past. (It is so too in the case of the prince, his incalculably deepened mirror-image.) But if not the 'steep and thorny way to heaven' his sister urged him also to take, there is a hard road to be travelled yet.

At first sight Laertes has all the fire and fury Hamlet lacks in his quest. Hell-bent on revenge for his father's death he confronts the same individual, 'O thou vile king!' (112), that the prince is no more than childishly rude to, 'Seek him i'the other place yourself' (IV,3,34). Laertes certainly does not seem to suffer from 'thinking too precisely on the event' (IV,4,41); but while Hamlet puts that to himself as a possible trait behind his desperately shameful inaction, in the deeper scheme of things he does all the thinking he needs to do and no more.

The underlying point at issue really is one of honour, which tends to be something measured by the outside world and therefore visible in its aspects. It is not always so; and there is only one place where it is truly gauged. In part the play turns on this point. The prince sees his continued tardiness as shameful, when it need not be so, since it arises from a need to send the King and his reputation to hell. The Ghost has irredeemably obscured his inner vision with the words, ' . . . this visitation / Is but to whet thy almost blunted purpose' (III,4,110–11). Given its situation the spirit might have known better; but one can hardly discuss it in such personal terms. Merely it *is*. Nevertheless it lays an inhuman burden on the prince's shoulders: to complete what can only be a full revenge while dominated by thoughts of his dishonourable delay. Even the brilliantly analytical prince cannot clearly see – for he does not yet have the experience – the fatal trap of honour. Too often it is defined not by our feeling but by others' seeing, and the globe is made miserable as a result. Shakespeare does not show his hand on the matter. The situation is complicated by Hamlet's undeniably flawed ego, which he is all too conscious of, and which – again – is with him almost up to his dying words. But it is easy to condemn him for the wrong crime.

Meanwhile we applaud Laertes for his defiance and we witness his unspeakable hurt on seeing his sister. After the very questionable death of his father, and the disgrace of his 'obscure funeral', this sudden and greater blow might well dislodge his own mind for a time. In two of the cruellest strokes of fate imaginable his family is no more. Yet after the initial shock ('O heat, dry up my brains! . . . '), as he begins to observe and understand the play of her mind, and she sings her lilting songs and gives flowers to all and sundry, an inexplicably tender episode passes before us. Finally he submits to the King's sympathetic but firm lead ('Laertes, I must commune with your grief,' 193), as also to his own steadying need to find the right way forward, and promises to await the detail of his father's death before proceeding further with his revenge. But that he will proceed appears certain. In a wonderful counterpoint to Hamlet's own suspended action Laertes' delay is something at once excusable, necessary even; and his intent is altogether more driven and determined. Or so it seems, as the fates of the two spirited young noblemen are drawn inexorably together. But there is a more significant difference. Hamlet has the King's measure and retains the initiative.

'They say the owl was a baker's daughter' (41–2). A baker's daughter of folk-tale refused bread to a begging Jesus who turned her into an owl. We may or may not pick up a hint of guilt in Ophelia's straying mind, as to her silence at Hamlet's love-letter, and the return of his 'remembrances', at a time when he was clearly suffering. There is more than a hint of awareness of a devastating transformation in her being. The allusion is followed by a sentiment of the purest clarity, 'Lord, we know what we are, but know not what we may be (43–4).' A simple statement of experience – but what experience! – from a mind cast adrift, one wonders if it could persuasively have been made by a sane character. Yet it is a wholly accurate observation, applicable to anyone able to understand it.

The writer takes advantage of an unusual focus in a wrenched perception to throw in a remark that for all its fine phrasing, would scarcely be more than trite in the normal way of things, reflecting a change in fortune perhaps. As it is it reflects more. We know less than we think. We can plan less than we think. Everything of the future is subject to the blind imprisonment of the moment. We cannot see what is coming next. Finally of Ophelia's non sequiturs that have a consequence of their own, one may return to her splendidly gracious first exit line, 'Good night ladies, good night sweet ladies, good night, good night' (69–70). It is addressed to a company almost entirely of men, but the superficial error may hide a deeper natural truth. She has goodwill towards her fellow-beings and little thought for herself. (So too in her final exit.) But it is a ruthless world.

Never is this felt more. The accidental hurt we are subject to, courtesy of a gigantically distorted scheme of things, seems to speak out in Ophelia's songs of loss and her wrecked existence. An indescribable beauty lies at the back of her wandering presence, however unseemly it may have become, and in the sporadic offerings of a generous nature. The flowers, the concern for others, glimpses of a free and open spirit she may yet have become, all is no more than a scrap of human tenderness crushed by the mindless barbaric wheel of events. It is not an easy episode to turn the page on.

In her confused state she uses only prose and song. The artifice of the sustained spoken pentameter may not sit well with the abandoned controls of a rudderless mind. A sidelight is cast on the normal dramatic speaking convention. A coherent intelligence is presumed always to lie at the back of it, more so than in other forms of presented speech, where the driving force of the organising mind may be less of a requirement. A song can be a matter of rote; in prose anything at all can happen; but as the eagle-eyed instrument of its verse, the iambic pentameter lent an incisive edge to the theatre of the time.

IV, 6

A brief transitional scene serves to re-introduce Horatio, last seen with Hamlet after the Players' play. (Many editions show him in IV,5 advising the Queen to allow the deranged Ophelia to come in, but the relevant couple of lines appear to be ascribed to him in error.) We are reminded of an improbable solitary figure, self-contained, with a certain presence to him, but without ego. He is like a character from another time, mediaeval in his loyalty, no part of this decadent age. Yet he is answerable to its true needs, part of the elusive goodness to be found in it and at any time. There is a sense in which we know Hamlet is good because Horatio is good. The prince values him beyond measure simply for who he is (III,2,54f); he needs him near, as if to learn from him. Even the king, who one would think would be suspicious of such a close friend of his enemy, calls him 'good Horatio' (V,1,275). Here his strange aloneness is again revealed, as he expresses his anticipation at the letters: 'I do not know from what part of the world / I should be greeted, if not from Lord Hamlet' (4–5). He is a barely credible figure; and yet there are such all round us. Less likely than his existence, perhaps, is his friendship with the prince. But nothing should surprise us about Hamlet.

The episode also serves to catch up on the prince's adventures. One supposes the 'good turn' he is to do for the pirates may be the promise of a reward from the King for delivering him safe and sound, an ironical twist the writer does not bother to develop. Of course it could be something more positive from the pirates' point of view, money from himself for example; though now that he is face-to-face with the King's outright hostility, the first barren alternative may suit better. He is learning to be ruthless, as we soon find out. Yet would he then mention the 'good turn' in a full-hearted letter to his friend? Again one is caught in a non-question. With this petty example before one, it seems to have turned into an occupational disease.

'[Sailor] God bless you, sir. [Horatio] Let him bless thee too. [Sailor] He shall, sir, an't please him' (6–7). A simple exchange of courtesies with the Christian echo affirms what at other times we are more conscious of, though it is never more than a background note, weaving itself more or less imperceptibly into the play's music. Everything is subject to God's will. A faith is held in common and taken for granted. The immanence of the divine is not absent from the play, beside which human actions can seem no more than a rickety structure. More apparent than in some of the author's works, it remains a sporadic and faint motif: a reminder, within the very promise of its security, of human fragility and error. One can do no more than notice it and pass on.

IV, 7

A master-class is continued in the steady gaining of ground. Laertes is satisfied the King had no hand in his father's death, and in addition that the true culprit went so far as to attempt regicide. One assumes a colourful rendering by Claudius of Hamlet's arras-stabbing intent, aided no doubt by the Queen's recollection of his words, 'I took thee for thy better' (III,4,32). As we listen to the explanation of why more drastic steps against the prince were (apparently) not taken we hear again of his popularity, 'the great love the general gender bear him; / Who, dipping all his faults in their affection, / Would, like the spring that turneth wood to stone, Convert his gyves to graces . . . ' (18f). Claudius is wary of the will of the people and their headstrong allegiance. ('Stone' may be there to suggest an appropriate surface for the unavailing arrows of the subsequent image.) Establishing a man-to-man sympathy with Laertes with his rueful account of the prince's untouchability in the Queen's and the public's eyes, and encouraged by the bereaved son and brother's open-hearted response, Claudius is interrupted by a letter from the prince himself. The shock must be palpable but he keeps nothing private from Laertes at this moment, sharing the contents, asking his advice. He proceeds to lay out an irresistible scenario, flattering the young man with a tale of the international renown of his swordsmanship – and suddenly pauses. 'Laertes, was your father dear to you? / Or are you like the painting of a sorrow, / A face without a heart?' (106–8) Deliberately he builds again towards the disclosure of his murderous plan, touching for good measure on the stigma of a dishonourable dilly-dallying; and finds Laertes more than ready to consent, and to add a refinement of his own. Though after the Queen's news he has to double back again, to ensure the shock does not rob his accomplice of the poise and precision that will be needed, one has no doubt he will do so successfully. In a minor pursuit, so to speak, the quarry is within the tracker's reach.

Laertes is docile. No longer breathing fire (though we may suppose a smoulderingly quiet demeanour), he is content to follow the King's lead, determined only that he may be the 'organ' (68). A compelling and attractive character in his way, there is little wildly exceptional about him (beyond his rapier-work perhaps). He is not so much a dominant or original personality as a conventional one. One hardly imagines him firing off a stream of verbal brilliancies, nor as having the remotest wish to do so; he is not caught up in his own individuality. Rather one sees him expatiating a little tediously perhaps, as in his homily to his sister; or looking to a body of outside opinion to validate a course of action (IV,5,194f and 208; and, if only as a form of words, V,2,223–7). But he is a forceful individual. Subdued now, he never seems to lose a certain energy and verve, if in happier days it was as a member of a vibrant family, or such as to make his father keep an eye on him in Paris. He is not about to slump into inaction, a fault it is almost impossible to avoid laying at the gate of his opposite number. Indeed the current contrast between them, so heavily marked by the parallel circumstance of an all-consuming need to avenge a father, makes us the more inclined to agree with the prince about himself. And that we do (in spite of ourselves) illustrates how neatly we are persuaded to trip ourselves up. Aside from leading us to think about various questions that can't be answered, the dramatist brings us round in a perfect circle on this overriding issue. The net result is for the spectator or reader to lose the balanced view of the outsider rather more determinedly than is usual, in the matter of artistic appreciation; and so we further lose ourselves in the play.

One should not over-emphasise the role of a character in relation to another. Laertes has a natural appeal to the audience. (Perhaps we sympathise with him more as one of the lost.) At the King's question, 'What would you undertake / To show yourself your father's son in deed / More than in words?' (123–5), his answer is superbly to the point: 'To cut his throat i'the church.' Where Hamlet had scruples Laertes has none. Hearing the King's plan he is at once forward-thinking, committed; one sees him eagerly nodding at the back-up of a poisoned drink; but with the Queen's entrance and her abrupt declaration, 'Your sister's drown'd, Laertes,' his 'speech of fire' (190) is out. He leaves, unable to hold back his tears. Manipulated he may be, and yet he is no puppet; something in him demands respect. If the actor is directed to be quiet in his words of weeping, accepting the final blow of fate, a moment of nobility (and not the aristocratic kind) may touch the stage. His is the greatest loss.

The Queen's announcement of Ophelia's death is very different from her description of it. Virtually blurting out the news, she moved by Laertes' question ('O, where?') to re-enact in words the sad adventure. It is anything but a blunt account; the whole thing is rather a decorative verbal construction of a scene with an otherworldly appeal of its own. The facts are naturally to be accepted with all the detail of the 'fantastic garlands' and the rambling 'melodious lay'; but in their presentation she creates an experience of a rich profusion, of entering an abundance of the Earth, so that at one and the same time the listeners see a tragic accident and are taken on a kind of spectral journey. Perhaps she simply cannot cope with the unvarnished horror of what has happened; perhaps the distant and elegant phrasing suggests more than a mere retreat from the present, and a certain romantic identification with the dead maiden is in the air. It is as if the circumstance is calling to her, a solution to her own Gordian knot. Whatever the author intended by the high style of some of the language ('pendent', 'envious', 'weedy trophies', 'which time she chanted' and so forth), we may take what we like from his words. But we should remember they include 'pull'd' and 'muddy' as the dreamlike sequence comes to an end.

She is left with the fact itself; and to Laertes' understandable need to confirm it has actually happened, she can merely repeat, 'Drown'd, drown'd'. There are aspects to the Queen we catch sight of only in passing, as at her succinct aside on the nature of sin and guilt when told of Ophelia's disorder (IV,5,17–20), or when she laughs at her son in affection ('He's fat, and scant of breath,' V,2,265). A complex minor character, one feels she is never quite revealed; but she is no less "real" for that. Here a fey side sheds an unusual imaginative colouring onto the text for an instant. In contrast to all the rest of the blank verse in the play the passage takes the medium into a kind of story-land, rich with its own tones. Again we see a touch applied to the iambic pentameter of something more than expertise; and we are reminded of its versatility.

'High and mighty, You shall know I am set naked in your kingdom. Tomorrow shall I beg leave to see your kingly eyes . . .' (42–3). As always Hamlet leaves the King guessing: how much does he know for certain? *The Mousetrap* may or may not have been an accusation; and in any case, even with the poisoning by ear, did it amount to more than a wild shot in the dark? Can he know of the letter to England? A barely concealed jeering note in his own letter is bound to re-awaken the 'hectic in my blood' (IV,3,64) that seethes in the King at his continued existence. Hamlet knows how to lead his opponent into making the next move. The prince is 'naked', intimating he presents no aggressive threat (unlike Laertes' recent storming of the castle); but the word says more. He is open and vulnerable, a state he instinctively seeks, to counter the unlimited strength of the other. It was so when he boarded ship; it is so when he goes into the fencing-match. He relies on his wits, and a blind hope that the right will prevail; meanwhile a decisive confrontation draws nearer. All his energies are directed towards that meeting, come what may.

'The general gender . . . / Convert his gyves to graces; so that my arrows, / Too slightly timber'd for so loud a wind, / Would have reverted to my bow again, / And not where I had aim'd them' (18–24). A botched aim or missed target is a not unfamiliar subject for metaphor. At this point the King thinks he has found a deadlier weapon than his 'arrows' of a direct proceeding against Hamlet, but the prince's letter tells him the England trip has failed in its purpose. He at once has another scheme to hand, 'now ripe in my device' (62); and as he begins to prepare Laertes for his part in it, he sets him at his ease with a little dig at the ways of the young, in the same breath admitting the old have their vanities too. The 'riband in the cap of youth' (76), though in his regard 'of the unworthiest siege [importance]' (74), is no less needful 'than settl'd age his liveries and his weeds' (79). One can imagine Laertes charmed by a self-deprecating smile or shrug on the part of the older man. (Interestingly Polonius makes a similar comparison between young and old to Ophelia (II,1,114f), in a dissimilar context, again it may be to put the younger person more at ease.) There follows an image of startling power to evoke the 'witchcraft' of the French nobleman Lamord: 'he grew unto his seat, / And to such wondrous doing brought his horse, / As he had been incorps'd and demi-natur'd / With the brave beast . . . ' (84–7). Over in a second, a visionary presence such as might belong to a number of Shakespeare's plays, with his typically swift and adept poetic gift of capturing a charged moment; then why should one feel it could belong only to *Hamlet*? Perhaps it seems to present an equivalent expression for the genius of the central character; perhaps it mirrors the author's own uncanny ability to become one with his means, the five-beat line, the five-act play. Despite *Hamlet's* length one senses such a unity, in the folds of its construction. It may be there is truth in the two together: for Shakespeare is surely, at some level, giving us something of himself in his lightning-witted lead. At any rate in Lamord's horsemanship we are offered a perfect metaphor for the act of artistic creation. The King's remark, ' . . . so far he topp'd my thought / That I, in forgery of shapes and tricks, / Come short of what he did' (87–9), continues, if one so wishes it, to reflect what can be felt in the presence or recollection of great art. Re-reading these last lines (87–9) more in context, one may hazard that without knowing it the King has his unfathomably artful nephew on his mind. But that to a degree runs counter to the dramatic situation as we have it, and as such may (finally) be a step too far.

'There lives within the very flame of love / A kind of wick or snuff that will abate it' (113–4). Claudius strangely echoes the Player King sounding out the strength of his wife's loyalty: 'What to ourselves in passion we propose, / The passion ending, doth the purpose lose. / The violence of either grief or joy / Their own enactures with themselves destroy' (III,2,178–81). He might well have included "grief" in his own exhortation. As with the repetition of a theme from Polonius's words to Ophelia mentioned above, there clearly are a few tropes in Shakespeare's mind that contribute in a scattered way to the play. This one is more germane to the action; as so often, Laertes' situation is made to reflect Hamlet's and contrast with it. Claudius proceeds to test the root of the young man's resolve with a merciless exposure of two innocent-seeming words: 'That we would do / We should do when we would; for this 'would' changes / . . . And then this 'should' is like a spendthrift sigh . . . ' (117–21). Thus cornered, when asked what he will do to show himself his father's son, Laertes responds with a vehemence no doubt highly satisfying to the questioner. Yet as he introduces the question the King seems almost to be afflicted with a verbal tic of the playwright's, 'But to the quick o'the ulcer . . . ' (122). Would the speaker wish to remind Laertes of the corrupt nature of their plot? Of course 'ulcer' might suggest merely the awkwardness or difficulty of the situation, asking if Laertes is prepared to "get his hands dirty" so to speak; nevertheless it is a slightly surprising word to choose. For the sake of a reminder of the rot and skulduggery at large, the audience is offered what is admittedly a fine phrase, but for once perhaps not the most apposite. It merely goes to show how unerringly the poet hits the mark with the other thirty thousand-odd words.

Also a little surprising, but in this case perhaps the more convincing for it, is the King's incidental character reference for the prince: 'He, being remiss, / Most generous and free from all contriving, / Will not peruse the foils . . . ' (133–5). Given the urgency of the situation he is likely to mean what he says: he will want to leave as little to chance as possible, and not to have the prince's suspicions aroused by an unlikely oversight. Nor does Laertes disagree. Nor the audience, as one supposes, despite the contrivance of the Players' play and the (yet to be revealed) alteration of the letter of commission on the ship. As Laertes, and despite evidence to the contrary, Hamlet too has a nobility transcending the accident of birth. A casual remark from his arch-enemy reminds the audience of his great capacity for good. So deftly are we turned then in the direction of the final Act, and to the resolution of the warring forces always at work, in an individual as in a country.

V, 1

Free from the confines of Elsinore Castle, and (for a moment) of the desperately straitened circumstances of two most noble families, we find ourselves with a couple of ordinary fellows to whom things happen, if they happen, within the ordinary process of time. Suddenly there is no crisis; no entropic disorder seemingly designed by fate; and as Hamlet and his companion come up against a less speeded-up world, a sidelight is thrown on what one may call the royal construct. In the person of the First Clown the prince's assumptions are challenged: in his anonymity he has no automatic right to any kind of superiority, he is not the foremost character in the conversation he conducts; and the other stays very much in charge of his own domain. Indeed it is tempting to see the Grave-digger as sovereign in his land, and the royal visitor as receiving a lesson in kingship. First, though, we are treated to an exchange between two working people and a perspective on life uncoloured by the outlook (inevitable as it is) of political power.

The working day is their master and within it they make their own time. Beneath their discussion of the ins and outs of a suicide's burial, drifting as it does into what appear the customary roles of a comic and his straight man, and beneath the light song boomed out from the grave-pit, lies the pathos of Ophelia's death. It is fact now: but while the two Clowns unwittingly remind us of it, they provide a welcome diversion. Shakespeare is adept at balancing the dark portent of a moment with one form or another of outright humour. (At a later pause, veiling a deeper urgency, we are introduced to the preposterous Osric.) The serious-sounding question from the First Clown, asking how a Christian burial can be justified – 'How can that be, unless she drown'd herself in her own defence?' (6–7) – marvellously sets the tone. They are both in earnest, as they look at the situation, and wryly resigned to the hand of unprincipled power behind it. This last is agreed to by the stronger character with a neat turn of wit: ' . . . and the more pity that great folk should have countenance in this world to drown or hang themselves, more than their even-Christen.' One imagines an innocent expression belying a conscious irony. It is followed by a poor joke, a better riddle and a devil-may-care song, from the one royally robust character of the play.

As they approach, Hamlet and Horatio might as well be back in Wittenburg, a couple of students passing through a churchyard. As the skulls fly up, the dominant onlooker dazzles the air with irreverent comments. Politicians, courtiers, lawyers, land-owners, all come in for it. In his exchange with the First Clown he is matched in word-play, every manoeuvre fully met, till he can only complain to Horatio of the presumption of the lower class these days: 'The age is grown so pick'd [over-refined] that the toe of the peasant comes so near the heel of the courtier, he galls his kibe [chilblain]' (126–8). Suddenly the prince's railing against the world of privileged careerists can seem a little shallow. The acute observer of society's ills is at the same time a youthful student mouthing the stuff of dreams. His fine words and inexperience betray him; he is scarcely someone who knows himself.

It is the stranger therefore that the playwright chooses this moment to reveal his age, which turns out to be thirty. He is virtually a middle-aged man. What has happened is probably a piece of rushed thinking on Shakespeare's part, who while uncannily true to the less visible path of a narrative, can be cavalier with the temporal framework. Perhaps feeling he needs a more mature character for his ending he has simply written one in, despite the youthfulness still so apparent. But everything about the prince in the final scene stems from the root and growth of the character to that point; nor is anything to be gained from the addition of years. If 'young Hamlet' is to come of age it is not to be by the recording of a birth-date. Perhaps Shakespeare wrote in the detail as a birthday-gift to an actor. At any rate the slight incongruity is scarcely noticed in the drama of the moment. The master-illusionist gets away with it again.

Not only does the First Clown easily hold his own in the brief duel of words, continuing to parry after Hamlet retires from the cut-and-thrust; but in his casual reference to the 'many pocky corpses nowadays' that rot before death (150), we are offered a withering comment on corruption at least as telling as the prince's more expansive witticisms. Again, his use of a deliberative chop-logic to prove points to his colleague is as cogent in its way as Hamlet's own (on Alexander, 189-92). We may by now be so taken with Hamlet's way with words, culminating here in the flourish of another impromptu quatrain ('Imperious Caesar . . . ', 193f), that we may not at once register the more subtle contrast with the commoner. But in its essence the comparison between the two is as clear as day. The latter speaks from the broad centre of an assured existence. The prince, through no fault of his own, is incomplete in himself, still a voice from the margins.

As the two rustics are forgotten, and our attention turns to the altered demeanour of a victim of circumstance suddenly returned to the past, we may see the child in the man awaken, an innocent presence. Perhaps it is not too fanciful to see the chance encounter as contributing in its way to a deeper wholeness of being. As such it may lend itself to the idea of an inner life somehow drawing on its every resource for an all-or-nothing challenge.

This is below the surface, so to speak. In front of us the questioner has forgotten the battle of wits, hearing his own name mentioned, and learning he is widely perceived as mad. Unperturbed he continues his casual enquiries, till all at once he finds himself face-to-face with Yorick's skull. For a moment the mystery of all things is on him. He holds death and love in his hand. As he recalls the jester's lightning wit, the 'flashes of merriment that were wont to set the table on a roar', and his mischievous irreverence, that might quite well be turned on himself – 'Not one [No gibe] now, to mock your own grinning?' – do we not catch an impression of a familiar cast of mind? Among the many half-thoughts or pixel-pictures that may flick across the mind is that of Hamlet facing himself.

The opposites crowd in on him: a simple loving warmth, an abhorrent cold rictus. He is quick to associate the latter with his anger at womankind; and from that accustomed mordancy to move to another, his reductio ad absurdum of the premise of power. Just as 'a king may go a progress through the guts of a beggar' (IV,3,30–1) so now the great Alexander is to 'stop a beer-barrel' (192). His idle cynicism re-asserts itself. One feels that in the company of Horatio – or perhaps any familiar company – it is more likely to do so than when he is alone. He still cannot resist playing to an audience. The soliloquy following the meeting with the Norwegian Captain (IV,4,32f) seemed to have a man of sterner stuff waiting in the wings. But the development of a character is not straightforward or linear. With Yorick's skull in the hand, something forgotten is re-awoken. For all the intellectual's fine phrases now, one cannot but feel an instant of significance has come and gone. Something has happened.

As the funeral procession approaches the freshly-dug grave, and Hamlet and Horatio retire from it, no doubt talking in whispers, a very different atmosphere takes hold. Through it a piercing note rings out, 'What ceremony else?' Laertes is answered by a harsh barking chatter from the priest. In musical terms this part of the scene is almost audibly scored. Laertes oversees the lowering of the coffin (or corpse) with a lilting softness, 'Lay her i'the earth, / And from her fair and unpolluted flesh / May violets spring!' As the Queen echoes him, in a minor key, 'Sweets to the sweet,' and proceeds with a theme of union, in a kind of double gentleness, it is countered by Hamlet's dawning realisation, a shocked murmur. This is turn is swiftly overborne by Laertes' sudden raging, first with the prince in mind, then at the world to do its worst to him, so long as he remains with his sister. Hamlet advances with a thunderous phrase of self-announcement; a mêlée ensues, including the voices of Queen and King; and the prince fills the heavens with his own swelling note of defiance. The note is accompanied by a kind of breathing rasp of hatred from Laertes; and it ends in a pause, and a whispered parody of its climax, perhaps with an off-key emphasis, as if to take the wind out of its own sails, 'Nay, an thou'lt mouth, / I'll rant as well as thou'. After another pause the Queen's identifying theme, maybe by use of the instrument or theme that marks the prince, somehow foresees that racket modulating to a harmonious tone, at peace with itself. In its own voice the prince's medley bows out, half-frenzied, half-resigned. Laertes' rasp has continued to interrupt proceedings since it viciously began (at 'The devil take thy soul!'). Finally, after a brief engagement with the voice of the King, it is the last thing to be heard.

It may be that a musical taking-note at some level is a part of how we respond to every dramatic narrative, be it song or poem, novel, short story or play. It is a kind of map-making to accompany a more literal sense-taking. The above is a self-indulgence; but one imagines that at an inchoate level the development of every fictional character has to do with a wordless intuition, in some respect kin to a musical progression; and we are free to form our own individualistic views of that. As a finite dramatic part Laertes presents a gradual increase, moving and hard-won. At first the meek recipient of a favour from the King, and a loving if somewhat unoriginal brother and son, later a thing of fury intent on revenge, its force, sharpened by a further terrible family loss, intercepted and all but expropriated by the King – here he sheds another skin. Far more alone now than when he stormed the castle with the Danskers at his back, he is passionate to remember his sister in a world of neglect. His powerful rhetoric, his leaping into the grave, carry the mark of a free soul. His silence, too, as Hamlet seeks to outspeak him and outface him, since there is only one contest he has in mind, says much. And still he is in the pocket of the King.

Last seen not so much delivering the news of Ophelia's death as re-living it in reverie, now the Queen is clear in mind and open of heart. We may assume, not that she is free from her earlier sense of guilt, but that she is less in thrall to it. It exists, maybe, as something she can do nothing about, and meanwhile other matters claim her attention. We are to see no more signs of her 'sick soul' (IV,5,17); rather we see an affectionate woman, concerned more for others (or at least for her son) than herself. A tender farewell to Ophelia here raises the question: if her hope was for her to become her daughter-in-law, could she not have used her influence in the matter? If she knew of the love affair she surely knew of Polonius's refusal to countenance it. Then again, a further question is fruitlessly raised: would not Polonius have been delighted at the chance of his daughter becoming Queen? But the play leaves us no time for such a wild-goose chase of the mind; and here, dispelling such irrelevancies, we have before us a composed and expressive person, free to be herself. Disengaged for a moment from the King, scattering flowers in a way that may bring back Ophelia's own flower-giving, she seems to stand in a cold time for the simple heart's affections, at a gentle leave-taking. That Shakespeare may have chosen to cast the Queen as a touch more independent-minded towards the end of the play is at the least not contradicted by her comment on Hamlet's state of mind. 'This is mere madness; / And thus a while the fit will work on him. / Anon, as patient as the female dove / When that her golden couplets are disclos'd, / His silence will sit drooping' (266–70). She could not have been more right or more wrong. Her understanding of the essence of his situation is complete. He is waiting, wholly intent on bringing something to fruition; committed, with all his being, to the delivery of a concealed outcome. The effort is nerve-racking, life-racking. But it is not mind-wrecking, 'mere madness', if unsettling beyond the norms of sanity. Nor is the end result to be anything like a pair of yellow fluffy chicks. In the irony of the Queen's misunderstanding of the externals all her vulnerability is for a moment on view. She was not present when the King used the same image (III,1,161f) to describe to Polonius a similar intuition as to Hamlet's inner situation. He was more correct as to the externals. But she seems to suffer with her son.

It is a remarkable image to use for a man (the more so, perhaps, for a man to use, as the King does). Evidently the author found it an apt one; and one reason, one may hazard, is the distance between the moment before and the moment after hatching. Unpredictable new life, to take over from the old: until it is upon us we are blind. Behind the pattern of events all is subject to a principle of never-ending change. The play is of its events but draws upon the principle, perhaps, in a way that is at once more abrupt than we are used to thinking of, and more accurate. The point is only worth making in relation to the appreciation of what happens in *Hamlet*. Meanwhile the main agent discovers a certain singleness of being, as the final event nears.

He is of course always incomplete, as are we all. A magnificently gifted personality, with an ego as visible as the brilliance and the warmth that promise so much, by unnatural means he is led towards a resolution of his disparate self. Shakespeare takes up a certain aspect of life, with an accent on the compressed mental world of studenthood, in order to cast a revenge drama as compact as it is protracted. At this latest turn of events, with the stark reminder of Yorick's distant death overtaken by the starker evidence of Ophelia's suicide, the prince leaps (again) into premature action.

He instinctively turns Laertes' dramatic claim to an undying love into a form of challenge. Responding sardonically in kind (but with a spell-binding rhetoric), the prince advances and declares himself: 'This is I, / Hamlet the Dane.' Six words announce the man. It is typical of the char-acter, and of the play itself, that a wayward moment includes a fundamental step forward: there is something of a two-way direction throughout (with the goal itself both clear and not clear). When the prince first meets the Ghost he is unsure if it is 'a spirit of health or goblin damn'd', but feels he must go ahead. 'I'll call thee Hamlet, / King, father, royal Dane: O, answer me . . . ' (I,4,40, 44–5). Now, of a sudden, he is his father's son.

His (presumably) muttered justification for his own bombast from the grave has been mentioned, 'Nay, an thou'lt mouth, / I'll rant as well as thou' (265–6). Reminding of a comment after an encounter with Polonius early on, 'These tedious old fools!' (II,2,212), one effect it has is to leave the audience in no doubt of the speaker's sanity – when on his own. In all his soliloquies he is in perfect control of his mind, if at times uncommonly agitated. It is with others that he can be a little more than agitated. Thus the Queen's 'This is mere madness' immediately following the present remark stems from his somewhat crazed actions in verbally and physically challenging Laertes. It is in his action at times that he is – if not mad – not quite in control.

Again he addresses the bereaved brother, again from a closed-in view-point: 'Hear you, sir, / What is the reason that you use me thus?' His scornful throwaway exit line, 'The cat will mew and dog will have his day,' shows little empathy. Yet the simple 'I lov'd you ever' is also telling. It is easy to forget the almost crippling burden the prince bears; and that he also is recently bereaved. By his mother's shocking abandon-ment of the family that was, and by Ophelia's rejection, he has suffered a double betrayal. He has shown no direct sign of remorse at Polonius's death; and is to show little for the discarding of the lives of Rosencrantz and Guildenstern, already signed off. Yet his comment on the latter seems to include the former (V,2,68–70), and we may suppose 'this canker of our nature' is not a thing easily borne by a warm soul. Most burdensome of all is the terrible constriction placed upon the forward movement of his being, the oppressive sense of being trapped in the moment, waiting for the further moment – and finally an opportunity to do what he must – until which "guilt" is too paltry a word for what he must endure at the King's continued existence. His ego may be flawed but it carries him on. He does not know when the decisive moment will be, but never appears to doubt it will be. Even with this last action – for all its brutal insensitivity – at some level he will know he has made it more nearly present. It is ever closer.

So he goes forward, still grievously at odds with the world as with himself, yet with something in place. He has taken upon himself the honour of his name.

Of course one reason for Hamlet's shouting from the grave is simply to tell the world, 'I lov'd Ophelia' (251). This is (also) behind his astonishing lines as he approaches Laertes: 'What is he whose grief / Bears such an emphasis? whose phrase of sorrow / Conjures the wandering stars, and makes them stand / Like wonder-wounded hearers? . . . ' (234–7). Such poetry as to vindicate the human tenure, when it is gone. Much hangs on the arresting simplicity of 'wonder-wounded'. A few lines back the Priest speaks of 'peace-parted souls' (218), with a similar construction at half-line.

In the first part of the scene, the conversation between the Clowns, Hamlet and Horatio, there are no formally-framed poetic lines as such, apart from the Clown's song and Hamlet's quatrain. Often the poet continues the impetus of his blank verse in prose for a spell, allowing the poetry to emerge as it will, as for instance in 'Is this the fine of his fines, and the recovery of his recoveries, to have his fine pate full of fine dirt?' (95–7); or ' . . . your flashes of merriment that were wont to set the table on a roar?' (173–4). So the dramatic medium, together with the mind of the audience, is refreshed.

'That skull had a tongue in it, and could sing once; how the knave jowls it to the ground, as if it were Cain's jaw-bone, that did the first murder!' (69–71). A further prosaic snippet illustrates, not so much the poetic potential of the medium, as the force of the familiar and everyday. Within the natural rhythms of the unstopped sentence a freer discourse has its own ways of making an appeal. The original murderer is obliquely referred to first as if by accident by the King himself. Advising Hamlet to cease 'these mourning duties to your father', he appeals to the law of nature ' . . . whose common theme / Is death of fathers, and who still hath cried, / From the first corse till he that died today, "This must be so"' (I,2,103–6). In the Christian tradition Abel is the first person to die. Claudius is more direct in his one soliloquy of any length: 'O, my offence is rank, it smells to heaven; / It hath the primal eldest curse upon't, / A brother's murder! / . . . What if this cursèd hand / Were thicker than itself with brother's blood, / Is there not rain enough in the sweet heavens / To wash it white as snow?' (III,3,36–8 and 43–6). This second reference of the King's in its latter part is a beautiful instance of an effect that can derive from the open song of poetry, when a regular form is embraced, in this case the unrhymed pentameter. An elevated note may attach itself to the human condition, whatever the sense of the lines; so that within the immediate world that is spoken of, a further one is discovered, in which every reader or listener may have a place. Otherwise the repeated form is mere verse. The content may be noble or ignoble; but there is something ennobling in the outcome. Whereas a passage of great poetic prose will include the reader as great oratory will, as powerfully and possibly more directly, but without quite the same unitary effect. Coming back to Cain, the three references taken together touch on a sense of the fallen human in the play, as following the original sin. As such they lend added point to the many images of rot and corruption. Yet even in so doing, and along with several other more or less conscious echoes of the faith (see for example note above to IV,6, final paragraph), they add a note of their own, faint but ineradicable, the trace of Christian piety.

'Now get you to my lady's chamber, and tell her, let her paint an inch thick, to this favour she must come; make her laugh at that' (175–7).

The grinning skull he holds sends the prince's thoughts flying off on a misogynous tack: so he raves at Ophelia (III,1,140–1), 'I have heard of your paintings too, well enough; God has given you one face, and you make yourselves another . . . '. 'Frailty, thy name is woman!' rings out silently, an unforgiving thought, from the moment we hear it (the first time we see him on his own). Nor does his final leave-taking of his mother, as she lies dead and he lies dying, carry any hint of filial warmth: 'Wretched Queen, adieu!' (though it should be remembered 'wretched' suggests a sad case rather than a sinner). His friendship with Horatio, and his apparent inability to be friends with a woman, bring a further question to mind, though to leap to the conclusion that a latent homosexuality is indicated would be to take it too far. Rather, given the almost insuperable difficulties that have arisen with the two women he would naturally feel closest to, one may take it – if one thinks of it at all – as further evidence of the constricted path that lies before him, as his adult nature unfolds.

Not that we should think of him as a child. 'Thou pray'st not well. / I prithee, take thy fingers from my throat; / For though I am not splenetive and rash, / Yet have I in me something dangerous, / Which let thy wiseness fear. Away thy hand!' (239–43). Needlessly inviting Laertes' murderous rage he stays ice-cool in the face of the storm. He creates emergencies but can deal with them; and the greater emergency is not of his making. The lines quoted are image-free, which no poetry is for long. But their quick measured clarity hints an image of its own, of the prince's ominous alertness under fire, in an encounter with the same opponent which we know is not far off. His over-wrought imagination – all his fancy-filled world – is ready at a trice to fall away, once he is put to the real test. But as yet he has no inkling of a further encounter with him; nor of how he will finally be able to turn on his true quarry, a fox with nowhere to hide.

The King has featured little in the scene but ends it with his customary aplomb, urging patience on Laertes, and at the same time feeding his appetite for revenge with a blood-curdling promise, 'This grave shall have a living monument' (279). He means (almost certainly) that Ophelia's death will be recompensed by Hamlet's; but the closeness of 'living' to 'monument', accompanied perhaps by a glance at the intended victim, suggests the sudden finality of the deed. What with the skulls, the funeral procession, the grappling in the grave, and now a visual suggestion to set the seal on all that these betoken, the stage is primed for its last Act.

And the King's few words here leave us in no doubt as to who is in charge. The fallen figure is to set the scene. It is unlikely that Hamlet's recent jocular reference to 'Cain's jaw-bone, that did the first murder' at all consciously recalls, in the mind of the audience, Claudius's agonised address to his 'limèd soul, that struggling to be free, / Art more engag'd' (III,3,68–9). But the enormity of his crime on both private and public grounds, the murder of an innocent man, a brother and a king; and the despairing would-be humanity of the criminal, as he is defeated by the price of staying on terms with his conscience – all is somewhere in our minds. Just as the two principal players have been circling each other for so long so it is with ourselves and the play's resolution. There is something of either of them in each of us. Finally, on the boards, we will discover the conclusion, or it will discover us. The preliminaries are all but over.

V, 2

It is entirely natural for Hamlet and Horatio to be together. It is as if the less stable personality requires the other's presence as a kind of ballast, to keep steady. While it is tempting, and easy enough, to imagine details of a backstory that would fit with the picture offered at III,2,48f – for example that the prince met the pauper some years back and is funding him through college – such an example shows how little it is needed. It is merely obtrusive. As it is Horatio's persona is curiously limited to its connection with Hamlet's: there is almost nothing beyond it. The character spends a good deal of the play apart from the prince but in more of a dramatic vacuum, so to speak, than the rest of the cast when not on view. On the other hand, when present and fulfilling his role as Hamlet's familiar, he has an individuality and a depth that touch a chord. We sense an independent being; the more compelling, perhaps, in that he knows how to be. He is not 'passion's slave' (III,2,64); and unlike the First Clown, of whom the same might be said, in his lack of concern for himself he seems to occupy a special place in a self-regarding world. He has been 'as one, in suffering all, that suffers nothing' (III,2,58); and yet, while such a reference to past experience raises interest, it stays a closed book. The present connection with Hamlet is the all and sum. As close as he is to the centre of the play's action (even wishing to accompany the prince into death), one feels he cannot in essence be altered by anything that happens. It is as if he has already undergone everything. He is a witness, a passive part of events; till at the last he is to be their chronicler.

Here he listens in growing amazement to the moves Hamlet and the King have made at long range. Hamlet is sharp and vivid: he lay 'worse than the mutines in the bilboes [mutineers in fetters]'; and who is not with him as he rises and steals forward? 'Up from my cabin, / My sea-gown scarf'd about me, in the dark / Grop'd I to find out them . . . '. Back in Elsinore, after sending a provocative letter to the King, he is at once keyed up, alert to the great danger he is in, and keenly at ease. He is glad of the daring that led him to the letter of commission: 'Our indiscretion sometimes serves us well / When our deep plots do pall'; no more does he accuse himself of cowardice or of thinking too much. His trust in 'a divinity that shapes our ends' allows him, now the time is close, to commit himself to his fate. In fact it is closer than he thinks, as the King is not going to wait for a report from England; nevertheless he knows it will be soon, and he is prepared. 'It will be short. The interim is mine, / And a man's life's no more than to say 'One' ' (73–4). The die is cast.

'So Guildenstern and Rosencrantz go to't' (56), comments Horatio on Hamlet's summary sending to their deaths of innocent men. Hamlet's two old friends and fellow-students, ignorant of the contents of the royal sealed letter, have done no more than follow the King's instructions in trying to sound Hamlet out, admitting as much when challenged, and accompanying him on his voyage. They have become whipping-boys for his displeasure; and now pawns to be sacrificed in a deadly game 'between the pass and fell-incensèd points / Of mighty opposites' (61–2). At such a high-handed justification Horatio is more pointed: 'Why, what a king is this?' The note of surprised disapproval would doubtless irk the prince; one imagines his next words, whether said coldly or shouted, as angrily confronting the questioner. He lists the King's foul deeds, again insists his conscience is clear . . . and backs down. 'And is it not to be damn'd / To let this canker of our nature come / In further evil?' (68–70). No doubt he would issue the same (forged) instruction again, for to him it is war, no holds barred, and the death of the King's two errand-boys will send a signal. At the same time he knows he has gone too far, as he did with Polonius (Ophelia and Laertes may also be in his mind); and to incur his friend's criticism may make him the readier to admit it. It is a telling admission. Before he has said half-jokingly to Guildenstern, 'My wit's diseas'd' (III,2,296); now he recognises 'this canker of our nature'. Before he has said to Rosencrantz, in a double-edged self-reprimand, 'A knavish speech sleeps in a foolish ear' (IV,2,22). But this is no semi-apologetic throwaway remark. The language is unambiguous: 'Is it not to be damn'd . . . further evil?' The sinner knows himself.

Again one returns to the wording. The 'canker' is there, a part of him; the guilt lies in its indulgence. But he is able to begin to put something right. ' . . . I am very sorry, good Horatio, / That to Laertes I forgot myself; / For by the image of my cause I see/ The portraiture of his. I'll court his favours . . . ' (75–8). Like a weather-vane his outward focus can shift now in one direction, now another. At the mercy of a mixed nature, he has taken a step towards its understanding. He may have been aware of his superabundant ego; now he is more deeply conscious of its effects. One senses him waiting the King's next move a little freer in his inner being, a touch readier for the challenge. Nor is this merely a matter of self-knowledge. To an extent the destined meeting is to be played out in human terms, good (in spite of all) against evil; an open and generous nature against a narrow self-calculating one. By his actions Hamlet seems instinctively to recognise the strength of a position that scarcely troubles to defend itself, ready to operate in the freedom of the human spirit. His intent to make some sort of amends to Laertes for his behaviour at the grave is a straw in the wind, a sign of a more liberated inner self, or of a person more flexible and able.

It is an act of reckless bravery for Hamlet to come back to Elsinore at all, let alone after advertising his return with a mock-subservient letter. Much-loved prince he may be, but the King is the King, with vast resources to draw on. As it seems to draw near, one may wonder what kind of encounter he envisages. The determination he expressed on forgoing the opportunity to dispatch the kneeling man at prayer says all, presumably, that he needs to say to himself: 'Up sword, and know thou a more horrid hent; / When he is drunk asleep, or in his rage, / Or in th'incestuous pleasure of his bed; / At gaming, swearing, or about some act / That has no relish of salvation in't. / Then trip him, that his heels may kick at heaven, / And that his soul may be as damn'd and black / As hell, whereto it goes' (III,3,88–95). He does not care for his own situation, which for its safety must require evidence of the King's guilt; his inner focus seems to be fixed on some kind of confrontation whereby the other dies as his father did, 'with all his crimes broad blown, as flush as May' (III,3,81). That the crimes will warrant an eternity in Hell will be enough. Yet the criminal will have a living reputation on Earth.

It seems the prince does not think past the essentials. So far from 'thinking too precisely on the event' (IV,4,41) he lets it hover, to assume what shape at last it will, provided only it is on its way. His attitude to forcing the issue, or rather to making it ever more likely, has been consistent. All he has done is to remind the King of his existence in as disturbing a way as he can; to put himself in harm's way; and to trust to his instincts, to chance and to God. The spirit of a gambler takes him on; and at last the background situation is beginning to coalesce, and he can sense the nearing resolution. It would be lacking in credibility for him to declare the condition of a revenge that safeguarded himself: to send the King to Hell, damned in the eyes of all. There is only the revenge. Now the pursuer in him is aware the other's frustration has been mounting for some time, and that the sheer nerve and nature of his reappearance may tempt the enemy into the open, to ensure that this time the business is dispatched. An instinct is guiding one to trap the other in an exposed space. The paradoxes in *Hamlet* never end. In commentating on the play there is a danger in ascribing too much to a clear motive. But even if he cannot say it the prince knows what he is doing. After so long we see him as ready as he can be, as composed as he can be; and still blindly finding the way.

Out of nowhere a gloriously comic scene is upon us. Hamlet's 'antic dis-position' is gone; he has no need to bear himself 'strange or odd' (I,5,169). A moment of truth beckons. Meanwhile the absurd pomposi-ties of a young rich land-owner making his way at court present an opportunity for ridicule. The prince does not hold back on his impa-tience with those who ape the manners of the great; and yet he is almost gentle with Osric himself, reserving the cutting edge of his scorn for remarks out of the courtier's hearing. There is no trace here of bitterness or a harsh intent, as there was at times (admittedly with personal rea-son) in his dealings with Polonius. But he is as always exasperated at the social distortions wrought by pomp or undue privilege, whether exhib-ited in an over-fanciful habit of speech or in a more corrupt and destructive way. It is tempting indeed to see him as many a modern rebel against a privileged upbringing; except that he has no great respect for those born to a life of labour, nor any wish to abjure his own inherited benefits. But he is profoundly conscious of the cruelty in soci-ety as it is, whether it is the England of Shakespeare's contemporary audiences or the universal human world of his later ones (and it is of course both). One need look no further than his lucid lines at a dark moment to be reminded of an outlook that transcends personal back-ground: 'For who would bear the whips and scorns of time, / The oppressor's wrong, the proud man's contumely, / The pangs of dispriz'd love, the law's delay, / The insolence of office and the spurns / That patient merit of the unworthy takes . . . ' (III,1,71–5). Now in lighter mood he is as quick as ever to draw attention to the faults in society he sees about him, which he does as usual with a flourish for his audience, and never more delightfully than here.

After leading Osric into an obsequious nonsense on the weather, exactly as he did Polonius on a cloud's shape (III,2,346f), he listens in alarm to the courtier's wildly affected vocabulary as he commends Laertes as 'the card or calendar of gentry', and pays him in his own coin. 'Sir, his define-ment suffers no perdition in you; though I know to divide him inventorially would dizzy the arithmetic of memory . . . '. To have this hat-flourishing embodiment of euphonious vacuity 'hoist with his own petard' is indeed 'most sweet' (to borrow from Hamlet's plans for the

King in very different mood, III,4,209–11). The prolix torrent is brought to a gulping standstill. The prince is a dab hand as a parodist of the grand style, as when on board he dashes off 'An earnest conjuration from the king, / As England was his faithful tributary, / As love between them like the palm might flourish, / As peace should still her wheaten garland wear, / And stand a comma 'tween their amities . . . ' (38–42). In truth he loves language; and again one sees his creator looking out momentarily from the character's costume. Certainly the prince has the touch of a Shakespearean devilry of wit about him.

His comments to Horatio out of Osric's range are biting. First a 'water-fly', a gaudy trivial nothing, the preening messenger soon becomes a 'chough [chattering bird] . . . spacious in the possession of dirt,' a scathing twist on the land he owns. After he leaves his bowing and scraping is dismissed with a merciless quip, 'He did comply with his dug before he suck'd it'. One sees a precocious infant practising to be a courtier before feeding, and glimpses a possible outcome for the speaker's wealth of talents. What a satirist he might have made! (And, as one may say, as the part of him that is the young Shakespeare included in what it became.) The potential in the prince that dies with him is many-sided. He proceeds to comment in more general terms on the 'drossy age', ruing its widespread superficiality. So many have 'only got the tune of the time and outward habit of encounter,' a phrase that says much. Finally, noting how for Osric and his kind a 'yesty collection' of frothiness lets them get away with 'the most fann'd and winnow'd opinions', he dismisses all such insubstantialities of mind and being: ' . . . Do but blow them to their trial, the bubbles are out.' We are to see no more of one of the most acute and mordant observers of society in literature. As he faces his own trial, the critical side to his nature drops away. No more is he to look for faults in others. The arrival of the lord, to ask if he is willing for the match to begin, puts every diversion out of his mind. As he says to Horatio, in answer to the other's concern, 'the readiness is all.'

As the drollery of the Clowns offers an interval of light relief between the report of Ophelia's death and the fact of her funeral, so the spectacle of Osric and his high-flown patter dances between the final moment of waiting and the final meeting. In either case an ominous note underlies the surface proceedings, unmistakably with the gaping skulls, more subtly with the courtier's surrender to the charade of power, which seems to have swallowed him whole. One is no less amused for the reminder of the context: in part the effect of the two episodes is to suggest a less harrowing perspective for the ever-present themes of death and corruption; and one is able to respond more freely as a result. But as well as releasing tension humour can tighten it. Laughter itself echoes with the shock of the unexpected. It is with a refreshed awareness, then, that the audience enters the closing stage of a long pursuit. Meanwhile Hamlet, who has himself derived a certain amusement from either occasion, takes it in his stride.

He knows, as soon as the lord speaks, that the time has come. The endgame is to begin, with a result one way or the other inevitable. The King sends a courteous message to which he replies in kind, with the respect due a monarch. His response seems as much for himself as to the lord, whom he may not expect to report back a precise rendering, word-for-word; but every word counts. 'I am constant to my purposes; they follow the king's pleasure. If his fitness [convenience] speaks, mine is ready, now or whensoever, provided I be so able as now' (179–81). It is a description first of method and then of present intent. Beneath the graceful exterior lies a simple crystallisation of his position, that has been long in coming.

If the words are reported with some degree of accuracy the King may gather yet another hint of the prince's implacable enmity: for they seem to have only one opponent in mind. But he does not know of the alteration to the letter of commission, just as he did not know of the true intent behind the Players' play, or indeed behind Hamlet's behaviour towards him throughout. He has been tormented by suspicion, Hamlet by knowledge. Despite the King's easy composure in public, he may be the less stable underneath, now that the psychological moment is on them.

'The king and queen and all are coming down.' It is turning out as Hamlet would have wished, even if he does not know it. Whatever happens – and this may be only the first of a series of decisive moves – is now no longer a purely private battle. The Queen has also sent a message, 'to use some gentle [noble] entertainment to Laertes before you fall to play.' Always she shows, or tries to show, a mother's love to her son. Hamlet accepts the point (which he has already made to Horatio). Now the two friends are left together.

It is not clear to what extent Hamlet has confided in his companion. We know he has passed on details of his father's death (III,2,68–9), and that Horatio was in league with him at the performance of the murder play. One does not know if the prince quoted the Ghost's words to him, 'If thou didst ever thy dear father love . . . Revenge his foul and most unnatural murder' (I,5,23–5). One does not need to know, but one may need to wonder, as the play again invites the audience to enter the mists of speculation. Those words with their terrible claim on the prince's being, that must ring in his mind with the force of a holy injunction – one may imagine Horatio has not heard them but guessed at them, and at Hamlet's intent, much as if he had been told. Now he is anxious; yet his first remark refers to the contest only as a bet ('You will lose this wager, my lord'). There appears to be something unsaid, a tacit understanding. The prince is already on his own.

He answers blithely enough, 'I shall win at the odds,' though to say that for some time he has been in 'continual practice' hardly fits with the sense we have of his life since the start of the play's action, nor with his complaint to Guildenstern that 'I have of late . . . forgone all custom of exercises' (II,2,286). Perhaps it is an authorial slip (or a scribal error in the text's transmission); or maybe it is intended as a touch of bravado. At any rate suddenly a premonition catches at him like a physical pain, 'But thou wouldst not think how ill all's here about my heart . . . '. He shrugs it off; it is 'such a kind of gain-giving as would perhaps trouble a woman.' The challenge is to his duty as a son but also to his masculinity.

A director might try to convey the presence (though it would be a tall order), unperceived by either of the two, of the Ghost standing by. At last, after unimaginable twists and turns, an answer to its dread words is somewhere near.

To Horatio's alarmed offer to delay the bout Hamlet is dismissive. 'Not a whit, we defy augury; there's a special providence in the fall of a sparrow.' Since augury concerned itself with foretelling the future from the flight of birds, the scriptural reference to the sparrow suggests not only that there is no way for us to sense the future, but that all is in the hands of God. Everything that happens, and specifically every death, has its significance. He continues, more to himself than to Horatio; and even more, perhaps, as if looking into the eyes of all who turn to the end of their journey, to meet it bravely. 'If it be now, 'tis not to come; if it be not to come, it will be now; if it be not now, yet it will come: the readiness is all. Since no man has aught of what he leaves, what is't to leave betimes? Let be.' A hero's words, but reflecting not the heroism of a prince, but the stoical death-right of the human being. It is the moment the play becomes universal. "It" at first may appear to be the crucial encounter with the King; the sentence following expands the scope; and one realises that in the mind of the prince, one has always led seamlessly to the other. From the start he has lived with the likely outcome. But he is a realist, not a fatalist; and as the others troop into the hall, he is wonderfully light at heart.

The King is suave, charming even, as he brings the two together who were almost mortal enemies an hour or so back. Ignoring him Hamlet at once offers an apology to the man he could scarcely have done more to harm. Directly responsible for his father's death, very much to blame for his sister's, destroyer of the sacred moment of her funeral . . . the prince has little hope, one would have thought, of achieving anything other than deepening Laertes' murderous resolve. He does not know of this, of course; though with a part of his mind he must suspect it. But he has chosen to take the whole occasion at face value, addressing the man who might have been his brother-in-law rather than the one who tried to strangle him ('I prithee, take thy fingers from my throat'), and whose last words to him were 'The devil take thy soul!' In a similar spirit he does not examine the foils but assumes fair play. It is his only hope: and with it he finds a freedom and warmth that – if the director so wishes it – can reveal a new person standing before us. If the decision is taken to present the character as merely disingenuous, unwilling or unable to be sincere, it will not be difficult to inform the speech with a touch of slickness, or negative tension; and an opportunity will be lost. For the final episode seems to have a slightly different person at its centre, someone no longer at the mercy of his own mercurial temperament; a character more open to the world.

The speech of apology is at the very least difficult not to listen to. Now Hamlet is at the heart of the maze, so to speak, he can see more clearly. He has already admitted Laertes' feelings are not dissimilar from his own ('For by the image of my cause I see / The portraiture of his' 77-8). To an extent now he can view himself as through another's eyes. He sees someone "taken out of himself", a different being. To attribute the deaths of Polonius and Ophelia to a madness on his part can be seen as a deliberate evasion, or as an honest attempt to explain a kind of possession of his nature by something inexplicable. He can hardly go into the details of the Ghost's appearance and command. Or, as at other times in the play, the situation can be viewed as partaking of the "either-and-both" syndrome where contradictions rule (see final note on II,1). It is an excuse, it is true. 'Was't Hamlet wrong'd Laertes? Never Hamlet. / If Hamlet from himself be ta'en away, / And when he's not himself does wrong Laertes, / Then Hamlet does it not, Hamlet denies it. / Who does it then? His madness' (210–14). There is surely truth in this. No-one can see things from all points of view. And there is a case for saying that once the Ghost's plea is heard, while for the most part the prince's brain runs itself perfectly, the need to keep making things happen is not under control in the normal sense. What more can Hamlet say? Who has not apologised with the ambiguous yet altogether sincere words, "I wasn't myself" – ? But there is more he can say to Laertes, and the speech's ending is both literally exact and imaginatively so. 'Let my disclaiming from a purpos'd evil . . . ' is crystal-clear. Whatever Laertes' thoughts at present, as a member of the audience one takes it as almost certainly true. ' . . . That I have shot mine arrow o'er the house / And hurt my brother' is no less certainly true. It captures something unreachable without the use of the imagination, a truth of the heart.

Laertes makes a "correct" reply, which is illuminating as to the aristocratic code of honour it draws on. It is a specious argument in terms of the real situation yet natural-sounding enough for us to suppose it is half meant. Despite himself the speaker may be moved by Hamlet's words; and the ending is strangely torn between what is and what might be. 'I do receive your offer'd love like love, / And will not wrong it' (228–9) is pure bogus. Yet at the same time, given the outward trappings of the occasion, the friendly excitement in the hall, and the other's far-reaching apology, the sentiment – and even the intention – may express a wish the speaker cannot conceal.

He is a good man. Yet in anointing a foil's unbated tip with poison he is throwing a code of honour to the wind. To assume the King is acting merely in sympathy with his plight, and out of a concern for his own safety, is to turn a blind eye to the violation he has devised of a noble custom. A fencing-match cannot be interfered with in this way, one would imagine, least of all by the monarch. Laertes knows nothing of the King's own crime. 'To hell, allegiance! Vows, to the blackest devil!' he snarls as he bursts into the castle; and now, as Hamlet has come out into the open, he is drawn more nearly into a self-destructive darkness.

One could argue, if one wished, that he too has gone partly mad; when all he has done is succumb to the pressure of events. His own story within the play, if secondary to Hamlet's, leading out of a mirrored circumstance, shares with it a catastrophic impulsiveness. The concluding episode is to show his own emergence from the shadows; and while the main thrust of the tension of the moment surely lies with the prince and the King, there is a sense in which the theme of a conscience at bay now rests in the nobleman.

Laertes finds himself less committed to his plan than he expected. After Hamlet's open acceptance of his guarded concession ('I embrace it freely, / And will this brother's wager frankly play'), and laddish raillery ('I'll be your foil, Laertes . . . '), he is almost back in a sparring session of the sport he loves so well. He goes through the motions, carefully choosing the right foil for the wrong reason, and quickly finds himself two hits down. The language the odds are framed in is now not clear; but this is an unfortunate start for the King, who though he has backed his nephew needs the better fencer to score a hit. Aware of his anxiety (but not presumably of its immediate cause, the Queen's drinking from Hamlet's beaker), Laertes mutters to him, 'My lord, I'll hit him now.' The King's reply shows what he thinks of his display, 'I do not think't'; and there is (or can be) a moment when everything is in the balance. At Laertes' admission to himself, 'And yet 'tis almost 'gainst my conscience,' there should be a pause of sorts, Laertes marking time, not knowing what to do; till Hamlet rallies him, 'You but dally . . . '. Both men become excited and both are done for. Laertes' wavering is crucial; in dramatic terms he is a still developing character.

Meanwhile the King has given a stellar performance. A persuasive figure from the beginning, at this late point in the proceedings his genial charisma is at its height. To the bystanders the fencing-match will seem the perfect solution to the recent animosity between the two young men, and his tactful gesture at its start will have drawn murmurs of approval. When Hamlet expresses doubt he gaily defends his splendid wager, hiding a host of misgivings of his own (H.: 'Your Grace hath laid the odds o'the weaker side'. K.: 'I do not fear it. I have seen you both; / But since he is better'd [considered better] we have therefore odds'). As they prepare to play, with a superb fanfare which recalls his first exit from the stage (then in a genuine goodhumour with his nephew, I,2,124f), to martial music and the music of great guns his voice rings out: 'Now the king drinks to Hamlet!' Even now, with the Queen dying before his eyes, he may yet triumph: after the wounding not only is Hamlet to perish but also Laertes who could prove a danger. There will be a world of sympathy for him if he can get by the next few minutes. The poisoned drink and rapier-tip can in good time be juggled off onto a false source;

and with his sovereign authority, his quick thinking and compelling charm, he will stand every chance. Sorry as he may be to lose his wife, his instinct for self-preservation will take over. Even after she dies, announcing a poisoned cup but unaware of the poisoner, he has a second's grace. But there is something he has been unable to calculate.

The Queen's death is almost lost between the intercharged dramas of the male world. As indeed her life is; and Ophelia's more so, until the deformation of her personality sets it apart. Gertrude's only speeches of any length in different ways are filled with empathy for another: her concern for her son when the Ghost appears to him in her chamber (III,4,116f); and her pastoral elegy (as it virtually becomes) to Ophelia on reporting her death (IV,7,166f). Otherwise her contributions to the dialogue, scarcely more than interjections, present a remarkably varied and full picture. As vibrant a character as any, she is created almost incidentally, a half-hidden yet unchecked presence. It is a breathing-to-life by understatement. Her only soliloquy is a mere four lines long (IV,5,17f). And yet somehow she is with us as much as any character, as knowable as any, and as unfathomable as any – in the literary or real world.

As a commentator it is something to beware – the trespass beyond the gates of privacy, the drift towards the indefinable. No-one can pluck out the heart of another's mystery, to take up the prince's warning to Guildenstern (III,2,337). Shakespeare's approach with a number of characters in *Hamlet* reminds us of this, where questions are posed and not answered; and with none more than the Queen. It is not only that we cannot begin to quantify her guilt; more broadly, it is difficult to class her as a "good" or "bad" person. For this reason she is an individual as realistic as any. Her warmth for her son is ever-present, if overlain briefly with anger at one point. She dies with his name on her lips – 'O my dear Hamlet!' (288). She appears to have fallen head-over-heels in love with Claudius and is affectionate and supportive towards him at all times, even courting physical danger to protect him when Laertes storms in. After the chamber scene (yet not necessarily because of it) we know she is possessed by thoughts of guilt and sin. She has been careless, perhaps more than careless, perhaps far more; and yet it is difficult to think of her as in any way evil. It is an expressive part, if a limited one; to an extent the author of her own predicament, she is overborne by events. Discerning, loving, she never quite seems to be allowed her own space. It is as if she stands for an unrecognised quality, a woman's eye in a male world. Finally, perhaps, she is someone we know and not someone we judge.

At the start Laertes and Hamlet are two of a kind, young aristocrats waiting to return to their studies abroad, with a glaring difference. One of them is at ease in a loving family. When he returns from Paris the similarity is increased by the destruction of his family, and his desperate need to avenge his father's death, and the difference sharply replaced by the way he takes to fulfil that need. As one becomes the target of the other the division seems to leap to breaking-point, and yet as they wrestle in Ophelia's grave the sense of something shared grows too, with either on fire to announce his love for the departed. 'That is Laertes, a very noble youth,' murmurs Hamlet to Horatio as the funeral procession comes to a halt; and one feels the respect between the two talented young men of the court will have been mutual before the start of things. The tension between the rift and the kinship, both aspects accelerated by Hamlet's declared love for Ophelia, is finally broken as Laertes answers Osric's 'How is't?' with, 'Why, as a woodcock to mine own springe, Osric; / I am justly kill'd with mine own treachery.' With words that wonderfully echo his father's rebuke to his sister ('Ay, springes to catch woodcocks', I,3,115), he comes back to himself; as Hamlet too, who 'from himself be ta'en away' (211), may be said at the last to return to Hamlet.

Laertes is of course a powerful figure in his own right. Yet what happens to him is crucially bound in with what happens to Hamlet, and indeed provides the key to the resolution of the long deadlock. The two young men share a divided journey. To a degree by contrast they define each other's errors; and at the end, as each emerges from a tunnel of destructive circumstance, by their deeds a victory is achieved against past and present evil. Laertes' path, gradually broadening in terms of an inner self-possession, yet alarmingly delivering itself into the ambit of a controlling power, finds its independent way. Its owner discovers a strength that is needed. Secondary to Hamlet for a great part of the play, at the end he is no less the hero.

Revealing the set-up to the prince ('The king, the king's to blame'), no doubt in the hearing of all, commending Hamlet's action when the others cry treason ('He is justly serv'd'), with his last gasp he attains the truth of a clear soul. With a beautiful reciprocal absolution the men's brotherhood, advanced by Hamlet, is accepted by Laertes, and confirmed by them both. 'Exchange forgiveness with me, noble Hamlet; / Mine and my father's death come not upon thee, / Nor thine on me.' 'Heaven make thee free of it! I follow thee,' says the prince to the dead body. They have killed each other, but surely are innocent and (with the exchange) in a state of grace. It is the last we hear of Laertes, though one imagines Horatio is to tell the court ('the yet unknowing world', 357) of the background to his story too, with an account of the King's original crime. That is for later on. Now the King is no more. His plan, executed by proxy, has had its meaningless effect. But it has not triumphed. Many of the earlier audiences will have seen his soul already descended to Hell, Laertes' already elsewhere. Polonius's son has an honourable tale to tell. He has avenged his family's deaths, not through Hamlet's dying, but by exposing the evil behind the events. And he has put aside hate for love.

The King is out. His bubble has burst. After the moment of would-be prayer, when he takes the audience (and perhaps himself) by surprise with the vehemence and clarity of his longing (III,3,36f), he appears to accept his earthly situation, 'My crown, mine own ambition and my queen,' without further ado. But he cannot enjoy it. As he meditates later (IV,3,63–6), brooding on 'the present death of Hamlet': 'Do it England; / For like the hectic in my blood he rages, / And thou must cure me. Till I know 'tis done, / Howe'er my haps, my joys were ne'er begun.' He is a shell of a man, but a vastly impressive one; and after we witness the brief flowering of his conscience, we can never quite dismiss him as merely no reason to doubt, he exhibits a warmth that one feels is not entirely false, or need not be so. His story is as much of the loss of what might have been, than of the joyless exercise of power; a comment perhaps by the author on the true threat to those who have thrust themselves into the public eye. The effort needed can dull the sensibilities to the difference between real and fake warmth in the self. He remains an intriguing character till the end, personable, quick-thinking, and altogether capable – except in one area.

He cannot cope with Hamlet. And it is not only in the battle of wits that he is always somehow on the back foot. There is a quality to the prince which he is well aware of and yet unable to appreciate for what it is. He judges the prince will take up the fencing wager in no meanness of spirit: 'He, being remiss, / Most generous and free from all contriving, / Will not peruse the foils' (IV,7,133–5). He judges rightly but not well. The prince's openheartedness has an effect on Laertes that is to lead eventually to catastrophe.

Of course it is not "cut and dried" in a formulaic fashion: there would be little room for drama in a deterministic universe. Laertes' innate qualities may have prompted a hesitation in the fencing-match and a dying confession regardless of his opponent's behaviour. But it is at least arguable that that had an effect; and more, that the playwright may have consciously played for a subtle irony, in having Claudius fall foul of his own foul intention. There is no truth to the matter; it is merely another unanswerable question, with the difference that to ponder it may provide if not knowledge, then, maybe, a kind of illumination in that part of the mind where conclusions are not needed. (As in the undramatic world one has a sense of the characters one knows and no full knowledge.)

And so one has a sense of the King as more than a thing of nothing, or of shreds and patches (as Hamlet describes him respectively to Guildenstern and the Queen). A lost good man subsumed in a gleaming evil, a deviser and calculator who has nowhere to turn to, in the uncalculating world that Hamlet brings to the fray. It has been the prince's method from the start, if one may call it a method: followed by instinct, of its nature not visualised, but at the last leading to an unequivocal facing of the quarry.

What this account has left to say of the main character, and then of Horatio and Fortinbras, will emerge from comment on a few snippets of text that in their own way add to the magical power of the poetic spell. The phrase 'a rhapsody of words' has been plundered from a speech of Hamlet's (III,4,48) to suggest, not the trivialising of the holy words of the service his mother's re-marriage is to him, but (with a shift of emphasis in the word's meaning) the free-wheeling torrent of glorious speech the play is to everybody. It is impossible to begin to do justice to this. Especially the poet's uncanny hold over the iambic pentameter, as if it had been invented for him alone, is left for readers to make their own enquiry into, if they so wish. It resists analysis, as any matter of aesthetics, but is recommended as a source of enrichment for the mind to dwell on. This commentary salutes the inspiration of the words – the poem of the whole – though able to say next to nothing about it. In general when a snippet is plucked out it has been for the image or another more easily accessible aspect of the meaning, rather than the power of the buried lyric; but always in the hope of the latter working its magic as well.

'Our indiscretion sometimes serves us well / When our deep plots do pall: and that should teach us / There's a divinity that shapes our ends, / Rough-hew them how we will' (8–11). Glad of his impulsiveness on board ship, Hamlet recognises the hand of the divine. If the first two lines are precise and clear as within the everyday dimension, the next two are so in the world of the image and the imagination. The listener or reader is informed at a deeper level. Such lines are not uncommon in the play, the purest gift poetry has to offer. One may talk for ever of the author's finesse with imagery, with sound and tone, one may add the philosophical note and the original conception, but there is always something more. A true art fills the understanding and goes beyond it, to be taken up again by minds far different. And still nobody can say for certain what is or is not a good line.

'Ere I could make a prologue to my brains / They had begun the play' (30–1). The prince describes his 'indiscretion' to Horatio in terms a theatre audience will appreciate, the more so as they remember his interest in the art-form, more still, it may be, as they remember

Shakespeare's. It is a knowing reference to the multi-track mechanism at work in an artist's mind. Some will recall Hamlet's eagerness for the showing of (a doctored version of) *The Murder of Gonzago*: ' . . . the play's the thing / Wherein I'll catch the conscience of the King' (II,2,574–5).

'The play's the thing.' While this discussion has rambled beyond the direct action on stage, it is hoped that it has preserved something of the freshness of a mind's engagement with a performance. The saying is part of the doing, the inspiration of the words included in that of the action. In *Hamlet* a volatile element on stage becomes a part of the spectator's experience, so strongly is the play charged with what may be, and what may come to be, as against what is. The business of existence is shown in its uncertainty, its unknowing as well as its knowing. It is certain enough at the end; but till then much of the drama draws on a recognition of the tenuous nature of things, that is dormant in each spectator's mind. In this respect the link between audience and stage has an unusual directness to it, nebulous as it is; and the commentary has tried to keep hold of that.

'Tis dangerous when the baser nature comes / Between the pass and fell incensèd points / Of mighty opposites' (60-2). There is no reason to suppose Hamlet's disdain for lesser natures, evinced amusingly enough for the most part over the play, but also chillingly in the case of Polonius, Rosencrantz and Guildenstern, ever quite leaves him. He is an aristocrat in an aristocratic age. While 'fell incensèd' relates to the duellists rather than their weapons in the speaker's mind, the reverse will also apply in the audience's, aware of the rigged duel to come. The prince expresses a flash of resentment on being passed over for the crown – the king has 'Popp'd in between the election and my hopes' (65) – which has come up before (if the words are taken at face value), when he growls to Rosencrantz, 'Sir, I lack advancement' (III,2,313). One imagines a situation of confusion following the old king's death, the reassuringly competent brother, perhaps supported publicly by the Queen, outranking the absent, untried son in the court elders' deliberations and the mood of the country, despite its fondness for him.

Given the prince's sense of self one might have expected the issue of the crown to have come up more often; except for that very sense carrying something selfless within it. 'The interim is mine,' he says to Horatio, awaiting the King's next move at his murder, 'And a man's life's no more than to say 'One' ' (73-4). In with the ego is the need for a true self-realisation, a touch of idealism always there, if not always apparent. Lying beneath his scorn for the foibles of society, his disgust at his mother's antics (as he sees them), it emerges now as the character meets the challenge with a simple nobility. A little later, when he suggests to Osric (131), ' . . . to know a man well, were to know himself' [self-knowledge is needed for the knowledge of another], one feels a point lurking beneath the casual remark, the hint of a theme of self-discovery. 'Stand and unfold yourself,' says one guard to another at the play's very outset. To the audience as to the character himself, while a complexity remains, a certain unfolding is at hand.

'If it be now, 'tis not to come; if it be not to come, it will be now; if it be not now, yet it will come: the readiness is all' (198–200). He is committed to the event. The randomness and lack of a clear vision, the self-doubt, the jarring inconstancy of the figure battling in the present moment, all is swept away. He has pursued an elusive role; but finally his action is to define him. The light yet steady path of the sentence, the sense of the quick short words gathering in 'readiness', and more, the four-word echoing clauses of consequence, suggest a conscious structuring of the prose-pattern such as is (or was) the norm in poetry. Yet it is as likely simply to have occurred, the author open to the resources of sound-play, without conscious deliberation. Something of this sort happens in all poetry, beyond the threshold of awareness, in the mind that creates as in the mind that re-creates. Author and listener share in the unexpected, a brush with the spontaneous, in the untold resources of a half-sung language to delight and musically define.

This is not to say the author does not plan, and plan carefully; but that however deep the artifice, something lies deeper. It is a gift of the language, refined by countless usage in countless users, operating through the mind of the artist and in any mind that meets the construct, but never to be fully construed.

To return to the construct of the chief character: as he waits for the action to begin, his mind is clear, his person is free, the thinking is done.

It is enough for him to be able to say to himself (as well as to Horatio), 'Let be'.

'This presence knows, / And you must needs have heard, how I am punish'd / With sore distraction' (205–7). As the final episode starts, and Hamlet gestures to the small party of onlookers as he begins his apology to Laertes, the larger group beyond may have a flickering sense of being included. Is there an invitation to the audience to cast themselves for a second in the penumbra of the play, a part of 'this presence' - ? In the same speech the words, 'Sir, in this audience, / Let my disclaiming from a purpos'd evil . . . ' allows the possibility a little more room; and later the invitation (if it may be considered one) is further pronounced: 'You that look pale and tremble at this chance, / That are but mutes or audience to this act, / Had I but time – ' (312–14). ("Mutes" are silent performers among the cast.) There is much in the play to bring the theatre audience closer to the stage, as it were, drawing as it does on the ambiguities that obtain as to direction and definition within the self. By this means the character of each main player has perhaps struck a chord in that part of a spectator's mind that is always, at some level, aware of its individuality. Now at the close it seems natural for the main part to bring his counterparts – every one of us – more directly into his hearing, to experience the shadow of death.

Modern existentialist drama, that explores an age-old question from a new angle, can refer directly to the audience, as indeed older scripts have done. *Hamlet* anticipates much of what has lately become a commonplace on stage, the isolation of the individual, the inexplicable surround, the indifferent universe. It is also a rattling good yarn. A means to encourage the dramatic illusion of reality has not yet become an end in itself. But it is worth looking a last time at the means, or at an aspect of it that goes to the heart of an underlying sense of disorientation. It is something concealed by the business of living but which has everything to do with it: the distance between an act and its consequence.

The invisible event. 'Sir, in this audience, / Let my disclaiming from a purpos'd evil / Free me so far in your most generous thoughts, / That I have shot mine arrow o'er the house / And hurt my brother' (217-21). Behind the beauty and pathos of Hamlet's exchange with Laertes, his plea for forgiveness finally answered with 'Mine and my father's death come not upon thee, / Nor thine on me' (308-9), lies an almost tangible sense of going astray. All the major characters (with the exception of Horatio) have erred; and at a number of points the play's imagery, with the idea of an aim or target included, has underlined the tendency as if it were endemic to the situation at large. Which it is: to any human situation, and will be so long as we are recognisably human. The play catches at the nature of the time capsule in which, instant by instant, we have our being. The image of a brooding bird, used by both the King and Queen, waiting for the conclusive next event (III,1,161–4 and V,1,266–70), lays weight on the state of unknowing between an act and its outcome, as things develop. *Hamlet* is also about success, which is also endemic in the story of the species, but to be fought for. The passage from the Ghost's command to its fulfilment, arguably the two events that overshadow all others and subordinate them to their sequence, illustrates the war of uncertainty within which a battle is won. From first to last the scope for error, in the blind time between events, fills the dramatic narrative, increasing as the moment of crisis nears. Finally, at terrible cost, it is reached and what must survive, survives.

If there is a tendency to go wrong, to be blindsided by fate, much in the play is to do with negotiating a path. There may be no answer to the situation, as with Ophelia, who nevertheless shows an awareness of what has happened: 'Lord, we know what we are, but know not what we may be.' Another line, from an idle backwater of the play, tells us more of the chasmic nature of change, the hidden theme of the whole. 'Our thoughts are ours, their ends none of our own,' says the Player King in a choric moment typically lurking within a wooden character and a string of tedious couplets. The play's structure in part reflects the deceptive matter it is made of. Hamlet's journey on one reading shows in close-up the lie of the land, as it were, when an answer is to be found to the interference of fate.

Literature is not concerned with the mechanical. Whatever the surface, acts of decision, acts of intent underlie it. At a significant, let alone life-changing level, these cannot be entirely straightforward in their operation, and a literary work cannot do other than reflect this. In the play Hamlet's act of will is not something he is master of initially, though it may be said he becomes so. The tragedy arises from the enormity of the Ghost's own act, which lays on the prince's shoulders an all but impossible burden. It is a necessary command (or enforcing plea): family honour is to be maintained; Denmark is to be saved; while on a universal level (or what we know of it), the distinction between good and evil is to be upheld.

Dramatic tragedy springs from the need to know this last irrefutably, in the direst circumstances. The traditional description of its effect on the spectator of a cleansing or catharsis, through the excitement of fear and pity, along with the resolution of the events that caused such emotions, has stood the test of time and is surely correct. Perhaps it might be deepened by a reference to the realm of uncertainty where the individual operates more or less freely and more or less blindly. A tragedy will succeed in part by reminding the audience of such an area at the back of the mind, in which is enclosed the knowledge of one's individuality. By a dramatic touch, even as it resists all definition, it is brought a little to the fore. If this is a part of the process of stage tragedy, it is nowhere more so, one would imagine – and whatever one's personal reaction to the play may be – than when witnessing the Tragical History of Hamlet, Prince of Denmark.

The title-pages of the first texts naturally carry the royal name in full. Expectations of a kind of behaviour befitting a prince are never quite absent in the mind of an audience, especially at the time it was written. As the dying Queen announces foul play ('The drink, the drink! I am poison'd'), at last the audience sees the man of authority. He takes immediate action, 'Ho! let the door be lock'd!'; he stabs the king, 'The point envenom'd too! – then, venom, to thy work'; he completes the job, 'Here, thou damn'd, incestuous, murd'rous Dane, / Drink off this potion! Is thy union here ? / Follow my mother'. In the throes of death he instructs Horatio to 'report me and my cause aright', seizes the poisoned cup from his friend and empties it (maybe dashing it to the floor); and does what he can to ensure an acceptable succession to the throne. The onlookers are frozen in shock. At their side, as it were, we glimpse him in his true colours, as if for the briefest of moments the prince became king.

A terrible anger has struck home. 'Here, thou damn'd, incestuous, murd'rous Dane . . . '. The Dane is the antithesis of a true one; in the word, it may be with all the scorn a whisper or shout can bring, and in the action with it, Hamlet takes full possession of his declared identity (see V,1,238–9). (The adjectival text before the word here is a little unclear but the line as given is as likely as any.) His disgust with Gertrude remains ('Follow my mother'). She is at where Claudius is bound. Such an unforgiving sentiment may be performed as an off-hand dismissal with a softer 'Wretched Queen, adieu!' (311), or with a venom to match that of cup and sword; but however the moment is directed it is clear he is still revolted by her betrayal of his father. The prince has not altogether changed: something of the callow youth may stay in a kind of verbal lightheadedness ('Is thy union here [pearl, marriage]?') that leads to the savage sneer. But he has faced the odds and met his challenge. Onlookers and audience alike attend the end of an inner journey, the latter knowingly at some level, as doubts are cast aside. There remains the unfulfilled telling of a story.

It cannot be told. Hamlet's 'O, I could tell you – ' (315) seems to promise more than the reporting of him and his cause aright (317). Horatio may do what another can to clear his name further; and the prince's plea to his friend not to follow him in death, but to show a greater friendship in the toils of life, is a burden of love. 'If thou didst ever hold me in thy heart, / Absent thee from felicity awhile, / And in this harsh world draw thy breath in pain / To tell my story' (324–7). But the undeclared story in 'O, I could tell you – ', the riches in the empty space of the dying words, 'The rest is silence', seem to withhold the key to the individual. Desperate not to leave a 'wounded name' behind him the prince appears to wish to offer up, so to speak, the uniqueness behind the name, to place it on record, to be understood. But there is no key and no such understanding.

In a way he is more deeply one of us than at any point before, in his final moment voicing such a wish, that may be buried at some level within the individuality of all. At the same time he stays entirely other (as all do). Of course it is possible to take his anxiety as he dies to be related solely to the outward details of his story being made known, with no call for anything further. But whatever remains untold the character remains incomplete at death; and as such, truer to life than if it were attended by some sense of a conclusive fulfilment. All moves on, with the path of the inner being cancelled at some point, but never in itself ended.

A minor poetic effect illustrates the ever-changing, and at the last deepening, outlook of the prince. The apprehension of a final certainty, as reflected in the light brief words of 'If it be now, 'tis not to come . . . ' (198f), is overridden by a slower, more rasping monosyllabic line, 'And in this harsh world draw thy breath in pain . . . ' (326). The certainty is on him now. Again, one supposes the poet may not have traced the last stage of the prince's journey by these means, or at least not consciously; but it happens. The resources of language to underscore subtleties of meaning are infinite.

'I knew you must be edified by the margin ere you had done' (143-4). Horatio has a dig at his fellow-student's needing a marginal gloss (so to speak) to allow him to understand Osric's abstruse language. One sees Hamlet enjoying his friend's aside, as later his observation, following the courtier's exit, 'This lapwing runs away with the shell on his head' (168). The shell may be the absurd hat but it is also the sense of being only half-born that the over-eager Osric carries about him. It is tempting to relate this use of a hatching metaphor to those by the King and Queen about Hamlet: the audience is given a background alert, as it were, to the process of his emergence from a kind of cell. Shakespeare may or may not have had it in mind; more likely the image came to him because of its recent use and for no other reason. Yet as if the play's imagery had a mind of its own, it works at a level of which the author may not have been fully aware. Even to say all this is to damage the spontaneity of the occasion. The comment shows a quick wit; yet Horatio is never caustic. He has a dry but easy sense of humour, as we see when he complains to Hamlet, 'You might have rhym'd' (III,2,264); or at the start of the play, when dragged to the battlements to see a ghost, he answers Barnardo's 'Is Horatio there?' with 'A piece of him.'

His attempt, foiled by the dying prince, to die with him, moving as it is, again reminds of a quality that is his alone. In Hamlet's presence he is not exactly a figure of action. Indeed he seems curiously not of the direct world where things are done; though when we see him before the prince's stage presence has begun and after it is over, a far more decisive character is on hand. The man who challenges the Ghost to speak is not the slightly hapless figure at the scene of the spirit's first appearance to Hamlet (see commentary on I,4, first paragraph). Nor is the thwarted suicide the authoritative figure of practicality and wisdom we see at the close. But even then his life belongs to another's; there is no sense of a locus of independence in the conception of the part. His strength derives in its entirety from a requirement of Hamlet's being, reaching beyond his death. It is a deeply human role, and yet not entirely so, in that there is a mechanical aspect to it that attaches to the play's construction. While as Hamlet's trusted friend he is able to know him as no-one else (ever) can, in a sense he is no more than peripheral to the world of change. He observes rather than participates in events, and finally is ready to chronicle them.

It is another paradox of the play. He is there and not there. But as Hamlet's friend he is the embodiment of a simple and true love, up to bidding him farewell: 'Good night sweet prince, / And flights of angels sing thee to thy rest.' And he is also a friend to all that is good in Denmark, taking charge of the immediate needs of the practical situation, and virtually handing over to Fortinbras. Indeed, does he not embody the good of Denmark? And still he is not a fully substantial figure. 'Blest are those,' says the prince, 'Whose blood and judgment are so well commingl'd, / That they are not a pipe for fortune's finger / To sound what stop she please' (III,2,60–3). Perhaps there is no-one really like this. Horatio is an ideal, but one of the deepest humanity. In a play of human error, he represents an understanding that cannot be.

Fortinbras enters 'with conquest come from Poland', after greeting the English ambassadors with a 'warlike volley'. He is clearly no longer 'of unimprovèd mettle hot and full' (Horatio I,1,97); nor is he the 'delicate and tender prince' of Hamlet's estimation (IV,4,48). At the sight of the dead his words are scarcely those of an untried creature of impulse: they are profound, commanding even. 'This quarry cries on havoc. O proud death, / What feast is toward in thine eternal cell, / That thou so many princes at a shot / So bloodily hast struck?' Death is after all the superior huntsman. Nor will it mistake or miss a target. So far as the less conclusive forces of life go, the Norwegian prince exhibits a fine balance of blood and judgement in advancing his country's interest ('I have some rights of memory in this kingdom'), while paying every respect to the regal proprieties of the dark occasion. If we remember the rash youth we hear of at the start of the play, we see a different character now. He looks a promising candidate for the throne of Denmark and we imagine there will be none other. Perhaps he is the more promising for the fault he has shown. As Laertes, as Hamlet, he too has escaped somewhat from his own shadow. He is fallible but he can learn; and by the end we have little doubt he can lead. From his transitory appearance on his way to fight the Pole (IV,4) we gather the impression of someone of a steady bearing, no more. In this brief but charged final episode the suggestion of a true authority begins to take hold. We see enough to be able to discern for the country the sweeping new start it must find.

Its old body is stripped away. The royal house of which the elder Hamlet and his brother and son are the last survivors is gone. Nor has another risen from within the land. After the Ghost's visitation the prince knows 'the time is out of joint'; to 'set it right' takes not only his life but in a sense, all the land can lose without losing itself. The metaphor is of a displaced or broken bone but a deeper surgery is needed. At last a natural development is possible of the living strength of the country, the people's inheritance. The rot is gone. Denmark itself can be seen as a silent character of the drama, in the way it reflects a bare hope for the future, in the unstated promise of its renewal.

'For he was likely, had he been put on, / To have prov'd most royally . . .' (375-6). Why should Fortinbras say this? On the one hand it is the courtesy of an outsider; on the other it may be a token of his admiration for Hamlet's decisive action in ridding the land of the evil at its head (assuming he has been told the bare details behind 'this sight', 340). Another possibility is simply that the author was intent to bring in suggestions at this time to his text of the attainment of a certain aristocratic ideal in Hamlet's life; thus both Laertes and Horatio call him 'noble' (307, 337). It is an ideal that transcends its immediate bounds and yet is defined by them initially: we should never forget the enclosed status of the highest rank of society at the time of the play's writing. The second possibility is probably the weakest and the third the strongest. At any event, minor though the matter is, the author has left us guessing once again, this time it may be through an oversight.

Fortinbras pays the Danish prince the respect due the pre-eminent royal. Claudius's body is passed over. However briefly, Hamlet has worn the mantle lost in death by his father. The final sound of the play, a peal of ordnance, is for him. As if in anticipation of 'the soldiers' music' the very words of the final speech sound with the heavy beat and measured tempo of a dead march. 'Let four captains / Bear Hamlet, like a soldier, to the stage . . .'. The change in status of the speaker is silently reflected in the words. After 'Let us haste to hear it' and 'Let four captains . . .', his last commands carry an authority of the open imperative, in 'Take up the bodies'; and in the play's final words, simple, charged and unequivocal. 'Go, bid the soldiers shoot.'

Afterword

Hamlet is a complex play. There is little general agreement as to how to approach it. The main character is an enigma of whom something can be said. While it would seem part of Shakespeare's purpose to have given rise to a stage role in which the mystery of individuality stays intact, a certain inner development can be noted that is a part of the story. After the prince leaves the court and muses on his situation, following the crossing of paths with the Norwegian army, we can see someone more settled in his intent, as if at last he has learnt to carry a burden more steadily. It would seem the 'antic disposition', assumed – and in part succumbed to – for purposes of concealment, is behind him. Matters are taking on a more practicable shape; he lives no more by disguise. Irresponsible and shocking – perhaps even sinful – as his behaviour still can be, at Ophelia's grave he says who he is and what he feels. The 'canker' of his nature, as he terms it, may never leave him; but he is closer to being on terms with himself now than before.

All along he has a deeper responsibility than to the appearance of things. It is notable that his references to the dead Polonius are all unkind quips; but set against this is the torrent of tears the Queen reports seeing him in over the body. One might detect a clue here (offered in tantalising fashion) as to a disregard, at the deepest level, as to what others may make of his behaviour and outlook. But in the central matter of gaining revenge he is caught between the inward eye and the eye of the many. He is governed by an outward definition of honourable behaviour that insists on a swift slaying of his father's murderer. It is illustrated by Laertes' response to his own loss; and if it is set in stone in the mores of the aristocratic world, it is written in fire in Hamlet's mind. And yet he is led by his very being to operate in such a way that only a full revenge will do.

When he sees the kneeling Claudius he discovers a compelling justification for delay. (That at the same time it can look like procrastination is a minor example of the play's juggling-act.) Claudius is to die 'unhousel'd, disappointed, unanel'd' as did his victim, thereby bound for hell for the murder, not for heaven by virtue of being in a state of grace. In spite of the excruciating guilt the prince so often feels, at this one point (later seemingly forgotten) he realises a further intent. The murderer is not to go to heaven.

At no point does he appear conscious of a strategic aim that is deeper still. The murderer is to be known as evil. His reputation is to die with him. To be known as a villain is a part of his punishment on earth, and fitting in the wider view; and insofar as Hamlet can be said to have a strategy, it allows for the possibility of such a fulfilment of his mission. It is notable that he does not appear to make the slightest attempt to kill the king 'when he is drunk asleep, or in his rage, / Or in th'incestuous pleasure of his bed; / At gaming, swearing' and so forth, surely seeking a more publicly damning occasion. The prince appears to be steered in part by what we now call the unconscious. His true purpose is never blunted.

In terms of a revenge tragedy, this is a line to take as one tracks the central character. It is tenuous and at the same time, for such a deftly-woven role, in danger of being over-prescriptive. To look at the character in more general terms is to run a further risk of going off-track oneself. But though it does an injustice to the nature of the work as an entertainment, I offer a final thought as to the construction of the protagonist and the play itself, with relation to the audience.

Whatever his commitment to the act of revenge Hamlet has virtually no idea of the form it will take or how it will come about. Barely an instant before the act itself does all become clear. Always he is isolated from the next step, unable to see beyond the moment. The playwright prepares an elaborate sequence of events to create a visible and tangible personality who inhabits the same diffuse world of uncertainties and contradictions as do we all. 'Our thoughts are ours, their ends none of our own', says the Player King in what may be a hint disguised as a cliché. It is in the blind time between events that the pulse in the mind that carries the sense of the identity, a familiar and easy enough presence for the most part, can sometimes play tricks on us, pound with pressure. It is when we are doing things that it does not have us in its hold, in however relaxed or otherwise a fashion, but the case is more the reverse – we know who we are. In a sense *Hamlet* covers two events and the time in between: the first appearance to the prince of his father's ghost, and his fulfilling of its demand. In between – on such a reading – an unconscionable moment passes of doubt, delay, disorder, mirroring in large an aspect of the transient working of the mind and being, an illuminated shadow.

To an extent all fiction does the same; but it seems that in *Hamlet* the pull is strong on a latent recognition, on the part of the spectator, of an indefinable aspect of the being, at least as it relates to the field of far-reaching action. We are reminded of our own blindness. To put it differently, there is something concealed in the mind of the audience, as it creates its nexus with the stage.

All this may well be irrelevant. It may also be wrong. It has long been recognised that writers on *Hamlet* are liable, as the Gentleman says of those who profess to understand Ophelia, to 'botch the words up fit to their own thoughts'. What matters is an ever-living quality, the dance of the play's long pageant, that every spectator and reader will discover differently. It may be that a tension of contradictions, in some way kin to that operating at the core of the self, gives *Hamlet* its key ability to compel and confound the attention. Yet to outline the idea can seem intrusive. One imagines the play will always be played and always resist a label. It will doubtless continue to throw up questions. Why did the playwright choose not to have Hamlet witness Ophelia's madness? Why is Claudius's regicide (and fratricide) not made publicly known till after his death (by Horatio)? External character dynamics, and authorial choice therein, will always be a rich field of interest. As an epic poem, too, the work offers scope for investigation in an area that has barely been touched. The astonishment when one looks at such a play and hears its poetry is unlikely to die down. But whatever the future enquiries as to its nature, the skills of dramatist and poet will lie in wait for more. Something of *Hamlet* is forever concealed.

Printed and bound by CPI Group (UK) Ltd, Croydon, CR0 4YY

13/04/2025

14656603-0002